Growth Games

Books by Howard R. Lewis

WITH EVERY BREATH YOU TAKE

THE MEDICAL OFFENDERS

(*with Martha E. Lewis*)

Invitation

If you're like most people, you are tapping only a small fraction of your potential for perception and emotion.

There is a whole range of positive feelings—like love, joy, warmth, wonder, zest—that you rarely experience but are nonetheless within you. You have sensations of excitement and pleasure waiting to be explored.

For just a small hint of what you're *not* experiencing, try this experiment to sharpen your senses:

Close your eyes.

Keeping silent, tune in to the sounds around you. Listen to them one by one, then all together. Don't try to identify them—just *listen*. This ever-changing symphony is always there for you to enjoy.

With your eyes closed, focus on your sense of touch. Feel the air against your skin, the texture of your clothing, anything within reach. Move about—touching, listening, smelling, tasting—all with your eyes closed.

Then, eyes again closed, have someone lead you on a silent, blind exploration, preferably outdoors. A tree, a rock, a face, are all new experiences when your eyes are closed. Before long you'll feel a close bond of trust with your leader.

Run with him across a field. Roll down a hill. Spin around. Jump. Skip. Crawl.

A new world will open up for you.

That's what this book is about.

GROWTH GAMES

How to Tune In Yourself, Your Family, Your Friends

by Howard R. Lewis and Dr. Harold S. Streitfeld

HARCOURT BRACE JOVANOVICH, INC. HBJ NEW YORK

Drawings by Carol Nicklaus

First edition
ISBN 0–15–137501–1
Library of Congress Catalog Card Number: 77–124838
Printed in the United States of America
A B C D E

The excerpts on pages 54, 55, 56, from *Altered States of
Consciousness*, edited by Charles Tart, are used by
permission of John Wiley & Sons, Inc.

The frontispiece is by Michael Mauney, *Life* Magazine, © Time Inc.

To Martha, David and Emily Lewis

To Virginia, Vicki, Susan, Andrew, Lisa and David Streitfeld

. . . the Peaks of Our Experience

Compared with what we ought to be, we are only half awake. Our fires are damped, our drafts are checked. We are making use of only a small part of our possible mental and physical resources.

—William James

Foreword
BY JANE HOWARD

Growth Games is an encyclopedic cookbook of the recipes by which the Human Potential Movement seeks to infuse its myriad followers with aliveness, awareness, and sensitivity they do not find elsewhere.

Earnest partisans of this movement, Dr. Streitfeld and Mr. Lewis, know their terrain well. They lament, with reason, that many of us lead needlessly guarded, resigned lives, protected by our inhibitions from risk but also from *joie de vivre* and growth. Veteran participants and leaders of many of the movement's encounter sessions, marathons, T-groups, and sensitivity-training workshops, they present here what some will think a radical and audacious notion. They say that a group isn't the only place you can learn to "get in touch with your feelings."

You don't need to pay a behavioral scientist, they suggest, to achieve the joyous growth that good groups generate. All alone, they think, you can learn to uncork anger, meditate on Zen koans, breathe more profoundly, enjoy your body as well as your head, and jettison some of the rubbish from the surface of your mind. Drawing on their eclectic knowledge of such various disciplines as Bioenergetics, Conjoint Family Therapy, Gestalt dream analysis and Far Eastern philosophy, they propose many routes to the movement's destinations—self-actualization and the peak experience. In your own living room, they say, you can stage such socially useful "games" as Chucklebelly, Eyeballing, Massage, First Impressions, and Fantasy Trips.

My own experience with this movement, a year's journalistic and personal odyssey through some twenty widely disparate specimens of the genus encounter group, exposed me to many of the techniques described in this book. Some of them seemed ridiculous at first, and some do even in retrospect. Do we really need humanistic psychology to tell us how enviable is a two-year-old's sense of wonder? Cannot automatic hugging and "eyeballing" be just as evasive and phony as never touching anyone, never meeting anybody's gaze? Does opening the senses of smell and sound to their fullest, on the streets of a city like New York, lead to exaltation? Questions like these are already being debated by critics of the movement and will continue to be by readers of this book.

But the obvious often eludes us. Some encounter activities are far more jarring and instructive than they might seem. I am the better, I think, for having practiced being sillier, quieter, more forthright, and more spontaneous than social conventions normally permit. Some of these games led to moments of euphoric liberation I can still, three years later, recall with wistful nostalgia.

The power of these games, as the authors wisely caution, is not to be belittled. Let the players beware; let nobody be drunk; let no amateur, however well-meaning, tinker frivolously with the fragile psyche of another. Readers who know this, who are serious as well as idly curious, will find *Growth Games* a valuable guide and introduction to the Human Potential Movement.

I know of no more exhaustive compendium of the movement's methods.

A Note from the Authors

This book seeks to bring you practical benefits of humanistic psychology, widely called the "Human Potential Movement," "sensitivity training" and the "encounter movement."

This exciting new field aims to help you reach your full growth in terms of your senses and emotions. It embraces a wide range of approaches to resolving problems in personal functioning and interpersonal relations and includes such frequently neglected areas as body states, sensory awareness and consciousness expansion.

The emphasis—on these pages, as well as in the field—is on your direct experience. The games presented here are explorations that can lead to new insights and more satisfying modes of living. Discussions and anecdotes are designed to supplement your actual participation in the activity.

For easy reference, games are indicated by an arrow (►) at the beginning of a paragraph. The activities suggested here represent a selection of those that have proved to be most successful in practice. A large number have been tested in leaderless groups. This book was written as a guide for you in working with others, as well as by yourself.

We wish to thank the many in the field whose work we have drawn on. Our citations and attributions hardly do them justice. Special credit goes to the principal figures in this movement: Alexander Lowen and the late Frederick S. Perls and Abraham H. Maslow.

We also wish to thank the participants, many in Aureon Institute workshops, whose experiences are here recorded. To protect their privacy, we have made it a rule to disguise identifying details.

We have personally reaped many benefits from the work described in these pages. As participants as well as leaders, we have learned the value of these growth games, and we are delighted with this opportunity to share them with you.

HOWARD R. LEWIS
HAROLD S. STREITFELD

Contents

Contents

I

FIRST
THINGS FIRST

Investigators in psychology find that most people have an untapped, often unsuspected potential for richer, fuller lives. To reach your full growth in perception and emotion, you can apply to yourself a wide variety of techniques, termed games.

1

Games for Growth

You are almost certainly much better than you think you are.

More than you now permit yourself, you can be happier, stronger, braver. You can be more loving and giving; warmer, more open and honest; more responsible and responsive. You can perceive worlds richer and fuller than any you now experience. You have it in you to be more creative, more zestful, more joyous.

All these prospects are within you. They are your potential.

This book seeks to help you to fulfill your potential—to grow—by applying to yourself findings from the exciting new field of humanistic psychology.

This discipline, also called the Human Potential Movement, has, through empirical means, arrived at a positive view of man's nature. An impressive body of evidence shows that the average person has untapped, often unsuspected resources of great extent and diversity. Moreover, the typical person has powerful healthy instincts and a strong drive toward growth. He has it in him to rise to his full emotional height. This hope for man is firmly rooted in a scientific basis.

The many activities suggested here are fruits of this new psychology of optimism. They have been tested and refined in practice and to help you achieve your potential, to encourage your growth by freeing your emotions and raising your level of awareness.

While professionals may find this book useful as a compendium of techniques, it is written primarily for laymen. The discussions are intended to be clear even if you have no special knowledge of psychology. Nor need you participate in organized sessions of the Human Potential Movement, though group members and workshop leaders may find they can put many of the ideas mentioned here into immediate use.

This book is for you, then, if you'd like to begin being all you *can* be, experimenting alone and with your family and friends. Essential before you start is this recognition: that you have a need and capacity for continuous emotional development; that though you physically have stopped getting bigger, you have not come to the end of your emotional growth.

Games for Grownups

Let us watch some children at their games.

Six-year-old Emily is playing Mother. She's experimenting, though she doesn't know the word, has barely heard it.

"You stop that right now, Nicholas, or I'll land on you," she snaps. And she experiences how it feels to act bossy and impatient, as her own mother sometimes is.

Then: "Very well, Nicholas. Anything you want, dear." In this dry run she senses what it's like to be the mommy of her dreams, forever soft and yielding.

Which feels better? What's right when? As Emily scolds, then spoils, then tests a middle ground, she moves forward emotionally, gaining a type of learning that may guide her years from now when she's a mother.

Karen is playing at a puddle. For fun, of course—but she's opening new doors of perception. Mud is soft; dirt, hard; stones, sharp. Water churned with an open hand makes a deeper sound than water splatted with a finger. A rotting leaf smells different from a rusty can. She peers down into the puddle—and sees that in every larger world there is a tiny world crowded with detail.

Joey is trying to dribble a basketball. His muscles and reflexes are slow to coordinate bouncing the ball and running. He's been at it for hours, and each small improvement leads him to conclusions that may stay with him for life: Accept challenges. Stay with a task. Use your body—movement can be exciting.

Games can also be important for adults—as learning adventures and as preparation for life. As used in this book, games are activities leading to emotional insights.

These are *healthy* games. They are close in spirit—sometimes in content—to the games children play. They are different from the maneuvers of the so-called advertising game or the insurance game or as in "Okay, I'll play your silly game." Such games are rituals: conscious exercises in role playing, in which you operate as is expected of you in a highly structured situation.

Growth games are also very different from yet other major types of games in psychology: those described in Dr. Eric Berne's widely read work on transactional analysis *Games People Play*. In Berne's special use of the term, a game is typically an unconscious maneuver in which one player seeks to win an emotional pay-off through manipulation. In the game Berne calls Indignation, for example, a woman entices a man to make a pass at her so that she can have the primary gratification of rejecting him. Many such games are even gamier.

By contrast, a growth game is wholly positive. Many are therapeutic and seek to liberate you from the need for subterfuge. Thus, the woman who persists in the ugly maneuver of Indignation may, through one or more growth games, become aware of what she's feeling, how she's acting and how she might be more honest and direct.

A growth game seeks to help you experience yourself, others or the world in a new way. The words "experiment," "experience" and "activity" are used more or less interchangeably with "game." "Exercise" is avoided, since its connotation of mindless, nonself-directed routine is antithetical to the spontaneity and experimentation that lead to growth.

Anatomy of Games

Some growth games are primarily exploratory, while others are directed toward a specific goal.

Exploratory games usually ask, in essence, "What are you feeling? How do you act?" Aside from a generalized sense of like or dislike, most people don't know precisely what they feel. Nor do they observe how they actually behave. Many games, therefore, aim to help you isolate an element of your personality, which you can then examine in perspective.

► A game can be extremely simple. One purely exploratory game asks you to describe yourself as an animal. This is one of the many games that can be played solo, and you're welcome to try it now. You're likely to start getting glimpses from your unconscious of how you really feel about yourself.

One housewife visualized herself as a race horse locked in a stable. She had a professional background as a speech therapist and for a long time had romanticized being a wife and mother. Actually she was bored, which led to a general discontent. Her visualization helped her become aware of how much she wanted to get back to work and quit being solely a homemaker.

One answer from the unconscious often leads to further exploration. The sales manager of a drug concern said he reminded himself of a pigeon. A moment later he added, "The kind that people throw rocks at." This, he realized, was his impression of himself on several of his jobs. "I keep looking for more and more responsibility. But I hate the feeling of being conspicuous and vulnerable."

The Kind You Throw Rocks at

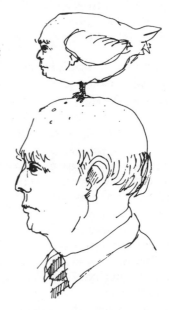

"What's your solution?" he was asked.

"I have none right now," he replied. "But a well-stated problem is half solved."

An exploratory game can be especially revealing if a feeling is painful and thus buried by rationalization. Members of a workshop observed to a participant named Steve, "You don't assert yourself."

His reply: "I do assert myself. It's just that this person I'm talking about happens to be my mother, and I don't want to hurt her." Later on he spoke of not wanting to "start in" with his aggressive wife ("It's important to keep peace in the family") and a pushy neighbor ("Look, I have to live next door to the guy").

▶ Games often simulate an emotionally evocative situation and bring into focus your characteristic responses. The most effective way of arousing your reactions may be to translate a figure of speech into physical terms. In an experiment dealing with Steve's lack of assertiveness, he was literally pushed around. Others in the group pressed their hands against him and shoved.

Heretofore Steve thought that if pushed, he'd fight back. What he found he was actually doing was fighting back his anger. "Hey, come on," he said, backing off. "Cut it out," he pleaded. Even when he was finally able to utter, "Goddamn it! I said stop," his voice had little conviction, and he made no effort to enforce his will.

The game was a replica of his life. He at last realized for himself what he'd been told many times before: His lack of aggressiveness lay in *him*, irrespective of his mother, wife or neighbor. "I don't stick up for myself, period," he said.

"How do you feel when you're pushed around?" the group leader asked, and shoved him.

Steve pondered a moment. "Like I want to run away."

"Tune in to the feeling. Capture it, so you'll recognize it again." The leader pushed him once more. "Where do you feel it?"

Steve worked at locating the feeling. It proved to be an emptiness in his belly and legs. Now aware of his problem, he was in a position to remedy it in daily life.

"But what do I do when I get this urge again?" he asked lamely.

"What do you think?"

"I don't know."

"That's a cop-out," the leader told him.

"I use it as a signal to take a stand?"
"Can you say that again?"
"I use it as a signal to take a stand."

Reworking a pattern of behavior often takes considerable courage. You may feel anxious over trying alternatives, or you may simply not know how to go about it. A directive type of game can help you. Unlike an exploratory game, in which responses are open-ended, the goals of a directive game are reasonably clear.

► Under laboratory conditions a directive game can offer practice in taking an emotional risk. Steve, who felt in peril if he asserted himself, was named Absolute Dictator of the group, with the task of telling the members what to do, how to sit, where to stand. At first he was extremely reluctant, then fell into the job with such gusto that others soon rebelled against his iron rule. Even this was instructive; it helped him sense the reasonable limits of assertiveness.

Many games combine both exploratory and directive elements, not only bringing you to a new awareness about yourself but also offering you the opportunity to act on it.

► Dr. Everett L. Shostrom of the Institute of Therapeutic Psychology in Santa Ana, California, has devised a game in which you lie flat on your back on the floor and ask your partner for help getting up. Most games won't work unless you're in the spirit of them. Before embarking on this experiment, therefore, imagine that you are as weak as a kitten, so helpless you cannot possibly rise unless your partner helps you.

Now. What do you feel when you have to ask for help? Perhaps you're afraid of being turned down. See to what extent you are, in fact, rejected. Can you now ask without this fear?

When you reverse roles, explore how you feel when you're asked for help. You may possibly experience negative feelings—scorn, resentment, guilt, glee at having the upper hand. Plunge into such feelings, and see if you can overcome them.

A game may also serve no other purpose than to be enjoyable. Pleasure, enrichment, delight, are the aims of many of the activities in this book. Conceivably they can be "improving"—they can help you relax or open up to merriment. But primarily the experience is to be enjoyed for itself, like a symphony or a painting. A moment of fun has great value, and it can never be taken away.

A Psychology of Optimism

Theologian Harvey Cox has observed that "while gaining the whole world, Western man has been losing his own soul." The swift social changes of the twentieth century seem, for many people, to have overtaken and bypassed conventional religion, which until now has provided people with a framework for their spiritual life. In the hope of reclaiming some of what has been lost, a significant and growing number of Westerners are experimenting with different ways of seeking inner harmony.

"Never before in history has a single society taken up such a wide range of religious and near-religious systems at once," *Life* magazine observed in a survey of major trends for the 1970's. Eastern religions are attracting large numbers of followers. Philosophies and systems of belief that were once of interest only to scholars and the occasional mystic are being taken up seriously by a large cross section of the population. There is growing interest in astrology, tarot-card reading, even witchcraft.

By far the greatest activity, in numbers of participants and in general influence, is taking place in humanistic psychology, in the Human Potential Movement. The aim of this movement is to help people reach their full emotional growth, to become fully functioning in terms of their own particular talents, traits and preferences.

The Human Potential Movement came to flower in the 1960's, with the founding of the American Association for Humanistic Psychology. This organization provided a forum for the growing number of practitioners and researchers who had come to see themselves as a "Third Force," whose theories and practices went beyond psychoanalysis and behaviorism, the two sets of theories dominating the psychological profession.

The Third Force developed in large part because many psychologist had come to feel that psychoanalysis and behaviorism embodied an unjustifiably pessimistic view of human nature. Orthodox Freudians tended to focus on animal-derived impulses—sex, aggression—and to consider "higher" feelings only in terms of cruder instincts. Behaviorists explained most mental processes as physio-

logical responses to outside stimuli. They went about curing emotional disorders by reconditioning behavior.

As the model of man in traditional psychoanalysis is the animal,
so in behaviorism it is the machine. Neither of these approaches in
its classical form deals with the essential, optimistic qualities that
make man human, or make an individual life worth living. Both
tend to pathologize—place their focus on mental illness—with the
result that little attention is given to what is normal, healthy or
positive.

Because the Freudians tend to think and write about mental
illness, and the behaviorists to concern themselves primarily with
questions that can be dealt with only in laboratory experiments,
little work was done studying the kind of human experience that
does not fit into existing psychoanalytic theory or can not be subjected to laboratory experimentation. Independent-minded, humanistically oriented investigators began to study the phenomenol-
ogy—the actual observable experience—of the normal. This research formed the basis of a new, optimistic school of psychology.

Another chief drawback of traditional psychological theory and
practice was that its fruits were available, on a practical level, only
to a relatively small part of the population. Psychological help was
sought only by people who were able to afford expensive therapy
and/or who were in desperate need of it. The Human Potential
Movement works to develop approaches that promote personal
growth more quickly than traditional psychotherapy, and that are
of help to the "normal neurotic"—which means that more people
are reached, helped faster and with less expense.

A major innovation is that many therapeutic groups are leaderless—no psychologist, psychiatrist or other professional leader is
present. This development came about after psychologists at the
Western Behavioral Sciences Institute in La Jolla, California, gathered data from interviews with 1,000 people who had taken part in
groups. These people agreed almost unanimously that they had
been profoundly influenced. Typical comments were: "It was the
most important thing that ever happened to me," and "It changed
my whole life."

Mentioned most frequently as producing this effect was a deep
exchange of understanding and emotion among group members.
These outstanding incidents did not necessarily involve the thera-

pist; in fact, he was responsible for no more of the high points than anyone else. To psychologist Richard Farson, this raised the possibility that a group could succeed without a leader, that it could be a form of therapy without a therapist.

Dr. Farson was warned by every therapist he knew that without professional guidance members of the group would quickly be at one another's throats. He went ahead experimentally, with extreme caution. The first leaderless group was watched through a see-through mirror by two professional therapists, ready to intervene if the group stalled or got out of hand. They found they were not needed. Every time the group seemed on the verge of serious trouble, the therapists were amazed to see a member step in and do exactly what they'd have done.

With this reassurance Farson set up an experiment comparing leaderless groups to groups led by therapists. It developed that leaderless groups behaved very much like led groups—members kept the session moving and did a good job of helping one another. "It may turn out," Farson concluded, "that our greatest resource for solving human problems is the very people who have the problems."

On this basis many of the experiments in this book are recommended for leaderless groups made up of you and your friends.

2

Ground Rules

You don't have to be sick to get better.

These games are intended for the "normal neurotic": the average person who is functioning adequately; whose emotional problems, to the extent they exist, don't severely interfere with his family life or work; who nonetheless wants to gain insight into his feelings and behavior; and who can profit from developmental experiences, without the help of a professional counselor.

For best results from these experiments follow these guidelines:

Take Responsibility for Yourself

Jim paused as he was leaving and looked searchingly at his therapist. "I've been thinking of going to Colorado for a while."

The psychologist—Dr. Stephan A. Tobin of Encino, California —responded, "Are you asking me if I think you should go?"

"Yeah, I guess I am."

"Jim, it doesn't matter to me if you go to Colorado or not."

"Yeah, well . . . you know I don't think I *really* want to go to Colorado at all. I feel more like going to the beach right now." Another searching look.

"I don't care if you go to the beach, either."

"You know," Jim started again, "I just about decided to stop screwing around. I've been thinking about going back to college, maybe medical school."

"Look, Jim," Tobin told him, "it just doesn't make any difference to me if you go to Colorado, medical school or Disneyland. You're still trying to get me to approve of your decisions."

"Yeah, yeah, you're right," Jim interrupted. He started edging toward the door. "Oh, look, I hate to ask you, but I'm broke and don't have enough gas to get home. Could you lend me a buck?"

Dr. Tobin cites Jim as a kind of person who declines to take responsibility for himself. Jim has had a great deal of therapy. Despite all the supposed insight he has obtained, he still leads a chaotic, unrewarding existence. "Instead of making his own decisions and supporting himself emotionally," Tobin comments, "he continually attempts to manipulate others into taking responsibility for his life."

Psychotherapists find that a patient like Jim almost never gets better. In essence, he brings in his brain at the appointed time and practically defies the therapist to fix it. He himself takes no responsibility for his condition or its improvement. He is much like the typical unmechanical automobile owner who takes his car to a repairman and says, "Here. It's your responsibility."

A point basic to this book is as follows: You need to take responsibility for what you are and for what happens to you. If you're fat or depressed or inadequate, it's *your* fat or your depression or your inadequacy, and no one else's. Possession is yours.

And so is accountability. Only you can get rid of a problem. It's inside you, and only you can get it out.

Thus, a question is implicit at every turn in this book: Can you take responsibility for your shortcomings and for your improvement?

In sensory awareness, for example, can you take responsibility for the blinders you're wearing? Can you take responsibility for increasing your perception?

Can you take responsibility for tensions that are shackling you? Can you take responsibility for resolving them?

Can you take responsibility for your guilt, anxiety, frustration, boredom? Can you take responsibility for overcoming them?

The achievement of responsibility is a giant step toward fulfilling your potential. "I can take responsibility" may be a new idea for you. Try it on for size. Say it, and feel that you not only can but must direct your own life. As the realization takes hold of you,

you'll almost certainly feel a surge of strength and self-confidence. Taking responsibility for yourself is hardly easy. It implies a preparedness for change. A wisecrack among therapists is that no neurotic wants to change; he merely wants to become more effective in his neurosis.

It's more generous, and probably truer, to say that change—even the alteration of an unsatisfactory form of behavior—is frightening. Most mannerisms you don't like in yourself developed to defend you against fearful pressures. Your defenses have worked— witness the fact that you're alive and functioning. (In Dr. Abraham H. Maslow's image: The house may rest on sand, but at least it's standing.) The greater the threat you still perceive, the more you'll resist abandoning your defenses.

In taking responsibility for yourself, you need to give up a lot of favorite villains: parents, incompetent therapists, people who put you down or keep you there. What they've done to you is minor compared to what you're doing to yourself. The analogy is sometimes made between an emotional problem and a broken leg. It's of only secondary importance how it came about. The main thing now is repair it.

You need to face up to many ploys whose purpose is to divest you of responsibility for yourself. One is to say, "I can't," when you mean "I won't." "I can't do that" often, in fact, means "I'd rather do something else." "I'd like to, but I can't" may be translated as "I'd like to, but I won't"—which can put your problem in focus.

Another stratagem is to explain yourself à la Freud. Why do you do such and such? "I can't help it. It's a compulsion." One patient always excused himself with "It's my neurosis." He quit after his therapist had him say instead, "It's my personality defect."

Everyday language can provide you with yet another way to habitually avoid involvement with yourself. By using what Gestalt therapists call "it" language (as opposed to "I" language), you stand apart from your feelings and actions and so escape personal responsibility. You might thus regard your voice and say, "It is choked." You are being perfectly grammatical—but you're treating your voice as some fragmented thing apart from *you*.

On the other hand, if you say or think, "I am choked," you are identifying with your behavior and assuming responsibility for it. Go one step further—"I am choking myself"—and you can experience yourself as an active agent who does things rather than as a passive creature to whom things somehow happen.

You can impose the impersonal form of speech on virtually every area of life. You may say, "It dropped out of my hand," instead of "I dropped it." "The train went off and left me," rather than "I missed it." In nearly every instance the depersonalized statement is a verbal hop and a jump, an effort to keep some distance between you and responsibility.

One student found the distinction between "it" language and "I" language an eye opener. He started to say, "It makes a great deal of sense," then corrected himself: "I can make a great deal of sense out of this."

A further cop-out from the need to change is to say, "Now is not the time." When *is* the time? Are you really saying, "Never"?

In sum, if you avoid this kind of responsibility, your prospects for achieving your potential are unfortunately dim. If you want to grow, you need to take responsibility for what you are doing to yourself.

Focus on Feelings

The emphasis in these experiments is on the "gut" (emotion, feeling, direct experience) rather than on the "head" (thought, reason, verbalization).

Constructive use of your intelligence—your power to analyze and logically relate information—is, of course, essential to your self-fulfillment. Without a well-developed intellect you'd be unable to abstract or generalize or deal with matters outside your direct experience. Your intellect can be an important tool for achieving psychological understanding and the realization of potential.

But your intellect can also provide a way of warding off feeling. In general, the closer you get to experiencing an event, the deeper is your emotional response. If an emotion is painful, you may blunt it by jumping into your head: You may filter the event through words, reasons, abstractions—each several steps removed from the actual nonverbal reality that you might otherwise feel.

This process, termed intellectualizing, can impair your emotional functioning. Experiencing something emotionally and understanding it intellectually are two different species of perception. In depth and color and richness, emotion is to the intellect as a living person is to an X ray.

The limits of the intellect were at last realized by Adam, a young man whose rational, analytical responses were devices for noninvolvement. His capacity for experience was severely limited—he'd conceptualize it out of existence. At one point his therapist had him close his eyes. He took Adam's hand and asked, "What do you feel?"

"Your hand," Adam replied.

"That's a conclusion," the therapist told him. "What do you *feel?*"

"That you're attempting a demonstration of some sort."

"Another conclusion. What is it you're *feeling?*"

"Let's see now. Your fingers. Your wedding band. Your knuckles. . . ."

"More conclusions. What is it you feel *before* your thoughts take over?"

It took some time. After giving more conclusions and explanations, Adam's face lit up and he said, "I feel pressure and warmth." Later on he said, "It's so simple, the feeling level. But I keep busting it up with thoughts."

While playing these games, stay with your feelings. An Irish legend holds that if you run from a ghost, he will continue chasing you, but if you run toward him, he will disappear. Breathing deeply and concentrating on your emotional response will help you intensify and thus become ever more aware of what you're feeling.

The notion of diving into a bad feeling—precisely what you want to be rid of—may sound like needless self-torture. Actually, becoming vividly aware of a painful emotion helps you come to grips with it. Much neurotic behavior is based on a desperate wish to avoid emotional pain. Concentrating on the pain—locating where it affects you, testing the limits of its severity, recalling past experiences associated with it—is a way of cutting it down to size. The pain will often become no longer dimensionless and overwhelming but merely a sensation that, once perceived in fullness, can be overcome.

A good way to strengthen an emotional awareness is to express it over and over, saying it louder and with more conviction. At one session, conducted by Dr. Ben C. Finney of San Jose State College in California, a woman said, "It is very hard, very unnatural, for me to ask for help."

"Say it again," she was urged by group members.

She repeated it, then said to each group member individually, "It is very hard for me to ask for your help."

Finally she was able to say, "It is hard for me to ask . . . but I am ready to accept your help."

Beware of intellectual obfuscating. Since open, direct feeling terrifies most people, they may erect walls of words as a barricade to emotion. When a feeling wells over you, you may jump from your gut to your head to ponder *why* you feel this way. Such probing for reason is, at best, a premature consideration until you learn from your gut *what* you're feeling.

You may likewise be disturbed by another person's uncovering of emotion. Avoid the common tendency to block feeling by interrupting him, possibly with an abstract question.

In one group a member named Mike expressed a long-suppressed longing for love. He stayed with the feeling, exploring it for the first time as an adult. "I want to be touched and felt," he said. "I have a great yearning for affection."

Oliver, another member of the group, shifted uneasily and asked, "Is this the way you usually are with your wife?"

The question was pulled from a hat in response to Oliver's own sense of being threatened. Mike, however, took it at face value and, leaving his gut, replied. By the time he finished, the feeling he was exploring was lost.

The intellect furnishes many other verbal devices to guard against emotion. "Interesting" is an unfeeling word, brittle even as cocktail-party chatter. "You've changed" is an empty observation. "I want to be me" and "I want to find myself" need to be closely clarified to be meaningful.

Watch out for intellectualizing that masquerades as feeling. A person can seem to make emotion-laden admissions, yet not feel a thing. The intellect can adopt the language of psychology, and so "guilty," "scared" and "lonely" can become as devoid of genuine content as "interesting."

The Human Potential Movement itself has given birth to a number of such clichés. "I care for you" is a vogue phrase, the encounter-group equivalent of the jet set's "Darling." "I feel" can also be over-used. In one group a woman punctuated every sentence with "I feel," climaxed by "I feel I have to go to the bathroom."

Vivian Gornick, writing in *The Village Voice* on new forms of psychotherapy, has described how she told an encounter group in considerable detail about her anxiety over being embarrassed or threatened by them. Afterward she realized: "I knew I was home free. I felt, as I looked around, that no one in this particular room on this particular night could say or do anything to alarm or hurt me."

Miss Gornick saw that she'd used her frankness as a dodge. By being open, she'd spared herself further risk. "How quickly and easily 'honesty' . . . becomes another cunning weapon in that bottomless arsenal of defense that is continually being re-stocked."

Psychologist Charles R. Kelley has summarized ways to focus on feelings with these six don'ts and a do:

Don't *block*—hold back, hold in or suppress a feeling.

Don't *turn*—censor, distort or redirect a feeling.

Don't *lead*—anticipate a feeling, get ahead of what you're actually experiencing.

Don't *fake*—force, dramatize or embroider a feeling; or pander to another person.

Don't *psyche*—intellectualize, verbalize, analyze, ponder or ruminate.

Don't *cop out*—defocus, divert your attention or drift away from a feeling.

Do *go to your core*—focus, connect to yourself and then to the others with you, and surrender yourself fully to the feeling from your core.

Engage in Feedback

In everyday life you get very little idea of how you appear to other people. As Dr. William C. Shutz of Esalen has observed, in our culture we have quite a few words for hypocrisy—"tact," "diplomacy," "discretion." In general, people are so polite that they'd rather see you go overboard than tell you you're slipping.

When people tell you how your behavior is affecting them, what they are communicating is "feedback." The term comes from engineering—a thermostat gives feedback to a furnace.

The benefits of feedback in groups were discovered accidentally. In the summer of 1946 a workshop on race relations was held at a Connecticut campus. Dr. Kurt Lewin, a social psychologist, arranged to have training sessions observed by research assistants, who were then to meet privately in the evenings to pool their reports and impressions. Some workshop participants were living on campus. Partly out of want of something better to do, they asked if they might sit in on the meetings. No one expected what followed.

The participants and trainers were electrified by the open discussion of their behavior. "Mrs. X attacked the group leader," a research observer reported. "Mr. Y came to the defense of the leader, and he and Mrs. X became involved in a heated exchange." The observation was immediately attacked by Mrs. X and defended by Mr. Y. Other members who'd been present took part in analyzing and interpreting the event.

Before many evenings had passed, all the workshop participants were voluntarily attending these sessions, some of which lasted for as long as three hours. Participants reported they were deriving important understanding of their behavior. To Lewin and his staff, it seemed clear that a powerful educational method had been hit upon.

Feedback can do more than tell you how you seem to others. You give as well as receive observations, and giving feedback can prompt you to scan your own perceptions and emotions. This introspection can put you in touch with reactions that, under ordinary social conventions, you may rarely express. Through feedback people can make themselves known to themselves and others through their actual behavior—what they say or don't say—rather than through an image that, in large part, may be a lie.

When playing games in this book with others, engage in feedback freely. One essential of helpful feedback is "leveling," letting another person know how you feel—either negatively ("I'm bored"; "I'm angry") or positively ("I like you"; "I'm sorry you're hurt"). Another essential is "confrontation," having it out with a person whom you dislike ("You didn't listen to me, and you cut me off").

Together, leveling and confrontation add up to "encounter," an honest dialogue in which you and another person tell how you feel about each other. Closeness and warmth often result even from exchanges that start out bitter and hostile. Dr. Carl R. Rogers, a prime developer of encounter groups, tells of a workshop member who commented on the "commitment to relationship" which developed on the part of people who did not like each other initially. This member went on to observe: "The incredible fact experienced over and over . . . was that when a negative feeling was fully expressed to another, the relationship grew and the negative feeling was replaced by a deep acceptance for the other."

For effective feedback, be direct and specific. By consciously avoiding generalizations and imputations ("You're insecure"; "You're too quiet") you'll become more aware of what you actually perceive ("It seems to me you quit talking when you're disagreed with. Like when Henry interrupted you"). You'll also be giving the other person feedback he can use.

Beware of the tendency to argue, which entails making points, defending yourself, recriminating others. Argument is generally repetitious and (superficially, at least) based on reason and logic, though it is often an indirect way of expressing anger and hostility. In encounter, by contrast, you own up to your feelings and go deeper into them, no matter how dangerous or painful they seem.

Also, don't gossip—that is, talk about someone who is present and who could just as well be addressed directly. You often gossip about people when you haven't been able to handle directly the feelings they have aroused in you. This no-gossiping rule promotes the direct confrontation of feelings. In one group Bill said, "The trouble with Ann is, she's always picking on me."

"You're gossiping," he was told. "Say this to Ann."

Turning to Ann, Bill said, "You're always picking on me"—and therewith plunged into the fears and conflicts he'd been feeling with respect to her.

General Tips

1. Be adventurous. Take risks. You may feel silly at the outset, so make the conscious decision: "What the hell. I'll give it a

whirl." You can't know precisely what will happen as a result of any of these games. Be open to what comes, unbound by expectations.

2. Even if you're alone, read over the instructions aloud to help you remember them and to clarify your goals. If you engage in a game with others, be sure you all understand the instructions and objectives. Confusion on anyone's part may dampen the experience for everyone.

3. Don't push the river; let it flow by itself. Respect your own rhythms, and be aware that somebody else's ebbs and flows of attentiveness are likely to be different. Whenever time periods are given, they're intended only as general suggestions. Stay with an experience as long as you find it rewarding, and no longer.

4. If an experiment doesn't work, try it again later. The moment may then be ripe. The games in each chapter are roughly arranged in order of complexity. If you've skipped intermediate steps, it may help to go back. You're unlikely to get good results zipping from one experiment to another.

5. Even after flashes of insight and sudden breakthroughs occur, additional practice is needed for reinforcement, especially in the application of an insight to your daily life. In *You Are Not the Target* Laura A. Huxley struck an excellent recurrent theme: "It works—if you work."

6. Come out of an experience gradually. Permit ample time for reflection. If playing with others, take time afterward to share comments and observations on what you've experienced, as well as feedback. This is often as enlightening as the experience itself.

7. While many of these games can be played solo, you're likely to get more out of them if you experiment in the company of others. The shared experience can deepen relationships, and subsequent discussion can heighten your experience. Just before a group breaks up, share what you got out of the session, what you wish had been different. Hint: Pretend you're on your way home and think of what you didn't say or do when you had the chance. Share these "afterthoughts" with the others.

8. Keep noise and extraneous talk to an absolute minimum. Anything that interferes with your concentration may weaken your experience. Especially beware of the tendency to joke and chatter, which are common attempts to cut off feeling.

9. Wear your most comfortable clothing. There is a Japanese proverb to the effect that underwear that binds keeps many a soul from enlightenment. If you wear glasses, experiment with taking them off. You may see yourself in a new light, and other people may perceive you differently.

10. Refrain from smoking. It's distracting and reduces anxiety. Instead, confront the source of your anxiety when you feel the impulse to smoke. No drugs or liquor, either. You're trying to tune in to *your* self, not some chemical's.

11. Innovate. The games in this book are springboards for variations of your own devising. Invent new games freely. For general principles and suggestions see Chapter 12, "Invent Your Own Games."

Proceed with Caution

The experiments in this book can promote greater self-awareness. But in the process they may release feelings causing temporary pain and anxiety. Please heed these words of caution:

• These games are no substitute for professional psychotherapy. They are not intended to resolve complex personality problems. If you are in therapy, confer with your therapist before experimenting with games that you may find even remotely troubling.

• Avoid pressure of any sort. Never play a game if you don't wish to, and never proceed beyond the point of a player's willingness. Wheedling and cajoling ("Come on. We did it. How about you?") are just as pernicious as nagging and browbeating. Experience shows that if a person approaches a danger point, he has an instinctive tendency to stop, absorb what he's learned, and reconstruct his defenses. If this wish is respected, there is little likelihood of an adverse effect.

• Be especially careful about introducing games to captive audiences. If a person is your student or your employee or a guest in your home, he may feel he has to do what you suggest, whether he wants to or not. Always be sure someone can decline to play without feeling uncomfortable.

• It is extremely rare for a person who participates voluntarily to become extremely upset in the course of experiments like these. In the infrequent emergency stop the game. Hold the person in your arms. Reassure him. Speak soothingly to him.

Calmly help him return his attention to the immediate reality. Ask him simple questions to bring him back into contact: "What's your name?" "Who am I?" "What color are my eyes?" "What's that on the table?" Let him sleep if he wishes. If he's still upset after an hour or so, seek professional help.

PART

II

COMING
AWAKE

Why use drugs? By sharpening your senses through experiments like these, you can make the world more vibrant. Through meditation you can expand your consciousness: free your patterns of perception and bring yourself into contact with your inner zone of serenity.

3

Games for Sharpening Your Senses

On St. Mark's Place in Manhattan's East Village there is a night club called the New Electric Circus.

The main dancing room, which seems as big as an armory, explodes with stroboscopic fireworks. Computer-run projectors rain down an automated Fourth of July of ever-changing colors and shapes. A flashing amoeba forms on the ceiling, drifts downward on cigarette smoke, engulfs you, then is gone. You are a living screen for a mad collage of film clips, a human sliver in a dazzling electric kaleidoscope, a fleck of rainbow in a swirling technological prism.

And the sound. Overpowering: Rock weighed by the megaton. Live from groups with names like Cat Mother and the All-Night Newsboys. Electronic squeals. Wails. Shrieks. Bleats. Moans. Crowd noises. Pandemonium so amplified it is not heard but felt.

And the mass of humanity. The rubbing of bodies. The feel of cloth and skin against your skin. Heat and sweat and smells and closeness. Or if you prefer another sort of tactile sensation, you can lie in a pit and be caressed by lush carpeting.

Overall (perhaps surprisingly) the effect is pleasant, and you're likely to go home feeling atingle, possibly euphoric. One aim of such go-go joints is to produce a nondrug turn-on. Even liquor is *verboten*. Through multimedia stimuli you are to experience the heightened perceptions and the sense of well-being familiar to users of marijuana.

You may indeed have a sensory awakening. But even an Electric

Circus—which *Playboy* calls the "Creative Plaything of disco-thèques"—can get boring. For all the sensory excitement it offers, more and greater stimuli are needed for the same result. This is largely because your senses are reacting passively, are being over-whelmed by stimuli rather than sharpened from within. The long-term effect is not to awaken the senses but to dull sensibility.

By contrast, true sensory awakening is active. Through experi-ments such as those in this chapter, you can tone up your ability to see, hear, smell, touch, taste. Without artificial aids. And certainly without drugs.

Wake Up! You're Dreaming

During World War II an American correspondent was working in Britain, where food was severely rationed. One of his favorite foods was pickled herring. He had not had any for a long time and finally succeeded in getting some. With great ceremony he sat down to eat this treat in the company of a friend. Conversation got ani-mated. Suddenly the correspondent discovered to his horror that he had eaten the herring without tasting it.

If you carefully observe your behavior, you are likely to find that you seldom make contact with reality. Like the correspondent, your mind—and your senses—are elsewhere. You take a walk in the country but muse over problems you left behind in the city. You make love but think mainly of chores that await you when you're finished.

"What is the Tao [the way, the truth]?" asked the disciple in a parable related by the Zen scholar D. T. Suzuki.

"Your everyday mind," replied the master. He elaborated: "When I am hungry, I eat. When tired, I sleep."

The disciple was puzzled. "Is this not what everybody else does, too?"

"No," the master replied. "Most people are never wholly in what they are doing. When eating, they may be absent-mindedly preoccupied with a thousand different fantasies. When sleeping, they are not sleeping. The supreme mark of the thoroughly inte-grated man is to be without a divided mind."

Chances are you spend much of the time intellectualizing your existence, rather than experiencing it. It is as if you were a figure in a dream, so far are you from being awake. You react to new situations not by accepting them for themselves but by following pre-established patterns, allowing past experiences to color the actual. Rather than being in contact with what is, you continually operate within a frame of reference of how things were or how things could or should be. Rarely do you experience the unique, evolving differences of each event.

When you were a very young child, you were at one with your environment. All perception was a totality, like the blend of musical instruments in a symphony. You made little distinction between what was inside and outside your skin. A bird in a tree was as much an experience as the beating of your heart. Only later did you differentiate them and conclude that one sensation was external and fleeting, the other internal and permanent. In so doing you lost your ability to fully experience the bird, to *be* the bird to the utmost of your senses.

Still later you learned where your body ended, and through fumbling, stumbling trial and error you learned to coordinate its various parts. Now skilled at maneuvering your body, you came to take it for granted. No longer did you wonder over your heartbeat or experiment with the touch in your fingers.

► If you wish to re-experience this early marveling in a small way, take your pulse, especially if you've never done it before. Press a finger to the pulsating artery on the thumb side of your wrist—and reflect on what a magic machine you are. (More body-awareness experiments are in Chapter 5, "Games for Enlivening Your Body.")

As you got older, you lost your sense of the immediate. "I think Freddy is schizophrenic," the mother of a little boy remarked. "One minute he's howling with anger. The next, he's all smiles again." To this extent Freddy is saner than his mother. When provoked, he's angry. With the provocation gone he reacts in a way appropriate now. Unlike Freddy, most adults are burdened by outdated feelings. Instead of responding to each moment anew, you may blur your senses with a reaction born long ago and carried forward by habit.

As a child, your natural sense of yourself and the world gradually and inescapably became smothered by learned responses to other

people's expectations. You saw and heard what your parents
wanted you to see and hear—though it meant shutting your eyes
and stopping up your ears. An interesting creature became a "filthy
insect," to be loathed rather than enjoyed. Joyous yodeling became
"noise," which "nice children" didn't make.

"We do not perceive ourselves and the world about us as they
are but as we have been persuaded to perceive them," Dr. Willis
W. Harman, director of an Educational Policy Research Center of
the U.S. Office of Education, has noted. "Our limitations are primarily not inherent but are those which we have [accepted]
through the suggestions of others. And our usual unawareness that
this is so is part of the hypnosis."

When you were delivered to the doorstep of your school, your
sentient days were numbered. As a matter of curriculum, your perceptions were suppressed. The emphasis was on verbal expression
rather than on physical reality. On the intellectual rather than on
the emotional. On working and playing well with others rather
than on developing your own potential.

And so, as an infant, you could bask with wordless delight in the
warmth of the sun. You could be the sunshine, both in it and of it,
as a fish is in and of water. Alas, society got hold of you, and by
the time you were in the third grade you were writing blah com-
positions about "Mister Sun."

As an adult, your contact with physical experience became ever
more dulled through years of exposure to an onslaught of perceptions. "The twentieth century is, among other things, the Age of
Noise," wrote Aldous Huxley in *The Perennial Philosophy*. "And
no wonder: for all the resources of our almost miraculous technology have been thrown into the current assault against silence."

Automobiles, for example, can be viewed as hulks of potential
noise, from the first starting of an engine at the factory to the final
shriek of brakes before the junkyard. There are more than 80,000,-
000 cars in this country. The noise level of urban life is exhausting
and irritating. As are the crowds. Stand in a bus or train terminal
during rush hour, and note the glazed eyes of passers-by. Life is
overwhelming. In self-defense people become zombies.

Radio and TV are cannon keeping the sensory barrage up everywhere. Thanks to the cheap transistor, there is no sanctuary. A

mountain climber labored up Mount Washington in New Hampshire. He found the climbers who had arrived before him listening to the World Series over a pocket radio.

"The din penetrates the mind," noted Huxley, "filling it with a babel of distraction—news items, mutually irrelevant bits of information, blasts of . . . music, continually repeated doses of drama that bring no catharsis but merely create a craving for daily or even hourly emotional enemas. And where . . . the stations support themselves by selling time to advertisers, the noise is carried from the ears, through the realms of phantasy, knowledge and feeling to the ego's central core of wish and desire."

In the global village wrought by TV both the marvelous and the appalling quickly become commonplace. Men walk on the moon. The dream of centuries is realized. Yet after viewing the first moon walk live for only a short time, millions found the event tedious and went to bed. Atrocities, burnings and deaths are brought into your living room daily from Vietnam. On our side are the perpetrators as well as the victims. Who can feel outrage every single evening? Who can help but eventually be bored?

Small wonder, then, that you've lost touch with the simple delights of a minute perception—such as becoming aware of the air against your face, or observing the subtle ballet of grass in a breeze, or savoring fully the aromas of spring. Your swaddled and weary senses restrain you in a land of suspension and removal, where the qualities of distance and separation seem inescapable. You may let nothing really touch you, and so you become a slave to automatic living. Thus, you deny yourself the fullness of living, which requires that you be able to open your senses fully and to direct your awareness.

"To be aware that we are asleep is to be on the point of waking; and to be aware that we are only partially awake is the first condition of becoming . . . more fully awake," an English psychologist, A. R. Orage, has written.

Sensory awakening is a method of unfreezing situations and yourself so that you may make sensory contact with the richness of each event. It seeks to rebalance the nonverbal aspects of your life that have long been overweighted by the intellect. In short, it seeks to bring you back to your senses. For starters, this game:

COCOON

In contrast with the insect world, humans start out as butterflies and end up in cocoons.

"Man is encapsulated," notes Dr. Joseph R. Royce of the University of Alberta. "If man wishes to gain a more inclusive worldview or to approach ultimate reality, it will be necessary for him to break through the several cocoons within which he is inevitably encapsulated. The first step in this process is to recognize that he is, in fact, encapsulated. Unfortunately, this first step is the most difficult."

To help you sense the cocoon you're in, you'll need a young colleague. Ideally, he'll be under a year old, a crawler getting into things with unrestrained curiosity.

► Take an object familiar in your daily life—a toothbrush, a shoe, a tomato. You see it every day. But this time study it as if you hadn't seen it before. Stop when you become bored. Restlessness demarks the wall of your sensory cocoon.

Study It As If You Hadn't Seen It Before

Now give the object to the child, and watch how he explores it. If it interests him, you may see him almost merge with it in the intensity of his awareness. What you're witnessing is unclouded perception, a natural gift you had until outside pressures took it away from you.

Follow the child around the house. See what he picks up to investigate. Does he turn it around and look at it, smell it, taste it, try to break or bounce it? Try to experience it as he does. At first this will be extremely difficult, for it is likely that your urge will be to ward off awareness. The capsule enclosing you is designed to shut out sensory stimulation.

Every rending of the cocoon is an accomplishment. If the going is slow, it may amuse you to know the words of a Mexican living in Los Angeles. He smuggled relatives into the United States and counseled them, "Look here, Americans are a very nice kind of people, but there is one point where they are very touchy. You must not let them know they are corpses."

Tune In to the Moment

This moment is all that exists. This fleeting instant—this *now*—is the only reality. The past is gone forever. The future is not yet born.

To illustrate: By the time you finish reading this sentence, two or three seconds will have elapsed.

Those seconds are now dead. Though represented by a finger's length of type, they are beyond reach, irretrievably lost to the past. All events are like drops of water running downstream. Not one instant that has swept by will ever come back.

Likewise, the future is unformed. The content of the merest microsecond from now will be the product of an infinity of alternatives still shapeless in eternity. Right now you can't experience even what comes next in this paragraph. If you took your eyes from these words to speculate, you'd probably guess wrong: Play it again, Sam. Bing-bang-boom and the hell with it. Bubble, bubble, toil and trouble. Cigarettes may cause cancer, but chewing gum gives me gas. End of paragraph—could you envision the claptrap that came up?

Your body is in the now. But if you're like most people, your mind is in the past or in the future. You grieve or glory over events of long ago. You harbor resentments and guilt and shame—hangovers from the past. You think of what you should have said or what might have been. You fear and fantasize over the future. You try to peer into your mind's-eye crystal ball in an effort to anticipate what will be.

All of which cuts you off from the present like a dark screen. You can physically see and hear only what *is* at this moment. You can have sensory awakening only if you experience the now.

If you bring your mind from miles away to the activity of the moment, if you abate the clatter in your head to focus on the physical reality around your body, you'll gradually experience a surprising sense of well-being. Indeed, tuning in to the now is one gateway to perceiving eternity. The philosopher Ludwig Wittgenstein observed: "If we take eternity to mean not infinite temporal duration but timelessness, the eternal life belongs to those who live in the present." By experiencing a moment for itself, you stop time. Time is defined as the interval between two events. When you are in the now, there is no interval. Only the event alone.

Perceiving the now is hardly easy. A Danish mystic once told the story of God's sending the angel Gabriel to earth to offer eternal life in exchange for a moment of man's time. But the angel had to return to God without delivering the gift. When he reached earth, he discovered that everyone was living with one foot in the past and the other in the future, and no one had a moment of time.

You may be baffled, even angered or exhilarated, by the implications of the seemingly simple idea of being in the now. You're likely to be intrigued by the many ways you keep yourself from immediate awareness.

You may leave the now by musing over the "if" or the "should have been"—imaginary reflections wholly unrelated to your present reality. The past subjunctive—"should have said," "should have been"—is the most useless verb form in English grammar and can well be struck from your vocabulary. When you use it, all you're doing is moaning that something you want to have happened didn't. You are describing a longing for a mythical, unattainable paradise.

You may seek escape from *your* reality by focusing on other people. This is common among parents who live through their children. The entire process, a cottage industry in some families, is likely to be one of selfishness, masked as generosity. A parent may say, "I'm sacrificing so you can go to college and be a success." What he often means is, "I'm willing to pay plenty to stay home and be a failure." If you live through someone else, you are having him live *for* you. If you have him be your eyes and ears, you are avoiding looking and listening on your own.

Hero-worshipers live through a mythical figure, be he Napoleon or a current football star. A fan burst into tears on reading that an entertainer and his wife were splitting up. "They seemed so happy!" she sobbed. However, she shut out the evidence that her own marriage was on the rocks.

Any type of fanaticism is an escape from awareness. The true believer, whether a political or a religious zealot, surrenders his senses to some others' view of reality, the codification of which is called orthodoxy.

Another way of escaping from your reality is to depersonalize your thoughts and feelings. Do you attribute what's on *your* mind to the generalized "you" or "one" or "people"? Thus, "You can't trust people" may be translated as "I don't trust anyone." A therapist at Esalen forbids members of his encounter groups to fuzz up their statements with "some of us" or "we" when they really mean "I," as in "Some of us think you're a shit."

"That's a cop-out," he declares. "If you think I'm a shit, take responsibility for saying so."

Perhaps you withdraw from a gut reaction to the moment by letting your head take over. Do you draw abstractions and conclusions—not seeing the present moment as it is but how it relates to a larger picture? The epitome of this tendency was reached by the fellow who dismissed his Joblike misfortunes with "Well, after all, earth is only a minor planet."

Since the Age of Freud, psychologizing has become a favorite form of intellectualization. Bandying about terminology lifted from clinical psychology is often a chilly attempt at putting emotions at arm's length. Do you interpret your feelings in psychological terms, instead of experiencing the feelings as they affect your gut? "I'm having a paranoid reaction," someone may say—in contrast with, "I'm scared. My shoulders are tense. My stomach is churning."

Wittiness is yet another way of withdrawing from a gut-level response. If you pun when talking about your feelings, it's likely that you're less conscious of what you're experiencing than of how cleverly you're expressing it. Punning can be a verbal defense against feeling. One unhappy daughter punned, "My parents and I have a financial relationship. We're partners in guilt-edged bonds." Punning can signal the dulling of even pleasurable feelings. Said a husband, stroking his wife, "You're a tactile sensation."

Wit and sarcasm are to humor somewhat as the two ugly stepsisters are to Cinderella. Humor is generally warm and devoid of bitterness. Wit and sarcasm are highly cerebral and often mask hostility. They can be useful as safety valves, when a painful emotion would otherwise be too uncomfortable to bear. Neither wit nor sarcasm responds spontaneously to the now. Humor almost always does, which is one reason why an episode you've found delightful or comical often falls flat in the telling. An entire scene was needed for Shakespeare to convey the smiles in Romeo's first approach to Juliet or Henry V's meeting with Katharine. By contrast, mere one-liners of wit and sarcasm can survive for centuries. Alexander the Great's deathbed witticism—"I die by the help of too many physicians"—is as durable as it is icy. It sounds almost as if Alexander were speaking of someone else, whereas he was witnessing his own life coming to an end.

Possibly you believe that you perceive the past, as well as the present. "I remember such and such distinctly," you might say. Actually, memory is a function of your mind right now. Recall any significant event of your life. Your recollection is in the present. The actual experience was in the past.

Moreover, however detailed a memory may seem, it is rarely identical with the event. On the scene you may have been inattentive or made assumptions, or misunderstood what was happening. Your initial misperceptions will gain credence as memories in much the same way that inaccurate newspaper reports acquire the luster of truth when written up as history. A memory is necessarily selective, since you always see life through the blinders surrounding your own situation. Yet listen to the memories people lay claim to. If taken literally, "I remember World War II" is a whopper. You don't even remember yesterday in reliable detail. What you recall is a keyhole view of a dimly lighted room, peeped at in passing.

An event, and the ensuing memory, is also subject to distortion, depending on your emotional make-up. You will see what you want to see—and this misperception will shape your memory. A friend of ours, who is a bit of a prude, read this chapter in manuscript. Our lead about the New Electric Circus was exactly the same as you've read. But George "distinctly remembered" a description of couples "screwing in a carpeted pit."

Much resistance to the concept of the now is the product of misunderstanding. Many people new to this existential view of reality translate it into a requirement: that you should live only in the now. Thus, they reject the concept by decrying apparent absurdities: "What about learning from the past? What about planning for the future?"

Of course, everything has its origin in the past, and the present inevitably develops into the future. In matters of the head, of the practical world, it is essential to derive reasonable expectations on the basis of experience. Otherwise it would be impossible to live. Some forms of mental retardation are so severe that the victims never comprehend fire. Striking a match is always a new experience, and—with no understanding of the consequences—they are forever in danger of going up in flames.

Nonetheless, the concept of the now has great validity in dealing with emotions and the senses. Now is a point in eternity at which you are in touch with the ongoing process. Past and future take their bearings continuously from the present and must be related to it. Without reference to the present they become meaningless.

In the analogy drawn by Dr. Frederick S. Perls, the developer of Gestalt therapy and a key figure in the Human Potential Movement, now is a phonograph needle. Life is the record. "If I play a phonograph record," noted Fritz Perls in *Gestalt Therapy Verbatim*, "the sound of the record appears when the record and the needle touch each other, where they make contact. There is no sound of the before; there is no sound of the afterwards. If I stop the phonograph record, then the needle is still in contact with the record, but there is no music, because there is *absolute* now. If you would blot out the past, or the anticipation of themes three minutes from now, you could not understand listening to that record you are playing. But if you blot out the now, nothing will come through."

NOW I AM AWARE

This is the most important single growth game. The idea of the now, of the immediate moment, of the content and structure of your present experience, is one of the most potent, most pregnant and most elusive principles in humanistic psychology.

▶ This game consists of stating explicitly what you are, at this moment, aware of. To firm up your contact with the present, begin each sentence with the words "Now I. . . ."

The game is likely to be most productive if you play it the first time or so with a friend. Remaining in present awareness is a taxing discipline that can usually be maintained only for short periods. A friend can help guide you into a now experience and also help restore you to the now if you slip out.

► First focus on the external world. Let your eyes roam about the room, settling on objects at random. State specifically what you see. Note how distinctive an object is when you see it as a unique thing of the immediate moment. What smells and tastes do you experience? What do you hear?

In the following illustration Carl is being guided by his friend Ron.

CARL: Now I look around this room. Now I see your desk. Now I see the clock. It's slow, no?
RON: Stay in the now.
CARL: Sorry.
RON: Now I . . .
CARL: Now I see the poster on the wall. Now I see a smudge on that poster. Now I see a tear in the corner. I think I did that. [*Catches self.*] Now I hear the clock.

► Now close your eyes, and concentrate on your bodily sensations. Start with the big toe of one foot. Sense the inside of it, then the skin around it, then the space between it and the next toe. Repeat for every part of your body, to the top of your head. To increase your awareness, try breathing deeply as you focus.

A friend serving as a guide can be especially helpful.

CARL: My mind's starting to wander.
RON [*taking the lead where Carl left off*]: Now feel inside your thighs. Now feel the skin, the hair. On top. Underneath. Now feel the space between your thighs. Now feel your pants' legs against the skin. Now feel your genitals. Go inside them.

► Lastly, tune in to your emotions. What are you feeling in the gut? Sometimes emotional responses will swell and recede in waves. Other times an emotion will deepen and grow ever more intense. Let them take you where they will. As you express negative feelings —guilt, resentment, jealousy—you're likely to find that they disappear. Conversely, positive feelings—love, warmth, joy—are likely to become stronger.

CARL [*referring to an argument with his daughter*]: Now I'm feeling sorry I gave her a snotty answer this morning. [*He later came back to this.*] I'm really depressed. Oh, God, I feel like such a bastard. Now I feel like crying.

RON: Stay with the feeling.

CARL: I am crying. . . . Now I feel better. Now I'm seeing my daughter again. God, I love that kid.

Silence Your Inner Voice

A cluttered attic is a special problem of highly verbal people. For an experiment suddenly ask a friend, "What are you doing right now?" He is likely to be talking to himself.

The mind is full of loose words, isolated phrases, commands, complaints. An inner chatterbox is perpetually lecturing, justifying, haranguing. There are unending rehearsals, recriminations, fantasy arguments, even puns and quips.

This malady is universal, but most prevalent in those who tend to intellectualize their feelings. Intellectualizers often confuse themselves with intellectuals. They may well engage in activities requiring the creative use of their ability to reason. But on the gut level the intellectualizer attempts to be objective about his personal experience, which largely means to theorize in words about himself and his world.

By this method he avoids contact with emotions and with non-verbal reality. He lives a substitute life of words. He is isolated from the rest of his personality and is contemptuous of his body.

The words flooding his mind thus wash out direct contact with the moment. Here are some ways to silence this inner voice.

LISTEN WITHOUT LABELING

Hearing is the critical sense in the now, for it's the sign that your internal voice is shut off and you're in contact with the fleeting sounds of the environment. The heightening of one sense is often accompanied by the sharpening of all the senses. So if you concentrate on your hearing, you're likely to find that you are seeing, tasting, smelling and touching more acutely as well.

► One way to make yourself more sensitive to sounds is to tap vigorously around your ear. The stimulation will tone up your hearing.

► Relax, close your eyes and immerse yourself in the sounds around you: the air conditioner, a bird, people talking, a plane passing overhead. First try to identify every one. Strain at this to become aware of your impulse to label sounds. Then realize that these labels ("vacuum cleaner," "footsteps") are not what you're hearing at all. If you wrote down symbols that more nearly represent the sounds you hear, you'd have "sssshhhh," "bzzzzzzz," "whnggg" and so forth. Note how inadequate words and symbols are for representing the richness and variety of auditory sensations.

► Now turn off the labeling part of your brain, and feel the sounds, with no thought of how they originate. It can be as if you're in the middle of a symphony orchestra.

BRING THE SUBVOCAL TO THE SURFACE

► Listen carefully to your inner voice, as if you were a member of the audience you're addressing. Notice how much of your subvocal speaking is one-sided, not an interpersonal give-and-take.

► Next, say aloud what's running through your mind, whispering at first, then speaking louder. Speaking it forth brings the subvocal to where you can deal with it.

To whom are you speaking? For what purpose? Are you trying to impress? Gain approval? Are you holding back something? Seeking to excuse yourself? What is your tone? Angry? Wailing? Bombastic? Continue talking until you have a clear idea of whom you're addressing and to what end.

► Now try to keep internally silent. At first this may be impossible for more than a few seconds at a time, for your internal blabbermouth will start up again. Notice the difference between inner silence and inner jabber, and alternate them by coordinating them with your breathing.

Be without words while you inhale. As you exhale, speak out whatever words have formed. If you persevere, you can look forward to training yourself to experience longer and more consistent periods of internal silence, with a corresponding clarifying of emotion and heightening of sensory awareness.

RELISH SILENCE

▶ Work at keeping silent while in the company of other people. Try it for five minutes at first, then ten minutes, then gradually for longer periods of time. Your internal voice is often the product of rehearsing what you're going to say. Freeing yourself from the need to talk also frees you from having to rehearse.

Listen to the chatter around you, with no thought of taking part. Notice how little need there is to respond to most social chitchat and how false much talk is: role playing, seeking to impress, saying what one feels one ought. All this becomes clear as you permit yourself to be a spectator to other people's games of verbal volleyball.

Recognize the different qualities of silence. How restful is the silence resulting from a freedom from chatter, as compared to the nervous silence of a social situation when you wish someone would talk to you. There is the comfortable silence between good friends, who need not keep up a running conversation to prove their friendship. Best of all is the silence that permits you to be alone with your thoughts and with your awareness of the environment.

The World of Things

Some people can't enjoy a garden unless they know the names of all the flowers. Similarly, there are those who can't evaluate a painting simply by looking at it. They have to know the title, the artist, his period and what the critics have said.

When you were very young, you were able to enjoy a thing for itself. When David Benjamin Lewis, age two, was taken on walks in Manhattan, he would rhapsodize over dog droppings as if they were fine sculpture. "Nice!" he'd exclaim, and try to take them home.

Later things were categorized and placed on a value scale. This approach is promoted by schools, through their easy-to-grade multiple-choice and short-answer exams—an emphasis leading to an accumulation of trivia disguised as knowledge.

Throughout the educational process there's an emphasis on the verbal as opposed to the nonverbal, on the written as opposed to the experiential. True knowledge is rooted in your emotions, fantasies and actions and is not merely deposited in your internal data bank. This is the difference between reading about revolutions and sensing what it is like to experience the anxieties and uncertainties of revolutionary change.

The following experiments aim to point up the thing behind the word.

WORDS VERSUS THINGS

► Pick up an ordinary object, like a pencil. Examine it closely for five minutes. Notice as many of its qualities as you can: the lead, the wood, the color it is painted, the texture, the scratches and rubbings and discolorations, the shape, the length to which it is sharpened.

Intermittently, every thirty seconds or so, say the word for it aloud. Note how inadequate the word "pencil" is to describe the thing.

EXPERIENCE A ROCK

Chances are you have a tendency to derive an impression from one sense alone. Something is predominantly seen or touched or heard but rarely experienced by a total you responding to a total it. This limited perception may be further narrowed if you feel a need to make judgments: to decide if something is beautiful or ugly, good or bad, useful or useless.

► As an illustrative exercise, experience a rock with all your senses. Look at it carefully. Taste it. Touch it. Hear the sound it makes in your hands and against other surfaces. Feel its weight. Smell it. Compared to the actual rock, note how shallow is an evaluation like "good" or "bad," or "beautiful" or "ugly."

Buryl Payne once had the members of a seminar experience rocks in this fashion. "As usual," he reported, "a number of persons fell in love with their rocks and wanted to keep them, a . . . common result of really being here-now with anything, be it a rock, a bite of food, or another person."

THISNESS

People often don't see specifics, because their minds are clouded by abstractions and generalities. A biographer once observed that Woodrow Wilson was so fuzzy-minded that he couldn't look at a railroad train without seeing a misty gray thing called Transportation.

By contrast, Aldous Huxley once gazed at a small vase of flowers after taking mescaline. Earlier that day he had merely noted the dissonance of its colors. "But that was no longer the point," he recalled in *The Doors of Perception*. "I was not looking now at an unusual flower arrangement. I was seeing what Adam had seen on the morning of his creation—the miracle, moment by moment, of naked existence."

"Is it agreeable?" a companion asked.

"Neither agreeable nor disagreeable," answered Huxley. "It just is."

▶ To approximate this sense of the uniqueness of things, take a look around you, and observe out loud *"This* room." *"This* chair." *"This* scratch." Try it on a walk outdoors. The most familiar things can assume new significance—a dazzling thisness, a concrete individuality, that causes them to leap out at you in full dimension.

Ralph Waldo Emerson once observed: "These roses under my window make no reference to former roses or to better ones; they are for what they are; they exist with God today."

Open Your Eyes

Just as you may be deafened by an inner voice, so you may be blinded by an internal watchman.

Many people have a self-conscious sense of always being stared at, often a result of having been looked at harshly in early life by parents. Carrying such a policeman around inside you can be extremely inhibiting. Such an encumbrance may restrict not only your behavior but your perception, permitting you to view the world only in ways acceptable to this internal dictator.

A person who behaves as if he were always being watched is generally frightened of appearances. To coin a term, he may be an inhibitionist, slow to try things for fear of seeming ridiculous. He feels constantly scrutinized and can't imagine that most people are either friendly or indifferent. He is sure that they must regard him with the cold, critical eyes of his parents.

Conversely, you may play the watcher rather than the watched, acting out the role of the unsleeping observer inside you. Such people look on, sitting silent in groups, being spectators instead of participants. They are critics, judges—always outsiders to the richness of experience. Life for them is a flower seen through the florist's window.

RELAX YOUR VISION

Instead of seeing, it's likely you spend much of your time staring.

Out of habit you may overfocus on detail rather than relaxing and taking in broader outlines. You may concentrate on the figure to the exclusion of the background. By so using your eyes, you can strain them and often miss more than you see.

An entire universe lies behind the world you habitually look at. To experience it, relax the muscles of your eyes.

▶ Become cross-eyed for a few seconds by staring at the tip of your nose. This approximates how you ordinarily overfocus. The sensation is much like chronic eyestrain.

▶ Now gaze off into the distance. Resist the temptation to rest your eyes on a particular thing. With practice you may feel your eyeballs loosening, somewhat like a woman taking off a girdle.

With your eyes thus freed, focus gently on relatively distant objects. When you stare, you see what's a few feet in front of you and nothing else. With your eyes relaxed, your vision can move easily from an object 10 feet away to something 100 feet away to a third thing 30 feet away and so on. You'll find that the world takes on new and enjoyable depth.

▶ If you suffer from eyestrain, try lying down and concentratedly exploring the tension in your eyes. After a minute or so cup the palms of your hands over your open eyes. Rest the heels of your hands on your cheeks, your fingers on your forehead.

Do this for a minute, then slowly remove your hands. Any relief? Do you wish to express the tension you feel in other ways—by stretching your arms, arching your back, yawning? Follow your impulse. Then repeat palming your eyes two or three more times.

Sight is often impaired by a blocking resulting from muscular tension in and around the eyes.

► For a quick demonstration of how the face muscles can limit eye movement, furrow your brow as much as possible, and see how it limits your gazing up, as if you were looking out from under a shelf.

One young woman had a habit of keeping her eyes turned upward. She saw herself as a guilty little girl, looking up all the time to see if her parents were watching. Some visual impairments are not so immediately evident. If, from childhood, a person never gets over a fear of looking into his parents' eyes, he may grow up unconsciously constricted in what he permits himself to see.

To help remove these blinders, here are two experiments.

► Rest comfortably on your back, and open your eyes as wide as you can. Turn your eyeballs as far to the right as they can go. Then look all the way up. To the left. Then down. Don't just whirl your eyes, but deliberately focus on a spot at each position. Breathe deeply with each movement. Repeat rhythmically for ten rotations.

► Open your eyes as wide as you can, and inhale deeply. Squeeze them as tight as you can, and exhale forcibly. Repeat ten times.

"How significant is the enormous heightening . . . of the perception of color!" exclaimed Aldous Huxley after his mescaline trip, described in *The Doors of Perception.* "Mescaline raises all colors to a higher power and makes the perceiver aware of the innumerable fine shades of difference, to which, at ordinary times, he is completely blind."

Without having taken drugs, mystics and sensitives have reported much the same experience. Dr. Shafica Karagulla, a neuropsychiatrist and researcher, has found a number of individuals with an evidently high degree of sensory perception. They claim to see energy fields surrounding people. These bands of colors reportedly vary with each person's emotional state and, sensitives say, can match the rainbow in splendor.

You may not be able to see the aura surrounding the body, but you can become more sensitive to color.

▶ For a whole day notice a particular color. Start out with a primary color, like red, and you'll soon discover how many shades of red there are. You'll also see how inadequate their names are. What color precisely is crimson or vermilion or magenta or scarlet? How many gradations of red cannot be described verbally? In the same way, focus on the other primary colors and on particular hues like turquoise or chartreuse or tangerine.

▶ Note how colors appear in combinations with other colors, how rarely colors appear in pure form. In school you may have gotten used to coloring apples red, bananas yellow, oranges orange. Examine these fruits and see what colors they really are.

Good painters are often able to overcome such "education" and remain well attuned to color. One unusually persistent child was banished from his kindergarten class for arguing that tree trunks are rarely brown, as his teacher had painted them, but are more often shades of gray and black. Look at a good portrait or still life or landscape, and see how many colors the artist has used to express the face, the objects, the countryside and sky.

PERSPECTIVE

By virtue of binocular vision you are capable of seeing in three dimensions. However, as a result of tension and trauma, most people, except on rare occasions, see a paper-flat world. An experiment to revive three-dimensional perspective is as follows:

▶ First, to point up a bad visual habit, stare fixedly at a tree. Try to grasp its precise shape and nothing else. Your attention is likely to wander.

But if you let your gaze play around the tree, defining its surroundings, you are likely to find visual excitement. The shape of the tree will become clearer. That's because (in the view of Gestalt psychology and Zen) the tree is not only its trunk and branches and leaves, but its surroundings. Now direct your gaze *behind* the tree. Watch how it leaps out at you.

Instead of looking at the branches of the tree, relax your vision, and look at the spaces between and around the branches. These shapes, possibly heretofore unnoticed, are also part of the tree. Painters and sculptors are especially aware of them and term them negative spaces.

It's *All* Part of the Tree

Walk about, and watch how perspectives change. All belong to the tree. The tree is many trees. Its surroundings are many surroundings.

If you keep at this experiment, you may have a rare and wonderful experience: The tree in all its perspectives, its multitude of surroundings, the field, the bushes, the sky—all may merge into one unified perception. In an illumination of the sort found in Zen you may glimpse the oneness, the integrity, the totality of all things.

Improve Your Touch

Touch is one of the neglected senses. Though used continually, it ordinarily is only marginally noticed. Only rarely are you likely to have an unalloyed, enjoyable touch experience. For example, are you truly in touch with the tactile possibilities around you right now? What about the book you're holding? The clothing on your body? The chair on which you're sitting?

In this culture touching others is discouraged. It is equated with sexuality and aggressiveness. Americans who work overseas often speak of being "manhandled" in lands where touching is an expression of warmth widely used even among casual acquaintances. Latin Americans are used to standing closer to one another than are people in the United States. Anthropologist Edward T. Hall tells of a conversation between a U.S. business executive and a Latin associate. The Latin, feeling too far away, kept moving closer. The American, feeling crowded, moved back, prompting the Latin to advance again. As the chase proceeded, both men became angry —the American because he found the Latin "pushy," the Latin because the American was "cold."

In a sermon entitled "The Human Touch—Who Needs It?" the Reverend Michael J. Young of the Palo Alto (California) Unitarian Church commented: "We adults have limited touch to three areas. We allow the handshake and similar symbolic, but safe, gestures. We may touch in sexual intercourse. And we may touch in hostility, where one feeling—anger—protects us from the others that might burst out. That is just about it! So far as a language of touch is concerned, we have condemned ourselves to a sort of pig Latin, where, when we touch at all, our meaning must always be veiled."

Here are some games to improve your sense of touch.

IN YOUR HANDS

You can get more out of the organs of touch you are most used to. To bring you into consciousness of what probably, by now, has become rote habit, try a hand-washing experiment.

► Slowly wash with water, experiencing the texture of water alone, of one hand against the other. Then wash with soap as well. Experience the sensations of drying your hands in the air. Compare this with drying them with a towel. Now, instead of using water, wash with table salt, then with flour, with soil, with pebbles. Compare the various sensations.

HANDLE YOUR SURROUNDINGS

You ordinarily touch things only with your fingers and palms and (in tasting) your lips. This shortchanges your sense of touch, for the entire surface of your body is covered with sensitive nerve endings. For a pleasurable sensation use to the maximum the tactile equipment available to you.

► Explore a room with all parts of your body. Your feet for example are extremely sensitive. Your face, too, can be exquisite in sensitivity. Keep your eyes closed to accentuate perception by touch. Note the differences of surfaces: the cool smoothness of a plastic tabletop, the warmth and roughness of a rug, the slickness of some metals, the fragility of some cloths. Notice the variety of curves and corners. Feel where one texture ends and another begins.

How does it feel to touch things with your cheeks and nose? How sensitive is the back of your hand or the sole of your foot? How does something feel when it rests against your belly? Or when you hold it between your thighs?

The way in which you approach the act of touch exploration may tell much about you. Albert Pesso, an authority on movement and emotional expressions, has seen that people in his workshops vary markedly in their approaches to touching. He noted in *Movement in Psychotherapy*: "Some touch with their whole hands in contact with the surfaces being explored. Some touch with the barest of fingertips. Some seem to be curious to find how it feels to touch with all parts of the body and are touching with their toes, their feet, and any part of the body they possibly can. Some remain standing all the while they explore, while some can be seen prone on the floor with their arms and legs outstretched, feeling with all that is in contact. Some climb on top of whatever objects of furniture are in the room. Some creep under all surfaces and feel the underside of tables and chairs."

SELF-TOUCHING

Touching yourself can be fun. But if you are unaccustomed to the idea of manual self-exploration, touching yourself may suggest vanity, masturbation, perverted self-love. Some hypochondriacs can envision touching themselves only when searching for palpable tumors. Albert Pesso has found that some people feel so guilty about sensual self-exploration that the experience produces in them the sensation of impending death.

Here is a self-touching experiment that is highly sensitizing.

▶ Relax on the floor, with your eyes closed. Lay your hand ever so gently on your chest, and focus on the sensation—it may remind you of a flower unfolding. Feel the sensation in your hand as well; *it* also is being touched, by your chest.

Slowly raise your hand, and sense the aftertouch. Explore all the surfaces of your body. Try varying the pressure of your hand, from barely perceptible to gentle to firm. Then try stroking.

On your face and head feel the change in topography of your brow. Rub your fingers across the faint ridges surrounding your eyes. Note the transition from hairless brow to hairline to fullness of hair. Notice the sensation as the hair is moved.

As you run your fingers across the bridge of your nose, feel the variations from rigid bone to softer cartilage. Feel the skin of your cheeks pressed across your cheekbones. Note the hollows beneath your cheekbones.

Explore changes in the shape and texture of your flesh, bones, hair, clothing and so on, so that you truly get to know yourself. At first you may feel uncomfortable in taking pleasure from your body. As this experiment proceeds, you're likely to find it easy to let yourself go and enjoy the fascination of your body.

Taste and Smell

Taste and smell, which are closely related physiologically, often succumb to the taboos against bodily pleasures. Both are highly sensual senses. Unlike seeing and hearing, they rarely serve purposes that a Puritan would find "practical." Like touch, they generally require proximity to the object perceived, thus are inhibited in a culture that makes closeness of nearly any sort unwelcome.

The sense of smell is particularly de-emphasized. There are primitive tribesmen—the aborigines of Australia, for example—who have a sense of smell almost as keen as that of hunting dogs and have many words to describe gradations and types of smells. By contrast, among most of us the ability to smell is underdeveloped from nonuse.

Body odors can be highly erotic, which may help account for the reason why uptight cultures deem them vulgar. In households that spend umpteen dollars each year on soaps and deodorants, children inevitably acquire a pronounced squeamishness about natural physical odors. One of the first expletives most children learn is "It stinks!"

Your sense of taste is likely to be a victim of culinary overkill. As a child, were you forced to eat what you didn't like, or more than you wanted? To tune out an unpleasant experience, you may have early acquired the habit of eating without tasting.

► Food is often overspiced. Subtle natural flavors, which would challenge and reward your sense of taste, are lost under a deluge of ketchup and an avalanche of salt. Increasingly, foods are becoming conglomerations of flavored chemicals that taste artificial. To glimpse the difference, have a cup of instant coffee sweetened with saccharin and lightened with a nondairy milk substitute; then sample a cup of freshly brewed coffee mixed with sugar and cream.

A child brought up on orange juice from a can simply does not know what the juice of a fresh orange tastes like. Cartoonist Mike Rokoff has depicted a mammoth soup factory. In front of a vat the size of a swimming pool stands a chemist sampling a ladle of soup. He's saying, "Needs more hydrolyzed protein derivative."

EXPLORE LIKE AN INFANT

As a small child, you put things in your mouth as a means of experiencing them. As you crawled on all fours, your nose was an effective organ for exploration. When you were broken of the habit of tasting things at random, you may have been rescued from possible accidental poisoning, but you nonetheless lost an effective way of making contact with your environment. When you learned to stand, you gained stature but lost out on the development of your sense of smell.

► To recapture your senses of taste and smell, shut your eyes. Touch your tongue to objects around you. (Don't worry about germs, which are ubiquitous anyway and for the most part harmless. Bacteriologists are amused at precautions taken by nervous mothers.) Note the great variety of flavors, textures, temperatures ("And germs," we can hear some mothers say).

Simultaneously sniff the objects. Close exploration with the nose will reveal that nearly everything has a distinctive odor. Indeed, the added dimensions of taste and smell will give a new identity to most things you thought you knew well. Smell the things in your cupboard, refrigerator, spice cabinet.

► Try eating with your eyes closed. Concentrating on tastes and smells can make food an experience beyond the mere eating. Even the lowly frankfurter can assume subtleties and shadings, and a meal can become like a symphony.

Orchestrate Your Senses

This chapter has sought to make you more alive to the world about you. At first, you are likely to experience the benefits of only one sense at a time. With practice you can become aware of an experience as a total entity, with your senses combined rather than fragmented.

► Take in the total sensations that you experience while doing ordinary household chores. Making the beds, washing the dishes and other routine activities can become enormously exciting if you treat them as sensory adventures.

► Absorb yourself in the experience of a walk. Look at a tree in all its perspectives. Listen to the rustle of its leaves. Feel the bark. Smell and taste a leaf.

A SENSORY CLIMAX

Dr. George I. Brown of the University of California at Santa Barbara and Bernard Gunther, director of sensory-awareness programs at Esalen, have developed total sensory experiences out of peeling and eating an orange. Do the following experiment in slow motion. The detail of the instructions reflects the slow pace at which to proceed.

► First, hold the orange in your hand, and experience it with your eyes closed. Sense its temperature and texture. Try to get to know what is different about it. See if you can really get to know it, so that if it were mixed up with many others, you could pick it out. Is it perfectly round? Where are differences in its contours?

Touch it to the flesh of your hands, your arms, your face. How does your skin feel after the orange has touched it?

Get to know its smell. Do various parts smell different?

Open your eyes. See if the orange corresponds with what you smelled and felt. What do you see of its shape, its color, the markings on its skin? How is your orange unique?

Can you pretend to be the orange? How does it feel to be stared at? Imagine your tongue and teeth coming at you. What, as the orange, would you like to do?

Now rub your tongue across the orange. Break the skin, and begin to peel it. Listen to the sounds. Watch the juice come out, and see the peel tear away from the flesh. As slowly as you can, break the orange in half. Take one section and eat it. Savor its juice and flesh.

If possible, have someone with you. Feed your partner a section of orange. Watch as he eats it.

Then—slowly, slowly—have him feed you.

4

Games for Expanding Your Consciousness

On the table was a blue vase ten inches high.

Marcia sat in an armchair some eight feet from it. She was taking part in perhaps the first psychological study of meditation. The eight participants in the experiment were in their thirties and forties, intelligent and well-educated. None had ever meditated before.

"Your aim is to concentrate on the blue vase," Dr. Arthur J. Deikman, the psychiatrist conducting the study, told Marcia (*Altered States of Consciousness,* edited by Charles Tart). "By concentration I do not mean analyzing the different parts of the vase, or thinking a series of thoughts about the vase, or associating ideas to the vase, but rather, trying to see the vase as it exists in itself, without any connections to other things.

"Exclude all other thoughts or feelings or sounds or body sensations. Do not let them distract you, but keep them out so that you can concentrate all your attention, all your awareness, on the vase itself. Let the perception of the vase fill your entire mind."

Deikman went on to explain that he would play a tape recording of a variety of sounds. "Keep the sounds out so that they do not disturb your concentration. Likewise, if you find you have drifted into a stream of thought, stop and bring your attention back to the vase."

Marcia proceeded to focus her attention on the vase for five minutes. In her second session she concentrated for ten minutes. Thereafter, for the experiment's ten remaining sessions, she was able to engage in contemplative meditation for fifteen minutes or more at a stretch.

One of the first effects she experienced while meditating was that her sense of time seemed to be bent out of shape. She would be sure that less time had elapsed than was recorded by the clock. Yet she would also have the feeling that somehow more time had passed than the clock showed.

The other participants shared Marcia's sense of time distortion. Furthermore, all the volunteers underwent a marked alteration in their perception of the vase. It would stand out from its surroundings like a source of light.

"The vase was a hell of a lot bluer . . . than it has been before," remarked Jerry, one of the participants. "It was darker and more luminous at the same time."

The vase also seemed to change shape and undulate. Marcia commented, "The outlines . . . seem almost literally to dissolve entirely . . . and for it to be a kind of fluid blue . . . a very fluid kind of thing . . . kind of moving." Jerry found the vase getting bigger and smaller—one moment, it filled his visual field; the next, "it didn't fill the field by any means."

Some of the participants felt as if they were merging with the vase. This was particularly true of Marcia, who recalled, "At one point it felt . . . as though the vase were in my head rather than out there: I knew it was out there, but it seemed as though it were almost a part of me." In subsequent sessions Marcia described a "film of blue" that developed as the boundaries of the vase dissolved. It covered the table and the light-green wall behind it, turning them blue. The film turned into a "mist," then into a "sea" of blue.

Marcia felt anxious because the vase "lost its boundaries and I might lose mine, too." She sensed herself swimming in a sea of blue and feared for a moment that she was going to drown. Once the anxiety passed, she found the experience very desirable.

Lionel, another volunteer, experienced a sense of departing from his body. "I felt this whole complete other plane where . . . my body was nothing. I wasn't aware of my body. It could not have been there and I wouldn't be surprised."

Lionel saw the vase turn many different colors, which started radiating toward him. "I was aware of what seemed like particles . . . coming from the highlights there and right to me. . . . I felt that it was radiating heat. I felt warm from it and then realized

that . . . everything was dark all around, a kind of brown, laven-
der, eerie color, and it was during this incandescent kind of radiating inner glow thing [that] I could feel my pulse beating in my
head and then there was . . . a twinge in my penis. . . .

"I felt that there was a light coming down from above, too, and
that something was happening up there and I started getting an
erection and this thing danced and it was very active. It moved, it
pulsated and also jumped around. . . . It seemed like many colors
around the edges of the table."

As a result of meditation the volunteers saw in a new way not only
the vase but the outside world as well. At the end of one session
Jerry looked out the window and was almost overwhelmed by the
familiar view. "Things look scattered all over the lot, not hung together in any way. When I look at the background, there is much in
the foreground that is kind of . . . clamoring for my attention."

The following day Jerry looked out the window and described
the landscape as "transfigured." He spoke of "a kind of lumines-
cence that the fields have and the trees are really swaying—it's very
nice . . . lean way over and bounce back with a nice springlike
movement."

Although the day was overcast, Jerry said, "The sky behind them
now is also very filled with light. There's a very blue patch in the
sky. . . . It's quite remarkable."

As the experiment progressed, all the participants became more
and more able to shut out distractions. Though the taped sounds
were clearly audible, Marcia experienced an interval of absolute
silence. "I am sure that . . . all sounds were obliterated. . . .
Somehow everything was out of my consciousness. . . . It was as
though the world was absolutely silent." At one session Marcia
found she was even able to disregard a distressing illness.

Initially several of the participants felt anxious. They feared the
loss of self-control, which meditation requires, and they were afraid
that they would not perform as expected. Without exception they
overcame their fears. All achieved meditation periods of fifteen
minutes or longer and concluded that the sessions were pleasurable
and rewarding.

But why? What is there about concentrating on an object that
can provide down-to-earth people with near-mystical experiences?
Deikman has theorized that through meditation you can un-

dergo a process called deautomatization, a shaking-up of your fixed way of perceiving the world. Everyone is to some extent an automaton, acting and thinking in a mechanical, habitual way. Automatization is necessary and useful insofar as it enables you to get through minor activities without excess thought and bother. But such automatic responding can make your thinking stale, your emotions rigid and your perceptions stereotyped.

Meditation exerts a force opposed to automatization, concludes Deikman. In contrast with transferring your attention away from an object or action, you concentrate on it. You thereby open yourself to an entirely new pattern of perception. Thus freed of your automatic responses, you can attain a new, fresh view of the world.

Your Zone of Serenity

Even though you may be able to cope successfully with life, there are likely to be areas of pain and defeat in which you feel helpless, easily overwhelmed, blocked. Besides expanding your sensory perception, meditation can help you encounter and master these areas, by promoting a sense of deeper personal resources, of solidity and strength.

Through meditation you can gain access to a zone of serenity and growth in the center of your being. As your daily life becomes more harassed, you may feel a pressing need for tranquillity. Longing for peace and quiet can be as urgent as gasping for air. Your first thought may be to escape by going on vacation. While a holiday may fill the bill, it is also possible that your inner turmoil will pursue you.

A clothing manufacturer tried to get away from his harrying business by visiting the Grand Canyon. One evening he walked to the rim to watch the sunset, one of the most awesome spectacles on earth. Across the canyon, vast and as old as time, the sky blazed a glorious golden red. "Suddenly I realized I must be nuts," he recalled. "All I could think of was: 'We tried that color in pajamas and it bombed.' "

Nor is there genuine relief in alcohol or drugs. The tale is told of a wealthy merchant in Baghdad who woke up one morning to find a demon sitting on his chest. The demon gave forth an earsplitting howl and raced around the room, jumping from the merchant's head to the walls to the ceiling.

Over the next weeks, never keeping still, the demon followed the merchant everywhere: on caravans to distant cities, even to a mosque where he thought he'd find refuge. The demon's shrieking and mad darting about kept the merchant from thinking and sleeping and drove him to distraction. At last he discovered opium. In the misty paradise he floated to on a cloud of opium smoke, the demon was gone. And so the merchant took to visiting the opium parlor ever more frequently.

One evening in the parlor the merchant reached for his pipe. It was gone, and when the merchant looked down, he groaned in horror. Sitting by his mattress was the demon.

"Sorry," the demon apologized. "When I'm here, I'm supposed to be in costume." And he turned into the opium pipe.

Meditation can help free you from your demons. The process of intense reflection is a way of profoundly experiencing what *is*. You temporarily suspend your intellect, and with calm detachment you observe the flow of being.

"It is as if I say, 'I do not know who I am, so I will watch myself unfold, moment by moment,'" Dr. Edward Maupin, a psychologist who has taught meditative techniques at Esalen, commented in "Meditation" (*Ways of Growth*, edited by Herbert Otto and John Mann). "I stay in the here-and-now, the present, instead of thinking about what is not present. . . . I watch my spontaneity spring out of a source I cannot completely grasp, and flow past like a river, which is never twice the same."

Meditation is a procedure for developing contact with your *Eigenwelt*, your inner, special, separate world. In the view of existential psychology you live simultaneously in three types of worlds. The *Umwelt* (the "around-world") is the world of objects. Your identity in the *Umwelt* is as a thing. To be treated as a statistic—as a person of a certain age or of a particular income or as one of X-many such and suches—is to be given an *Umwelt* identity. Similarly, you assume an identity as an object when you present yourself as a patient with an illness to be remedied, or when you are a warm body fleshing out a company's organization chart.

The *Mitwelt* ("with-world") is your social world, you in relation to the people you are with. The roles you play generally belong to the *Mitwelt*. You are a person who does this, who doesn't do that, who is a parent, a son or daughter, a husband or wife or lover, who works as a teacher or salesman or bookmaker, who is charming or agreeable or generous (or the opposite), who is a good host, friend or colleague, or a bad one.

To experience yourself only in terms of the *Umwelt* or *Mitwelt* is to be either a machine or a cluster of roles and surfaces. For completeness you need to experience your *Eigenwelt*, your own unintruded-upon world. "*Eigenwelt* presupposes self-awareness, self-relatedness, and is uniquely present in human beings," postulates the existential psychologist Rollo May. "But it is not merely a subjective inner experience: It is rather the basis on which we see the real world in its true perspective, the basis on which we relate. It is a grasping of what something in the world—this bouquet of flowers, this other person—means to *me*."

Meditative contact with your *Eigenwelt* rescues the inner you from your intellectualized ideas about yourself. It helps you separate thinking from being. Your experience of what is outside yourself is enriched by awareness of your own responses.

Meditation is sometimes referred to as "effortless concentration." The fact that this seems paradoxical—how can you concentrate without effort?—points up the difference between the meditative experience and ordinary, wordy activity. Meditation is *non-doing*. It is passivity combined with perception. It is as if you departed from your body and turned off your thoughts and became, instead, pure perception: a disembodied awareness.

Nondoing requires effort of a negative sort, much like the kind of exertion needed to relax a chronically tense muscle. "We always say, 'Just sit,'" the master Suzuki Roshi told Zen novices in San Francisco. "And if you do, you will find that Zen practice—just to sit—is not easy. Just to sit may be the most difficult thing. To work on something is not difficult. But to work on nothing is rather difficult."

If being passive is a great challenge, so is maintaining mental silence. You need to shut off the voice in your head and be mentally alert without words. The merest attempt to translate meditation into verbal terms is to depart that much from its meaning. Meditation must be experienced to be understood. Alan Watts, a philosopher who has done much to popularize Eastern thought in the West, has likened meditating to learning to ride a bike. You know when you do it right, and when you do it right, you know.

Many Westerners approach meditation with suspicion, associating it with the Orient, with self-hypnosis or with daydreaming, and feeling it's vague, mystical and incomprehensible. Brought up in a culture that places great value on activity, they find it hard to accept a procedure that, they think, suggests withdrawal from the external world.

Actually, neither retreat from the outside world nor mysticism need be part of meditation. Arthur Deikman, Edward Maupin and other investigators have found conclusively that ordinary people can realize dramatic effects after only short periods of meditation. More than 700 years ago the great Chinese master Mu-mon offered these words of encouragement, still valid today: "If a reader is brave enough and goes straight forward in his meditation, no delusion can disturb him. He will become enlightened, just as did the patriarchs in India and in China, probably even better.

> "The great path has no gate,
> Thousands of roads enter it,
> When one passes through this gateless gate
> He walks freely between heaven and earth."

Much of the writing on meditation is derived from Eastern thought, particularly from Zen. The basic doctrine of Zen, an offshoot of Buddhism, is the belief that enlightenment can be achieved by meditation and the realization of your inner self.

In general, humanistic psychology gives Eastern philosophy much more serious consideration than does Western psychology at large. The feeling in the Human Potential Movement is that there is a treasure trove of insight in the East that can be tapped for the West. For 1,000 years or more practitioners of Eastern religions have delved into questions and explored answers that only recently have become of interest to Western psychologists. Compared to Mu-mon, Freud was a Johnny-come-lately in matters of the human spirit.

Thus, humanistic psychologists part company with more conventional colleagues but pick up where William James left off. Around the turn of the century James speculated on the pertinence of religion and mysticism to the study of psychology and set forth many of his conclusions in *The Varieties of Religious Experience*.

For several decades afterward psychologists' interest in the East lapsed, to be renewed with the rise of humanistically oriented investigators. Dr. Hubert Benoit, a psychiatrist, has suggested that Zen is not a religion but a "universal point of view," not so much a system of philosophy as a practice of intelligent existence, one which contemporary civilization can use as an example to secure a harmonious and peaceful life, free from anxiety.

Meditative experiences are, of course, highly individual. Techniques that may bring peace and heightened perception to one person will often only bore and frustrate another. Here, then, in roughly increasing order of complexity, is a selection of methods. Experiment freely, and choose those that best suit you.

FIND THE RIGHT POSITION

The sitting position used in meditation should allow you to relax while remaining balanced and alert. The relaxation is more buoyant than when you're lying down. With your body immobile thoughts are not stirred up by physical activity, and your mind becomes tranquil more easily.

► Choose a position that allows you to forget about your body. Cross-legged positions are customary in Asia, but you can meditate effectively in a straight-backed chair, even in an easy chair. Use cushions on the chair to make yourself comfortable. Plant your feet wide apart and flat on the floor.

**Choose a Position That Allows You
to Forget about Your Body**

Philip Kapleau, head of one of the largest Zen meditation centers in the United States and editor of *The Three Pillars of Zen*—the best introductory work for Westerners—tells of his first attempts at cross-legged meditation, at a monastery in Japan. He was so racked by cramps that he could think of nothing but the pains in his legs. Only after he was advised to sit on a chair was he able to reach a meditative state.

► You may care to experiment with a cross-legged position. The simplest of all is to sit on the floor, tailor fashion—legs crossed, so that your right foot is more or less under your left knee, your left foot under your right knee.

The full lotus—the traditional Oriental position, which most Westerners associate with meditation—is extremely difficult to master. You need to cross your legs so that your right foot rests on your left thigh, your left foot on your right thigh. The resulting cramps make the full lotus impractical for most Westerners, and the position is mentioned here chiefly for the record.

The half lotus is slightly easier. You need get only one foot on one thigh. The other foot is underneath the opposite thigh, close to the buttock.

Half Lotus

Full Lotus

► In any of these cross-legged positions, raise your rump with cushions, so that your knees and buttocks form a stable base. Now let your back settle onto this base so that your backbone is a column that requires no strain to keep straight.

"Tailor"-Fashion

Generally, keep your back straight, whether you are sitting cross-legged or on a chair, with your ears in line with your shoulders, and the tip of your nose in line with your navel. Sit with dignity and grandeur, urges the Zen master Dogen, like a mountain or a giant pine. Rest your hands in your lap, thumbs touching. Keep your head 'erect, your eyes open and directed, without focusing, at a point a few feet ahead of your knees.

After getting into position, sway back and forth for a minute or so to settle in. Take a few deep breaths, and relax by focusing your attention on various parts of your body, especially the parts on which you are resting.

The next phase is to relax deeply, by concentrating on your respiratory process.

FOCUS ON YOUR BREATHING

Breathing is a passive process, requiring no conscious effort on your part. By focusing on this automatic mechanism, by merely letting it happen, you can achieve a blissful state of deep relaxation and detached awareness.

Breathing can become a "vehicle of spiritual experience, the mediator between body and mind," Lama Govinda wrote in *Foundations of Tibetan Mysticism*. "It is the first step towards the transformation of the body from a more or less passively and unconsciously functioning physical organ into a . . . tool of a perfectly developed and enlightened mind."

► First, become aware of how you breathe. Allow yourself to inhale and exhale in your usual way. You may discover that you breathe smoothly or hesitantly, deeply or shallowly, rhythmically or erratically. Don't change how you breathe. Just watch and allow.

► Now note if your in-and-out breaths are of equal length. Do they flow smoothly and easily, or is there gasping and other forms of unevenness? See if you can smooth irregularities in the flow and balance the rhythm without strain or force.

► Become aware of the depth of your breathing. Are you using all of your lungs, or are you breathing shallowly? Can you gradually increase your depth of breathing?

► Now concentrate on the rate at which you are breathing. Can you gently lessen each inhalation and exhalation so as to slow your breathing?

► Continue this experiment for a few minutes, to establish a pattern of smooth, deep, slow breathing. When you breathe in, can you feel an inflow of energy that fills your entire body? Psychologist Paul Bindrim suggests that you may be helped by imagining that this energy is in the form of light emanating from a source directly above and in front of you and shining on your forehead.

As you breathe in, visualize this light flowing into your body. After breathing in, imagine your entire body glowing with light. As you breathe out, imagine this light flowing out through your fingertips. You may be able to release tensions by imagining they are flowing out with the light energy that accompanies the out breath.

► Lastly, experiment with this classic Zen technique: As you exhale slowly, completely, think "one." Inhale again. Then exhale slowly, and think "two." And so on, up to ten. Then repeat.

You may find this counting difficult, because your mind will wander from it. Keep at it, striving to bring your mind back to the process of counting. When you are able to do this with reasonable success, play the following game.

► As you think "one" and are slowly exhaling, pretend that this "one" is going down, down, into your stomach. Think of its remaining down there as you inhale. On the next exhalation bring the "two" down, and place it in your stomach beside the "one." Eventually you may sense that your mind has descended into the middle of your glowing body.

GO WHERE YOUR MEDITATION TAKES YOU

Stray thoughts and random interruptions are inevitable. Trying to avoid them may make you tense. The very task of preventing mental wandering may only distract you further.

► Don't try to prevent distractions. Accept them. When distracted, patiently return again and again to the meditation. Gradually your attention, focused on the vase, leaf or other object of your meditation, will overcome the distractions.

► Again, try releasing discordant thoughts when you breathe out, allowing them to leave through your fingertips, along with the outflow of light and energy. Imagine your mind to be like a lake, and your thoughts like wind causing ripples on its surface. Let the wind die and the lake become clear. Now you can see into its quiet depths.

Do, however, resist preconceiving what should happen. Expectations are like static, and there is no surer way of putting interference into a meditation than to be wondering, "Is this right? Am I doing as much as I can?"

► Instead of anticipating what will happen, allow yourself to be aware of what *does* happen. Go willingly wherever the meditation leads you. Being in touch with your moment-to-moment experience itself often induces a kind of exhilaration. So it is far more constructive to settle into a meditation than to strive for a particular result. If ye seek, ye shall not find. The benefit of meditation must come from the meditative experience itself.

"In this culture," Edward Maupin notes in *Ways of Growth*, "you may well find yourself . . . beating yourself over the head . . . to do a good job of meditating." Try to stand apart from yourself and observe your tendency toward self-criticism, Maupin advises. "There is a kind of friendly neutrality, which you can bring to bear on any experience which emerges."

BE A SPECTATOR TO YOUR THOUGHTS

Ordinarily you are swept up by the thoughts, impressions, feelings and experiences that constantly flow through your mind. You and your mental activity are one. A memory arises, and mentally you are transported to the scene recalled. A plan develops, and for the moment you are transported to that future occasion when you might conceivably put the idea into effect. You sense a preference or a dislike. For an instant this response takes over, leaving you aware of nothing but your desire or your distaste.

► A form of meditation consists of watching this stream of consciousness, without being carried away by it or interfering with its flow. Let the procession of your thoughts proceed as it pleases, but be a bystander rather than a marcher.

Through meditation you can see into yourself. Detached and free, you can move "upstream" from your thoughts, fantasies and involvements to the states of mind that produce them.

To achieve this inward glance, do nothing. Make no effort of your own. Relax completely, and let go of your mind and body. Step out of the stream of ever-changing ideas and feelings that constitute your conscious mind. Watch the onrush of the stream as an interested observer, but refuse to be submerged in the current.

"Watch your ideas, feelings and wishes fly across the mental firmament like a flock of birds," advises H. Chaudhuri in *Philosophy of Meditation*. "Let them fly freely. Just keep a watch. Don't allow the birds to carry you into the clouds." In *Ways of Growth* Paul Bindrim offers a related metaphor: "Imagine that your mind is a room with open windows and your thoughts are like birds that fly in and out freely while you yourself remain inside."

MEDITATE TO SOUND

A mantra is a sacred sound transmitted in some forms of Buddhism from a master to a disciple. When the disciple's mind is properly attuned, the inner vibrations he feels from this word symbol, together with its associations in his consciousness, are said to open his mind to higher dimensions.

"Om" is regarded in India as the greatest mantra, representing God in His fullness. It is widely used in non-Buddhist meditation, not for its sacred symbolism but for the vibrations induced by chanting it. If continued long enough, the effect is like an internal massage, heightened when you experience it in a meditative state.

► Om can be divided equally into three prolonged syllables, covering a range of sounds. For the first part of an exhalation make the sound "owww," as in "cow." Glide into "oooh," as in "chew." Conclude with the final syllable, "mmmm," until you run out of breath. Inhale and resume.

With practice you'll be better able to divide the syllables evenly. Your first attempts are likely to be shallow and hurried. Practice will help slow your breathing and will also deepen the origin of the sound, so that you'll be chanting from the bottom of your belly.

► There are other sounds that you can meditate on. Push out "eeee" at as high a pitch as you can, and concentrate on centering it in your head. Sound "ayyy" from your throat and "ahhh" from your chest. Have "oooo" set up vibrations in your hips.

These sounds can be remarkably effective in group meditation. Overtones build up from the many voices, heightening the vibrations. After being brutalized by the Chicago police, protesters at the 1968 Democratic Convention were surrounded in Lincoln Park and in danger of yielding to panic. In an inspired gesture the poet Allen Ginsberg started a group chant of Om. For hours the thousands of angry, frightened young people were not only calmed down but transported. In an article in *Playboy* Ginsberg recalled his own experience:

"I began to feel a funny tingling in my feet that spread until my whole body was one rigid electric tingling—a solid mass of lights. It was around 8 P.M. now and I'd been facing the John Hancock Building, which was beginning to light up. I felt like the building, except that I realized it wasn't alive and I was. Then I felt a rigidity inside my body, almost like a muscle armor plating. With all this electric going up and down and this rigid muscle thing, I had to straighten my back to make a clear passage for whatever flow there was; my hands began vibrating. Five or six people were touching them. Suddenly, I realized I was going through some kind of weird trance thing like I'd read about in books. But it wasn't mystical. It was the product of six continuous hours of chanting OM, regularizing breathing and altering rhythmic body chemistry."

► Counterpoint is an interesting variation in group chants. Women may chant, to be answered by men. Children may respond to adults. Undercurrents produced by the chanting may be surprising. At a meeting on the American Association for Humanistic Psychology some 700 women shrieked like the wind, and a like number of men returned with roars like thunder. With a slight change in sound the women became harpies, and the men beasts. Many of these highly respectable professionals were disturbed by the primitive sounds they were making and were relieved when they glided into a counterpoint more soothing and sensual.

► The internal massage brought on by chanting can help rid you of minor muscular stiffness. You're likely to be invigorated by going through these sounds before getting out of bed in the morning.

► Yet another form of meditating to sound is to move with music. Lie on the floor, and immerse yourself in a musical composition.

Play it over and over again, and follow individual instruments, the rhythm, the melody. Let the body move as it will. Even if "unmusical," you're likely to transcend a merely auditory experience and feel the music throughout your body. Try listening not only with your ears, but with all parts of our body—your armpits, fingertips, genitals and toes.

Follow through on the first movement that comes to you. Make it wider, larger, stronger, softer. Let more and more of your body move. Your hands, shoulders, legs, have something to express—let them speak.

As you emerge from your mummy wraps of self-consciousness, you may achieve an exciting feeling of integration. Your body and feelings may become one in a complete form of expression, and long-suppressed emotions may rise to consciousness. After moving freely to music for about five minutes, one career woman found herself sitting on the floor, with her arms folded, as if she were rocking and crooning to a baby.

"I broke into terrible, uncontrollable sobs of grief for the child that was not there," she recalled. "Up to that time I had not wanted a child." Now she confronted "fear, selfishness, the refusal of commitment, not liking being a woman"—emotional demons she'd futilely sought to escape.

PRAY MEDITATIVELY

Meditative prayer, if you are someone for whom prayer has significance, is a form of deep contemplation, as well as communion with God. It requires that you be committed to God or to a spiritual theme while engaged in an act of continued concentration.

▶ Dr. Herbert A. Otto, of the National Center for the Exploration of Human Potential, in La Jolla, California, has described meditative prayer as consisting of four stages.

First, make an act of commitment: Establish a schedule of daily prayer—perhaps fifteen to thirty minutes once or twice a day.

Second, select a spiritual subject from the Bible or from another source. A single line that has meaning for you is suitable.

Third, fix your whole being on your selection. What does it mean? What are its applications to your life? Herbert Otto has called these questions the "two arrows of meditative prayer."

Finally, with practice you may attain a sense of oneness with God. A dialogue with God may develop. You may get in touch with an inner secret voice that, Quakers hold, is the voice of God responding to your questions.

For example, your thought for meditation may be "Love thy neighbor as thyself." You then ask, "What does this mean?" Your inner secret voice may provide an answer. Believers in meditative prayer hold that this may be the God inside you.

MEDITATE ON A KOAN

A koan (a Japanese word, pronounced with two syllables: *ko-an*) is a problem that baffles logic and points to ultimate truth. It cannot be solved by reasoning but only by awakening a level of the mind deeper than the intellect.

Koans aim to stop your mind wandering and word drunkenness. To the uninitiated, especially the intellectualizing Westerner, koans may seem like gibberish, like a trivial, meaningless toying with words. But precisely one of the purposes of koans is to point up the limitations of words, as opposed to the completeness of being.

There are many right answers to a koan, and there are also none. The koan itself is the answer. It is a formulation representing a state of mind, and its intent is to help you break the shell of a limited mind and perceive not what is thought but what is.

Nyogen Senzaki, a Buddhist scholar, and Paul Reps, an American student of comparative religion, have translated a classic Zen tale illustrating the use of koans:

"You can hear the sound of two hands when they clap together," said the temple master. "Now show me the sound of one hand."

His protégé came back the next day and began to play the music of the geisha.

"No, no," said the master. "That will never do. That is not the sound of one hand. You've not got it at all."

The boy retired to a quiet place to meditate. "I have it," he imagined. When he next appeared before his master, he imitated the sound of dripping water.

Again this was rejected. Many times more the student came back

—with such offerings as the sighing of the wind, the cry of an owl, the sound of locusts. All were wrong.

At last the boy entered true meditation and transcended all sounds. "I could collect no more," he explained later, "so I reached the soundless sound."

Thus he had realized a Zen principle: that sound and no sound are two parts of the same entity, much as the tail and the head are two parts of the same cat. Meditation may help you perceive such continua, indeed the *one* continuum—the wholeness and interrelatedness of the entire universe—which philosopher Alan Watts calls It.

Here, adapted from a translation by Nyogen Senzaki and Paul Reps of Mu-mon's *The Gateless Gate,* is a selection of koans that are likely to prove most rewarding to beginners.

► *Expressing the Truth*

A man was asked, "Without speaking, without silence, how can you express the truth?"

Replied the man, "I always remember springtime. The birds sing among innumerable kinds of fragrant flowers."

► *What Is Moving?*

One monk argued, "The flag is moving."

The other disagreed. "The wind is moving."

A patriarch passed by and told them, "Not the wind, not the flag; mind is moving."

► *The Stick*

A master held out a short stick and said, "If you call this a short stick, you oppose its reality. If you don't call it a short stick, you ignore the fact. Now what do you wish to call it?"

► *Give and Take*

Said a teacher to his disciple, "When you have a staff, I will give it to you. If you have no staff, I will take it away from you."

► *Skill*

A wheel maker made two wheels of fifty spokes each. Suppose you removed the hub uniting the spokes. What would become of the wheel? Had the wheel maker done this, what could he be called?

CONCENTRATE ON AN OBJECT

► For one minute look at the second hand of your watch, without losing your visual focus or mental attention. This practice in emptying your mind to increase sensitivity is almost impossible to do the first few tries. Your mind will seem not under your control. Only after you've had practice will you be able to avoid thinking about other things.

► Here is another experiment in meditating on an object. Concentrate on your hand. Observe the lines, the color, the texture, the shape in space, the shapes of the mounds and bases. Feel the warmth within the hand and the sensation of air around it.

Meditate on your hand so that it fills your entire consciousness. You are likely to arrive at a sensation of being in two places at once: at one with your hand, since you will be exquisitely sensitive to it, yet unconnected to it, observing it detachedly from a distance.

► One more experiment: Concentrate on an object that pleases you—a piece of sculpture, a vase, a flower. If you're concentrating on a flower, try to see the total flower as it exists in itself—devoid of all associations, labels, connections with other things and places and times. Exclude from the meditation your ideas and experiences concerning flowers, and avoid analyzing the flower, separating it into its parts or however else you may treat it intellectually. Keep the object of your meditation pure. Concentrate on it alone. Let your perception of it fill your mind.

TAKE FANTASY TRIPS

While meditating, you can transcend your physical location.

► Imagine yourself leaving the room. In your mind's eye go through the city and over the fields. Come to a meadow covered with fresh grass and flowers. Look upon the meadow with pleasure. Stay in the meadow, and meditate on it.

► You can achieve a more expansive feeling by visualizing a mountain in the distance. In fantasy go into the country, and slowly climb a mountain. Pass through a forest. Scale the heights until you finally reach a peak from which you can view the countryside.

► Yet another meditative use of imagery can take you to a chapel. Fantasize yourself walking through a grove and into a chapel. Enter it and meditate. In this setting you may achieve a state of sublime reverence.

► Meditate on a photograph or a painting of a beautiful place.

► Meditate on a memory of a lovely place you know.

RECEIVE ANOTHER PERSON

► Concentrate on the face of a partner. Distortions may appear, telling you what you project into the relationship: angels, devils, animals, all human possibilities. Before long you may move past these fantasies into the genuine presence of another human being.

► A meditative encounter can also enrich sexual intercourse. Take a position in which you can gaze eye-to-eye for a long time. A sexual meditation can last for hours and can lead the partners to a profound sense of oneness.

ACHIEVE A PEAK EXPERIENCE

Peak experiences are the most wonderful episodes of a lifetime. They are moments of the greatest happiness, ecstasy, rapture—the kinds that occur when a person falls in love or gives birth to a child, creates a work of art or climbs a mountain. In the words of Dr. Abraham H. Maslow: "Peak experiences are one part of the operational definition of the statement that 'life is worthwhile' or 'life is meaningful.'"

In peak experiences your conflicts of life tend to be transcended or resolved. You may feel you've found the ultimate truth, the secret of life. There is often a sense of having "gotten there," of having reached an end of striving and straining, of having satisfied all desires and hopes.

You may perceive a unity in the world, and you may move toward a resolution of personal conflicts. Peak experiences may improve your image of yourself and may help you fulfill your potential. Maslow has found the effects of peak experiences sometimes "so great as to remind us of the profound religious conversions which forever after changed the person."

A peak experience can occur spontaneously, in the course of ordinary life. Maslow told of a young mother scurrying around her kitchen, getting breakfast for her husband and young children. The sun was streaming in. The children, clean and nicely dressed, were chattering as they ate. The husband was casually playing with the youngsters. As she looked at them, she was suddenly so overwhelmed with their beauty and her great love for them that she went into a peak experience.

Psychologist Paul Bindrim, in his work with groups, has developed a "sensory-saturation" method for facilitating a peak experience. You may experiment with it alone, but you are likely to get the best results by engaging in the experience with another person or with a group of friends. Allow at least two hours, and follow this procedure:

► In preparation gather together five "peak stimuli." These are things you most enjoy touching, smelling, tasting, looking at and listening to. Such objects tend to lift your mood. In combination they will elevate your spirits higher than any of them would do individually. The stimuli need have nothing to do with one another. For example, you may choose to taste chocolate, touch silk, listen to a recording of Beethoven's Ninth Symphony, smell perfume and look at a picture of a beach.

Recall a specific peak experience that you would like to relive in fantasy—an event in which you felt joyous, free, at one with the world. If you are with others, tell them of this experience and how you felt. You and your companions are likely to stimulate one another's recollections.

Pick a partner, preferably a member of the opposite sex, whose eyes you can gaze into with openness and warmth. Sit opposite each other, close enough to be able to touch fingertips comfortably.

Get as comfortable as you can, using meditative methods for relaxing through breathing. Deepen the relaxation, by feeling that each part of your body is heavy and sinking of its own weight.

With your eyes closed, slowly make use of your peak stimuli. While listening to the music of your selection, smell, taste and touch the items you've brought. At the same time imagine your visual stimulus—your picture of a beach, say—as though you were looking at it through the middle of your forehead. Allow these sensations to flow together into the center of your being. In groups where it is impractical to play all the preferred recordings, Bindrim recommends a classical or semiclassical work that is emotional in quality and builds to a climax, like the Prelude to Wagner's *Tristan und Isolde*.

Recall in fantasy your peak experience as vividly as you can. Discover the event as if it were entirely new, letting sensations emerge by themselves.

After a period of silence, in which you enjoy the peak experience, open your eyes, and engage in eye-to-eye meditation with your partner, with your fingertips lightly touching. Play a musical selection as background. Stay with this feeling until you've reached the fullness of the experience. Then engage in feedback.

"The general outlines of this experience are not unlike those of drug-induced, hypnotic or Zen-meditated trips," Bindrim noted. Many participants report a sense of traveling beyond the boundaries of ordinary experience, and of approaching "God," "warm, white light," "birth," "the beauty of the whole thing," "the stream of the universe."

These experiences seem to have a lasting effect on many participants. After one workshop Bindrim did a follow-up study and found "an increased sense of inner worth, a sense of having completed a crucial psychic or spiritual cycle." Some participants were helped to a better understanding of their marriage partners. In one case such awareness led to an amicable divorce. In another case a "remarkably beautiful woman, whose husband had made childish and petulant fun of her body, was able to help her husband to stop playing little boy and to move the entire relationship onto a much more stable, mature and mutually satisfying level." Several participants reported that for the first time in years they had friendly, adult relations with persons of the opposite sex.

Beyond

One of the last uncharted terrains in the universe may well be man's own consciousness. For all that is now known about the jungles of Africa and the mysteries of interstellar space, the world you carry around inside you is still mostly like a dark continent, illuminated here and there by an occasional flash of insight.

Dr. Jean Houston and her husband, Dr. R. E. L. Masters, codirectors of the Foundation for Mind Research in New York, have charted the major levels of human experience, the stopping points on a mind trip.

The first is the level of sensory awareness, the level on which you function simply as a response to stimuli from outside your own body. The next level is where your personality exists as you experience it in ordinary consciousness. Here is the part of you that forms relationships with other people, loves and hates, experiences freedom and conflict.

Beyond these first two levels is the level on which archetypes exist. This is the part of you that transforms ordinary experiences into powerful symbols. Myths and rituals originate from this level, as well as that part of you that responds to the experience of universal themes. Rituals of birth and death and resurrection arise here. Legendary figures, like Oedipus, Faust and Don Juan, are creations of this third level of consciousness: embodiments of timeless themes.

On the fourth level mystical experiences take place. Most descriptions of this state have been given by people who have undergone profound religious experiences or drug-induced mystical experiences. It is almost always described in terms of the subject's being immersed in a torrent of preternatural light and in contact with or at one with the source of everything: a sense of God or eternity.

The Human Potential Movement contains a number of workshop leaders who conduct participants through "transpersonal" experiences—so called because such mind trips carry you across that which is personal to you and into a realm of the unconsciousness shared throughout humanity. Valerie, an editor in a publishing house, attended a workshop conducted by Dr. Charles T. Tart of the University of California at Davis. Josh, a clinical psychologist, was at one led by Jean Houston. Here, containing experiments for you to try, are their verbatim accounts.

THE OBSERVER

▶ "Dr. Tart [recalled Valerie] instructed us each to hold a conversation with somebody sitting near us. Only, during this conversation we were to hold a small part of our consciousness off. This part was to observe—not to judge, just watch—what we were doing. We were then led on to a series of such conversations with different people, and one nonverbal conversation. Each time, we kept 'the observer' with us and reminded each other to keep doing this.

"It was a weird experience—at first I had thought it couldn't be done. I felt the way I do when I try to talk when I've been smoking grass—as if the person talking (me) is just something I'm projecting, like a movie on a screen—not exactly phony, because it/I says what I would want to say and as much of what I feel as can be verbalized.

"But also I know, and I knew during this experiment, that there is a part of me that is only me and only mine, and that stays in. Sometimes—and it happened this time—I have an almost sly feeling about knowing this fact—as if I have a wonderful secret no one can ever find out.

"Dr. Tart went on to explain that the observer can learn to think, but in a different way from how the 'self' one is usually conscious of things. The usual consciousness is a data processor, responding to stimuli. The awake self, with the observer present, notes what's going on, as well as responding to internal and external stimuli.

"Later, at dinner, we had a good, long, relaxing meal in a Chinese restaurant. While we ate and talked, we tried to keep the observer with us. It didn't work all the time—this is a sophisticated technique, something students of the philosophy of Gurdjieff spend their lives trying to achieve—but at those moments when it did, the experience of eating changed. Again—this reduces the experience, but it's the easiest analogy to give—it was like being stoned. Tuned up. Tuned in. Turned on."

WAKING DREAMS

"After dinner [Valerie continued] Dr. Tart talked about 'lucid dreams,' which are like being in a normal state of consciousness.

" 'How do you feel in a lucid dream?' " somebody asked.

" 'The way you would feel if you found out, right now, that you were dreaming,' Tart replied.

"Some people have dreams like this, where they know they're dreaming and can even control what happens. You can try to make this happen to you.

"Tart had us lie down on the floor on our backs and follow his instructions. We were to achieve a state of deep relaxation, in order to facilitate going into the hypnagogic—i.e., lucid-dream— state.

▶ "This is how it's done: One at a time, raise each arm. Then each leg. Then your head a few inches from the floor. Focus all your attention on the raised limb until it gets unbearably heavy. Let it drop, and immediately raise another limb, and focus your attention on it. *Don't* think about the arm or leg you've just dropped. After you've done your right arm, left arm, right leg and left leg, raise your head. As soon as it gets heavy and drops, focus on your breathing. Just think, 'In, out, in, out.'

"Then, to keep yourself from falling asleep, raise your arm— either on your elbow or straight up. Straight up is easier—there's no strain. If you start to drowse, the arm will fall and wake you up.

"I kept feeling I was spinning around in a bed—a feeling I remember from childhood. I saw an image of a golden spinning wheel against a dark background. It was big big big. Later I figured out that this had something to do with the fact that I had been reading and thinking a lot about India—the spinning wheel is a modern symbol of India—and it all seemed too big to grasp. But beautiful."

GUIDED FANTASY

"Jean Houston took us on guided daydreams [Josh recounted]. After we had been put into a light trance state, she gave us a post-hypnotic suggestion—a key word ('eagle') that would take us into a trance more easily the next time. At the beginning stages of a trip she's fairly explicit in her directions about what to visualize.

▶ "Jean took us down into a deep cavern, where there was a room with four walls. At her suggestion we opened these walls one by one, to find four different images.

" 'Find the most concrete basic symbol of yourself as you are,' she said.

"I came up with the Egyptian ankh, the sacred T-shaped cross surmounted by a loop [☥]. As I was watching it, the oval on top swelled and burst and flopped on its left side. I realized later that I was seeing my image of my body. I had always been concerned that my left shoulder was much thinner than my right. I'd worked to bring it back to strength, but there was still always a difference.

► "After we shared our experiences of the cavern, we were put into another trance. Jean told us we would have two minutes in which to travel around the world, starting on a big white horse.

"Wowie! I found myself racing around the world on an elephant in India, a dog sled in Antarctica, a boat in the South Seas. It seemed to last far longer than two minutes. Although I had never done any of these things in real life, they all seemed like real experiences—as real as the experiences in dreams.

► "The last exercise of the weekend was a death and rebirth trip. We went down into a vortex, and this time we were told that there was a white light at the bottom. When we arrived at the light, there were stairs going down still farther, into deep water. Wearing breathing masks, we swam deeper and deeper, to find a profound symbol of ourselves.

"Earlier in the day, when Dr. Houston had instructed us to meditate on an object and ask it a question, I had started to come to some resolution of the problem represented by the ankh. Concentrating on a rough-hewn stone pendant, I seemed to receive the message 'Everything in nature is not symmetrical.'

"Now, at the depth I swam to beneath the stairs, I found my old friend the ankh again, which had continued to mend after its collapse at the beginning of the weekend. This time it looked very solid, and then it changed into a new symbol—a ring of fire.

"I'd gone to the weekend in the hope of finding new ways to overcome some of my communications blocks. I found within myself legendary figures with whom I could strengthen my identification—like Demosthenes, addressing crowds. Afterward I started having less trouble expressing myself.

"I visualized myself as a giant striding the earth, setting up a giant communications network. The ankh symbol was replaced with a new and deeper symbol—a crown of sparks. Jean told me this seemed to be my archetypal symbol, and from here, under hypnosis, she was able to lead me to a vision of blazing light. It only lasted a moment, and then the shadow of a man obscured it. But I think that with further work I will be able to go past the man—who is me—to really 'see the light' and stay longer in its presence."

III

BODY GAMES

Your emotional state is inseparable from your physical self. Chances are you're out of touch with your body—and therefore with your feelings, emotional as well as physical. These games can help you bring your body back to life and release emotions now imprisoned by tensions.

5

Games for Enlivening Your Body

Martians have the power to "discorporate." The Martian's physical self is irrelevant. He can dispense with his body and function as an unconnected mind.

This fantasy, from Robert A. Heinlein's science-fiction novel *Stranger in a Strange Land,* is shared by many earthlings. Possibly you conceive of yourself principally in terms of your emotions and intellect and attach relatively little importance to that mass of tissue below your head. You may feel that your body is a thing quite apart from what's upstairs.

If so, this chapter and the next may at first disturb you. You may feel disoriented, as if you were shown that round is square or black is white. For you are asked to look at yourself in an entirely new way: as a mind-body totality. Your body is not an appurtenance. It's not like a house in which you live or a car in which you ride. It's *you.*

"You don't exist within your body," notes psychiatrist Alexander Lowen, a principal figure dealing with physical manifestations of emotional stress. "The body is a person."

Your person. And only by perceiving yourself in terms of your body can you fully know yourself.

Self-awareness entails awareness of your body. Ideally, you sense what is going on in every part of your physical self. You feel the flow of sensation associated with breathing. You feel your tensions and constrictions and thus can come to grips with them.

If you lack such contact with your body, you are likely to have whole areas that are numb. They are missing from your realm of consciousness. You may act and feel awkward. In a literal sense you lack self-possession.

Getting in touch with your body may be a surprising experience, a bit like making a good new friend of someone who's long been only a distant acquaintance. The procedure may be slow and painful—but the pain is a positive sign. Dr. Alexander Lowen uses this analogy to help patients understand the role of pain in the healing process: "When a finger is frostbitten, it is not painful. The person may not even be aware of the condition. However, when the finger begins to thaw out, the pain is often very severe."

Mind and Body Are One

The volunteers urinated into specimen jars, then gathered to see a movie. Afterward (in this experiment conducted by Dr. Lennart Levi of Stockholm, Sweden) they gave follow-up urine samples.

A routine travelogue, chosen to serve as a control, produced little emotional response, and urine tests showed no important change in chemical content. But over several days the audience also saw a comedy, a horror film and a war tragedy. These evoked strong reactions—joy, fear, sorrow. Urinalyses disclosed correspondingly marked alterations in the audience's production of hormones. Emotion alone (and experienced through a movie at that) had caused profound changes in body chemistry.

Mental and physical phenomena are always interrelated. Your body and your mind are inseparable parts of a single biochemical unity, the sum total of which is you. There is but one process going on inside you. You may be aware of some of its manifestations in your tissues and organs. You may discern others as thoughts or emotions. Because of language and custom, you may call one manifestation "body," the other "mind." But in actual operation they are as intermixed as the yolk and the white in a scrambled egg.

To divide human functioning into the mental and the physical is to make an artificial distinction. You are, in fact, one integrated being, functioning as a whole. Every physical state, be it comfort or disease, has emotional components. Similarly, every mental response, whether an emotional reaction or an intellectual activity, is part and parcel of a physical process. It is insufficient to ask, "Is this mental, or is this physical?" Rather, you need to consider, "What of this is mental, and what is physical?" The two always go together.

You may find this concept hard to accept, because language sometimes works against you. Words are rife to distinguish between "mind" and "body," "mental" and "physical," "psychic" and "somatic," and these distinctions are certified by dictionaries that define such couplets as antonyms when actually they're functionally inseparable. The most revered of maxims is "A sound mind in a sound body," which generally conjures up the picture of a pea in a pod. Only if taken in a certain sense—soundness of mind is soundness of body; physical illness has mental components—does the maxim have validity.

Dr. David T. Graham of the University of Wisconsin Medical School calls mind-versus-body terminology "linguistic dualism." For many day-to-day purposes it is convenient to conceive of, say, doing a multiplication problem as "mental" and catching a cold as "physical." But it is important to remember that this is nothing more than a linguistic convenience—it is in direct opposition to the way you actually work.

Doing a multiplication problem is an operation entailing (at minimum) the cerebral cortex of your brain, a physical entity. Your ability to multiply is the result of a complex biochemical chain of events, all of which take place on a physical level. An alteration of body chemistry, the severing of a nerve with a surgeon's scalpel, the displacement of a few cells in an accident—all physical phenomena—could render a victim incapable of multiplying 2 by 2. Such obstructions of the biochemical process need not be at all exotic. If you've drunk too much or gotten too little sleep or if you're hungry or ill, you're well advised not to do a sticky computation, like your income tax.

Your ability to multiply, then, exists as a physical fact. It's not off in the blue somewhere, because you classify it as "mental"; it exists in your body cells.

Likewise, your body chemistry is unceasingly manifested in mental or emotional expression. Merely recall the last time you had a bad cold. Chances are you were gloomy and short-tempered and lost your usual enjoyment of food and reading and company. These "mental" effects were as much a part of your cold as your runny nose.

Indeed, during influenza epidemics some companies urge employees to stay home at the first sign of illness. Not only might they spread infection, but—befogged by flu—they might commit costly errors on their jobs.

" 'Psychological' and 'physical' (and their synonyms) refer to different ways of talking about the *same* event, and not to different events," noted Dr. Graham. "The difference between 'mental' and 'physical' (or 'psychic' and 'somatic,' or any of the other corresponding pairs of words in common use) is not in the event observed, but rather in the language in which they are discussed."

People who intellectualize commonly cling to the notion that the mind and body are separate things. The more you depend on intellectualization ·as a way of protecting yourself from painful feelings, the greater is your stake in believing that your mind is the real you and that your body is something apart that is your burden to lug around.

"You're smart or you're shit," is the motto of Phil, a college instructor. Phil is overweight, from nonstop eating. He has a facial twitch. His shoulders are stooped. He shuffles when he walks. Yet, clutching his copy of *The New York Review of Books* like a shield, he maintains that his body and mind have little to do with each other. In conversation he uses the phrase "me and my body."

"How can you distinguish between the two?" he was once challenged. "Where's the 'me' you're talking about?"

He pointed to his head. "Up here."

PHYSICS OF EMOTION

When you're depressed, you're depressed not only in your head but all over. Your respiration is shallower, vitality decreased, skin color poorer. Your muscles may be less coordinated and movements unsure. You're likely to be depressed even in your legs and feet.

Conversely, when you're joyful, you feel good all over. Your breathing and circulation are improved, and you look and act bouncy.

Is depression—or joy—then a physical or an emotional state?

The answer, of course, is that it's both. Mind and body are one, in constant interaction.

► To convince yourself of this, observe yourself the next few times you feel any particular way: happy or sad, companionable or lonely, interested or bored. Notice how these emotional states are part and parcel of physical sensations. Boredom is not only a wish to do something else; it may also be a tightening of the chest, a constriction around the neck and shoulders, an itching in the legs and feet.

A long list of physical ailments may result from emotional turmoil; for example: asthma, ulcers, colitis, hypertension, heart disease. In *Guys and Dolls* Adelaide, whose boyfriend had been putting off marriage for years, was medically astute when she sang through a stuffed nose:

> The av'rage unmarried female, basic'lly insecure
> Due to some long frustration, may react
> With psychosomatic symptoms, difficult to endure
> Affecting the upper respiratory tract.
> In other words, just from waiting around
> For that plain little band of gold
> A person . . . can develop a cold.*

Feelings Are Physical

Proprioception (from the Latin for "taking one's own") is the term for your ability to sense stimuli originating within your body.

You experience a proprioceptive sensation every time you suffer from a stomach-ache or a Charley horse or muscular lightness after exercising, or enjoy a satisfied feeling after a meal, or an orgasm. Changes in the tissues activate "proprioceptors," tiny specialized nerve endings found in muscles, tendons and joints. The proprioceptors help tie you together as a body-mind unity.

► Your emotions are proprioceptive sensations. If this surprises you, where do you feel this surprise? Along the sides of your neck, the backs of your hands, in your belly? The locations of such proprioceptive flickerings differ from person to person. But every emotion you feel—you do just that: You *feel* it, physically.

Common figures of speech may already have given you your first inkling of the proprioceptive nature of emotion. Language is a liv-

* "Adelaide's Lament" by Frank Loesser. © 1950 Frank Music Corp. Used by permission.

ing record of the experience of generations. Expressions you use every day came into being because they were descriptive and are carried forward because they are still valid.

So "a lump in the throat" reflects how large numbers of people through the years have perceived sadness. What else is fearful anticipation but butterflies in the stomach? Anger makes your blood boil; disappointment, your heart sink. Frustration is a pain in the neck; if severe enough, a pain in the ass. When tense, you may have a proprioceptive sensation of being "on edge," as if you were teetering on the edge of a cliff. Confronted by pressing alternatives, you feel "torn apart," possibly with the sensation of being ripped down your midline.

All of the foregoing describe the physical sensations associated with painful emotional states. You speak of having "painful experiences," of your "feelings being hurt." The ache of rejection is no less an ache than the ache of a crushed finger.

Much of the pain associated with emotions is felt because of your effort to *keep down* a deeper feeling. Thus, a "lump in the throat" indicates not only that you are very sad or deeply moved, but also that you don't want to give in to this feeling completely. A father feels a lump in his throat at his daughter's wedding, because he doesn't want to give in completely to his mixed feelings of joy and sorrow by breaking down and sobbing.

The contraction of the stomach muscles—"butterflies in the stomach"—that you perhaps experience when you are frightened is another way of keeping a more powerful feeling from emerging: If someone really lets his fear take over, he might tremble violently or give in to his urge to run away. Or so he believes.

Sometimes, of course, it is necessary to block deeper feelings in this way—you probably don't want to be carried out of the church sobbing when your daughter gets married, and you might have trouble living it down if you suddenly dashed out of your boss's office when you were about to ask for a raise.

Your tendency, when you experience one of these "blocking pains"—the lump in the throat, the butterflies in the stomach—is to take an action that will free you of that pain: If you have a lump in your throat, you may try to think of something to be happy about; if you have butterflies in your stomach, you may think of or do something that restores your confidence or relieves your tension.

If you feel angry and bottled up to the extent that you get a head-ache, you may take an aspirin.

But if this is the only way in which you deal with painful feelings —by relieving the physical tensions that block them—you will keep yourself from much richness of experience, and you'll probably find yourself repeating the same patterns over and over. Your anger will never get further than the inside of your head, and it will still be there after you've taken the aspirin. And as long as the anger is still there, you won't be free to experience much that is pleasurable.

In brief: if you block disagreeable feelings, you block pleasurable feelings, too. If you don't allow yourself to experience a feeling fully, you force yourself to undergo the long process of waiting for it to subside before you are free to feel anything else.

STAY WITH THE FEELING

"As a sponge absorbs water," Laura A. Huxley observed in *You Are Not the Target*, "so do physical pain and mental distress absorb our awareness."

Observe yourself the next time you do something self-destructive, like overworking, or agreeing to do something you don't wish to do, or worrying, or driving carelessly, or eating or drinking too much. Pause to analyze what you're feeling. You're almost certain to find that you're seeking to relieve a pain that is blocking a more powerful feeling that you may fear will be even more painful.

▶ Stay with the pain. Concentrate on your sensations, and allow them to develop unchecked. A deeper feeling is almost certain to emerge, and, with it, a deeper awareness of the situation you are in and how you are responding to it.

Margaret, a woman who was both busy and satisfied with her career and her family, was never able to say no when a persistent woman from her church group called to ask her to make cookies for church functions, even though she hated to bake. Once she decided to pay attention to what was happening to her, Margaret realized that whenever the woman called, she felt a sudden mild clenching of her stomach muscles, and that she could relax them after she'd agreed to do what the woman asked, though the prospect of a Saturday morning fussing around in the kitchen didn't appeal to her.

By focusing on the pain and allowing it to deepen, Margaret found herself flooded with rage. When the feeling developed fully, she was reminded of the feeling she'd had as a small child when her mother had threatened to punish her if she didn't help with the housework.

As a child, Margaret had been forced to hold her feelings in check, because she would have been punished if she hadn't. As an adult, she was still letting this old pattern keep her from knowing how she really felt and from making a mature, adult decision about what to do. Once aware of her reaction, however, she was able to tell the woman calmly and politely, "I don't enjoy baking. I'd rather help out in some other way."

RESTORING CONSCIOUSNESS

► A frequent reaction to pain—emotional pain no less than physical—is to anesthetize yourself through muscular tension. Observe what you do the next time you encounter someone you dislike or embark on an activity you hate. You tense up, just as you do when you sit in a dentist's chair, for instance.

Since early in life, your emotions have been under a more or less constant state of siege. The tension with which you've responded, termed character armor or motor armor, is generalized and only dimly perceived. The deadening often continues long after the original painful stimulus has vanished.

"Almost all persons in our society have lost the inner sense of large areas of their body," noted Ralph Hefferline, Paul Goodman and Fritz Perls in their classic work *Gestalt Therapy*. "The loss was not accidental. It was, when it occurred, the only means of suppressing intolerable conflict."

People commonly lose contact with their legs, buttocks, back and shoulders. You may know intellectually that these areas exist, but possibly you don't feel them as alive parts of your body. Right now, chances are you can't tell if your legs are contracted or relaxed, if your shoulders are raised or lowered.

A part of the body lost to consciousness may also be impaired in function. If you don't feel your legs, for example, you are likely to lack a sense of security for want of the inner conviction that your legs will hold you up. People who are extremely dependent often report that they're not sure on their feet—they need the help of someone to hold them up.

Restoring conscious contact with your physical parts can free you from habits and blocks, often from aches and pains. Once aware of a tension, you can make it dissolve. You can become *interested* in the sensation, and—no longer oppressed by it—you can watch it disappear. You are likely to realize for the first time that most of the answers to your problems lie within you. You have creative self-directive powers. Whereas formerly you needed the advice or support of others, now your most reliable source of information and guidance lies within yourself.

A TRIP THROUGH INNER SPACE

► Lie down on the floor, and seek quiet and comfort. Charlotte Selver has noted that the sensations from within "are like the stars, which only appear when the artificial lights are turned off." If you are enough at peace, the feelings within you can be very precise.

How do you feel on the floor? Light? Heavy? Free? Constricted? One person may feel the floor pressing against him; another, that he is sinking into the floor. These are personal reactions—the lightness or heaviness, pressing or sinking, come from you.

You may wonder, "What am I supposed to feel? What's right?" Can you now overcome such expectations, evaluations, labels? Let the sensations arrive just as they are. Don't watch them as an outsider, but experience them. They are you.

Some years ago there was a science-fiction movie called *The Fantastic Voyage*, in which a submarine was shrunk to microscopic size and sent on a journey through the bloodstream. Imagine yourself taking a similar trip through inner space.

► Enter your body through the bottoms of your feet. Try to locate any sensations in your feet, toes, heels and so on. Go slowly up your legs, getting in touch with any sensations emanating from the inside. Continue to explore upward until you have made contact with every part.

Examine pains and twinges ordinarily ignored: their sizes and shapes, how they affect you. They may evaporate under your scrutiny. Act on any urge to yawn, stretch, change position.

Determine how the various parts of your body relate to one another. Can you feel your body as a whole? Where your head is in relation to your torso? Where your genitals, chest and limbs are with respect to one another?

This exploration bears repeating over many days. Most people lack adequate proprioception and substitute visualizing in its stead. For example, you picture where your legs are but don't *feel* them. With a map of your body you can deliberately walk, kick or run. But for free, spontaneous functioning you need to feel your legs themselves.

Fragmented Body

Just as you may fragment your conception of yourself into "mind" and "body," so also may you conceive of the parts of your body as separate things, somewhat like sovereign nations in a loose alliance. Thus, when you reach for something, what do you reach with? Your arm?

▶ Try it. Reach for an object a few feet away, and see what parts of your body move. You'll find that you reach not only with your arm, but with all of you, from head to foot. Even a close-by reach involves your opposite shoulder, your back and your hips. Likewise, you see not only with your eyes, but with a network of nerve and brain tissue. You eat not only with your mouth, but with your entire digestive system, in fact with every cell that is living and therefore metabolizing.

You are a unified whole, and all your activity is interrelated. But the labels applied to various parts of your body can mislead you into believing the arm, the eye and the mouth are separate entities. "Arm," "eye" and "mouth" are descriptive terms for areas of tissue. The parts themselves—the real-life flesh and bone the names are supposed to stand for—never function independently.

Believing they do, however, may cause you to use only part of your resources. Most people picture pushing as an activity of the hands, and this conception limits the effectiveness of their pushing.

▶ Try this experiment with another person: Touch palms, and start pushing. Chances are your first inclination will be to push only with your arms. See how little you accomplish. Gradually mobilize the rest of your body. Notice how much better you push when it becomes an activity of your whole body, from fingertips to toes. If you're able to employ your brain as well—consciously come in contact with each part of your body—you're likely to get the best results of all.

PUPPET

Are your movements mainly gestures, disconnected efforts, rather than coordinated motions?

► Deliberately treat yourself like a puppet, and see how familiar it is to move as though your limbs were pinned onto your body. Let your body bend forward, knees slightly bent, your arms and head hanging downward. Be relaxed, as if a puppeteer were letting your strings hang slack. Now let the string pull your right arm upward, and suddenly release it. Repeat for your left arm, your legs, your head and neck. Have the strings pull your various joints: elbow, waist, knees.

How often do you move in this disconnected, fragmented way?

"There is very little pleasure in performing doll-like movements," noted Warren Lamb, an English specialist in posture and movement. Lamb found this experiment revealing:

► Spend half an hour trying to do only gesture movements. Deliberately move in a forced, jerky way. Exaggerate these erratic, disconnected movements to bring them into awareness. Then follow with a half hour of movements that are coordinated and well composed. Lamb likened such movements to a piece of beautiful music. "There is no question which is the more pleasant."

If you run your life with your head—reasoning, thinking, understanding, controlling—all the while underplaying your heart and gut, you may have a physically visible quirk that is extremely common. It takes the form of a head that is always held on to, that moves very little, as if it were not a part of the body, moving easily with the rest, but somehow different and separate. There is tension of the neck and shoulders, causing marked stiffness of gait and carriage. Look for this robotlike quality in friends first, so that then you may be more aware of it in yourself.

Mary Whitehouse, a dance therapist in Santa Monica, California, remembers one young dancer who had a very wide range of movement. Her dancing looked marvelous. But there was something wrong. "It was not free, no matter how much she moved. I looked and looked, and finally I caught it. She was like a mario-nette; the arms and legs lifted, fell; the torso bent over and back. She crouched down, sprang up, but there *she* was, sitting up in her head, manipulating everything else, with the result that the head and neck hardly moved."

Reclaim Lost Parts

Start reclaiming lost parts of your body now. To become more awake and reactive, stimulate yourself with tapping, slapping, stretching, shaking. Respond with your whole self. You'll realize the wholeness of your body and how all is interrelated.

Moving your legs and pelvis more easily may free your head and eyes. When your feet get more alive, your hands and abdomen may become so, too. Not only does the immediate sensation feel good, but the stimulation is likely to continue, affording inner release and clearer perception.

▶ A good way to begin is to take a mighty stretch. Overcome your good manners, and yawn your head off. The urge to yawn is a sign that your breathing is beginning to respond.

Some suggestions for the following experiments: In general, keep your eyes closed. Before beginning, experience how you feel. Tap or slap each area of your body for about twenty seconds, long enough to derive benefit but not get bored.

Work in as much variation as possible. Jump freely from one type of experiment to another: from, say, slapping one part of your body to shaking a second to touching a third. Intersperse fast and slow. Alternate being vigorous and soothing.

Come back to any area that seems to ask for more. Let the movement subside gradually, and before opening your eyes, experience the aftereffects.

Slap and tap with both hands *simultaneously*. You'll get twice the stimulation than if you used one hand, then the other. Also, keep breathing. You may resist coming alive by tensing up and blocking respiration.

When slapping, allow your hands to be flexible enough to take the shape of the area being slapped, your wrists loose. Don't beat yourself up. Use a vigorous, gentle slap that slightly stings but doesn't hurt.

In tapping, bend your fingers at the joints, and tap (don't jab) with bouncelike motions of an inch or so.

HEADS (AND SHOULDERS) UP!

▶ *Tap* with a lilting motion, like rainfall, all over your head, cheeks, jaws. Tap the back of your head, around the ears and the sides of the head, then the forehead. This can be especially invigorating if you and a partner do it to each other.

▶ *Slap the top of your head*, using a bouncing motion, raising your hands about an inch. Now slap the back of your head, then the back of your neck. Next, slap the side of your head and over the forehead to the cheeks, nose, jaws. This, too, is especially effective if done with a partner.

▶ *To free your neck and shoulders*, imagine a piece of chalk attached to the extreme tip of your right shoulder blade. With it, write your first name on an imaginary blackboard behind you. Repeat with your left shoulder blade. Next put the imaginary chalk in the right ear and write a word. Repeat with the left ear.

Follow this with a series of neck and shoulder movements. First push your head as far as possible toward your right shoulder blade. As the strain on the muscles of the left side of your neck brings pain, slap the muscles with the flat part of your right hand until the tension and pain disappear. Stand still, and feel the difference between the right and left shoulders and neck muscles. Now repeat, leaning your head toward your left shoulder.

▶ *Shoulder slapping.* Have a partner slap the entire area from the beginning of your shoulders at the edge of your neck clear down to your fingertips. Move up and down three times. Do an especially good job over the shoulders. Then go over the shoulder blades.

AWAKEN YOUR UPPER BODY

▶ *Use your other hand.* For a half hour use your left hand exclusively if you are right-handed, your right if you are left-handed. Keep your eyes open, and do everything as well as you can with your weaker side: Write, eat, dial a phone, throw a ball. Be aware of your feelings. How easily are you frustrated? Is encountering your weaker side like meeting a stranger?

► *Shake your arms.* Begin by wiggling the fingers of one hand. Then explore the movement possibilities in the wrist, twisting it in all directions. Extend movement into the forearm, the elbow, the upper arm, twisting and turning every way. Include the shoulder and all its possible movement. Finally, vigorously shake the entire arm. Follow the same procedure on the other arm. Then do both arms at once.

► *Be touched.* Have a partner stand behind you and place both his hands on your shoulders, next to your neck. Allow twenty seconds of firm, gentle touching. Have him slowly take his hands away, and for twenty seconds, digest the effect of this contact. Continue the touching symmetrically on the shoulders and sides and front and back, over the rest of the upper body.

► *Slap vigorously* the entire area of your arms, chest and rib cage. Move down to your stomach, hips and buttocks. Now work upward. Try doing this with a partner as well.

ENERGIZE YOUR LOWER BODY

► *Shake a leg.* Supporting yourself on one leg, wiggle the toes of your other. Stretch and contract the foot. Explore every movement possible in the ankle, calf, knee and thigh, twisting and turning in every way. Work up to the hip. Then shake the entire leg, causing it to vibrate vigorously from hip to toe. Then do the same to the other leg.

► *Touch your buttocks.* Then lift your hands slowly, and touch the back of one thigh, then the sides of the calf. Repeat for the other leg.

► *Slap one leg,* starting with the foot and working up to the calf, thigh, hip and buttocks. Slap both the front and the back, as well as the sides. Go up and down the entire area at least three times. Stand up, and experience the leg you have just worked on. Contrast it with the other leg. Now follow the same procedure over that leg.

► *Get a lift.* This exercise helps you come to awareness of your legs and hips. Your sensations will develop most fully if you proceed in slow motion. With each movement experience how you feel—and what you're perceiving in relation to your body, its motion and the floor.

Lie down. Slowly bring both knees up close to your chest; then lower them back slowly. Do this with each leg in turn.

Finally, still lying down, with knees bent and feet flat on the floor, very slowly raise your spine as high as you can. Let yourself descend one vertebra at a time. Repeat, but this time raise your spine only an inch or so. Slowly straighten your legs, and get up.

► *Footnote.* With both hands feel the tip, sides and bottom of one foot. Explore the sole. Become aware of its softness. Pull out and wiggle each toe. Scratch the foot. Rub it. Now, standing up and walking, feel the difference between this and the other foot. Then do the same to the other.

BRING YOUR BACK TO LIFE

► *Touch.* Settle comfortably on your stomach, and have your partner first lay his hands over the area of your shoulder blades. The two hands should touch simultaneously and lie flat but easy in position. Have him lift his hands and move to your middle back. Next, the lower spine. Notice where your breathing comes from. Be aware of how his touch affects you. After you change places, be conscious of his breathing and how he feels to your touch.

► *Slap.* Again lie on your stomach. Close your eyes, and settle comfortably. After about a minute, have your partner slap your shoulders, entire back, sides and buttocks.

► *Hang loose.* Stand up and bend over, arms hanging down, fingertips toward the ground, knees straight but not locked. Have your partner vigorously slap your back, sides and buttocks. Go over the whole area three or four times. Have him also slap your legs, arms and head. Straighten up slowly, one vertebra at a time, and experience the lightness you feel.

Image of Your Body

Sam is very fat. But he pictures himself as "well built." Guided by this body image, he continues to dig his grave with his teeth.

Your body image is your picture of your physical self. It devel-

oped along with your personality and serves as a model for what
you believe you can and cannot do. You normally rehearse subcon-
sciously before attempting to perform an activity, visualizing the
sequence of movements in terms of your body image. A body
image may facilitate one type of activity and impede another. For
example, a baseball player can clearly see himself hitting a ball with
grace and coordination, but he may be unable to picture himself
dancing with equal grace. An inadequate body image can handicap
your performance.

Your image of yourself, for better or for worse, interposes itself
in your functioning—urging here, restraining there. It can be a film
that has grown between you and reality. The notions that it is in
character for you to do this and not to do that or to feel this and
not to feel that compel or censor your activities and diminish or
distort your experience. Only in moments of true connection with
yourself is the image absent, permitting you to be as you really
are.

SELF-PORTRAIT

As a first step in rectifying your body image, you need to see what it
is and where it's awry.

► Start by drawing a nude figure of yourself. Even if you've little
artistic ability, it's likely to suggest how you see yourself. The
shoulders, for example, may only dimly resemble shoulders—but
your sketch will show if you see yours as broad or narrow, sloping
or straight.

By the same token, the figure may show how you'd *like* to see
yourself. If fat, for example, you may draw yourself either as very
fat or very thin. Either departure from reality is likely to be revealing.

► Now, in the nude, look at yourself in a mirror. Really look—at
your shoulders, genitals, hips, legs—all over. How does your body
compare with what you've drawn?

YOURSELF AS YOU ARE

► In the nude take a pose before the mirror, and see how it feels.
Move; change position. Try not to assess your flaws or attributes,

but confront yourself with your own image, and feel the impact you make upon yourself.

Let your body talk to you. Watching yourself in the mirror, touch your body all over. Just let it happen, and experience yourself as you are, right this minute.

► Lastly, talk to yourself out loud about your body. Studying yourself in the mirror, start at the top of your head, and go down to your feet, saying what you like or don't like about yourself. Can you accept how you really are? Can you see how your dislikes about yourself have altered your body image?

Body in Space

The space around you is not static in its meaning for you. The same distance, itself unchanged, can expand, contract, grow fuller or emptier, become friendly or menacing—all depending on your situation at the moment. You can explode many static notions about space with this simple experiment:

► Choose a spot about a dozen feet from a wall, and stand there. Explore your location visually, so that you will see how far it is from the wall in terms of distance and space. Walk the distance with open eyes, and see how different your concept of this space is. Actually experienced, is it longer? Shorter? Wider? Narrower? Then walk it with your eyes closed. Again it will be different.

Where are you? How much space do you have around you? What direction are you facing? Where are other people? As these experiments show, such spatial concepts can have great bearing on how you feel about yourself, about what's right or wrong.

ROOM WITH A VIEW

Your evaluation of a room varies according to your comfort or discomfort, familiarity or unfamiliarity with that room. The place you choose on entering a room is no accident. It is an expression of your relationship to everyone else in the room. As you grow used to that space, you develop a strong emotional investment in holding on to it. Albert Pesso, a pioneer in psychomotor therapy, noted in his *Movement in Psychotherapy* that the place you occupy is "an anchor and a location in space, a point of reference which has become stabilized and which gives [you] security." You become accustomed to seeing the room from a particular angle. You may get used to presenting one side of your body to one person, another side to someone else. How you feel about a room you visit briefly can point up your feelings about home and stability.

► Occupy a seat for a while. Settle into the spot. Then change places. Note your reactions.

When working with groups, Albert Pesso often finds that members resent him for asking them to leave their comfortable locations. They feel uneasy, that they have lost something. They don't like the person who now occupies "their" space.

How do you feel in your new spot? Observe how the room looks different from this new angle, how it may take getting used to. If there are others about, you may feel uneasy toward the new people around you; you may also feel a challenge to your security. Notice how you seek to orient yourself to this new location, that for the moment you are not as comfortable as you were.

► After a few minutes return to your old place. How do you feel as you get up to go? If you've been given sufficient time to orient yourself to the new spot, you're likely now to be reluctant to leave.

On the other hand, you may regard your old place as home. In Pesso's groups people are often cheerful about "getting back." They fall at once into a posture that they developed in that space, like settling into an old shoe. There's little need to orient themselves, since that was accomplished before.

OUT OF SIGHT, OUT OF MIND

Experimenting with space can help you see the difference between conception and perception, between abstraction and experience.

► With a group of friends form a circle, or line a room with people. Experience how you feel. Usually your front will feel warmer, and you will feel somewhat hemmed in at the sides. This comes close to symbolizing what you get from living in a community: warmth, with restrictions.

► If you turn around, your sense of the circle is likely to disappear. You may know intellectually that it still arches out behind you, but possibly you need to turn around to experience it. Your sides may now feel freer, and it may be your back that is warm. Symbolically, by turning away from closeness, you've gained freedom but put warmth behind you.

SOCIAL CIRCLES

How do you feel when in close contact with other people?
► With friends form a circle. Share your impressions. Do you find the circle confining? Do you resent the restrictions it imposes? After a few minutes do you feel better about the circle? Does it now give security and a sense of togetherness? Albert Pesso has observed that some people remain agitated and unhappy about being in a circle. "Their feet are further out from the circle than others and they can be seen looking elsewhere than at the other group members."

Do you feel crowded by the proximity of others? You may find yourself standing with your arms folded across your chest or with your arms behind your back, suggesting that you feel your arm movements are restricted. Folded arms can also indicate that you are shy of too much intimacy with your neighbors. You'd probably be more comfortable if you placed your arms around your neighbors' shoulders—but this expression of closeness is difficult in our distance-demanding culture.

The amount of space between people can strengthen or weaken the sense of group. Are all the spaces in your circle equal? If not, you may wish to see all the people equidistant, so that there are no holes in the group.

Equal distances suggest that no one is missing and that everyone has the same standing. If a large space surrounds anyone, he seems to stand out from the circle, disturbing the sense of group equality. If openings on either side of a person are equivalent to several spaces, the circle no longer seems like a circle but like two opposing lines.
► Become aware of the space your circle creates, and note how different enclosure is from being elsewhere in the room. Your feelings about the circle are likely to be more intense than your impressions about the rest of the room.

▶ The center of a circle generally seems considerably warmer than the outside. Place your hands toward the center. A usual comment is "This feels like placing my hands over a campfire."

▶ Take charge of the circle, and change its size from the smallest to the largest possible diameter several times. Tell the group to stop at any point, and explore the feelings each setting of closeness or distance offers you. Which feels best?

Some people desire such closeness that the circle they control is forced to turn sideways in order to make the diameter as small as possible. By contrast, some leaders keep the circle moving backward until the members are unable to take another step without climbing backward up the wall.

This experience often reflects how a person governs an organization or group he leads in the outside world. Do you cramp and crowd your employees or friends? Do you keep people at a distance (and maybe make them climb up the wall)?

▶ Finally, break up the circle, and return to where you originally were. Do you experience a feeling of loss? Relief? Some may comment the room feels colder, some that they feel freer and happier. Your conclusions may reflect your feelings regarding individuality, your need for others, your feelings about this group in particular.

▶ Front and back can also have emotional significance. Have members of the circle turn clockwise, so that everyone is facing another's back and has his back to someone else. What do you feel about the person in front of you? Do you sense him as a leader or as an authority figure whom you love or hate?

Your feelings about the back may be of supreme importance. Do you imagine the person behind you to be a loyal follower? An incipient back-stabber?

▶ Now have everyone turn the other way. Has your former leader, who was in front of you, become a lackey now that he's behind? Has a former hatred or love or suspicion been transferred along with the switching of places?

It is not only the person but also the position of the person that determines your response to him. People who don't like leaders often feel like pushing aside the person in front and taking over his place. If a woman is in front of a man, his attitudes toward having a female in a position of power may come forcefully to mind.

OUTER SPACE

The space you command is not limited to what's inside your skin. Realizing the true proportion of your body in space may help you feel less closed in, less constricted in how you hold yourself and in what you do.

► Lie on the floor, and close your eyes. Follow your breathing for a few minutes, deepening and slowing it to help you relax.

Sense how wide you are, how your chest expands as you take in air. "I feel like an enormous cavern," one person remarked.

► Now spread your arms out as far as they will go. Do this slowly, and sense the volume of air you pass through. Spread your legs out also. See if you can sense the distance you now encompass. One impression: "I'm straddling the ocean."

Concentrate now on how long you are, from the top of your head to the bottoms of your feet. ("I'm a long train." "A huge canyon.") Raise your arms as far off the floor as they'll go, and bring them down above your head. Sense your length now. Can you feel the length of your arms, your sides, your legs?

SPACE CARVING

A businessman who had no fondness for ballet dozed off in front of his television set one evening. An hour or so later he half-awoke to a program featuring ballet.

"Coming out of my fog, it was as if I'd never seen dancing before," he recalls. "I'd only been watching the dancers and had found it pretty boring to see this arm come up, that leg go down. Now before me I saw that dancers do much more: They carve shapes in space. Their bodies, their costumes, the air around them —they create a kind of instantaneous, ever-changing sculpture."

► As if your body were a knife in clay, see how much space you can carve out of the air surrounding you. All that space belongs to you. Touch its perimeters with your hands, feet, body, head. Crawl through the space. Jump to explore it.

This activity is often most successful in groups. Though members may be stiff and awkward at first, they will gradually warm up to the exercise. The group's support is of great help to people too inhibited to experiment on their own.

At a workshop conducted by psychologist Stewart B. Shapiro of the University of California at Santa Barbara, a colleague remarked to him how much this experiment reminded him of the back ward of a state hospital. "I agreed," says Shapiro, "and felt that this observation was highly significant in that this activity was, in a sense, a regressive activity, far more primitive and basic than the usual verbal stuff in which these people spent most of their time. I saw it as regression in the service of growth."

Moving through Space Together

For group sessions Shapiro sets aside a rectangular floor space and has students move through this space in pairs, in trios, and finally all together. They carve their space in any way they want—running, twirling, crawling, tumbling, jumping—and at any pace or pattern that suits them. Invariably, there is a lot of activity.

► Try it on your own and with friends. Make the space you carve larger and larger and your movements more expansive. Done outdoors, it's even more exhilarating.

► In another space-carving experiment, devised by dance therapist Sally McClure of Los Angeles, students use elastic jump ropes as stretchers and shapers. The object is to keep the elastic taut at all times—stretched by your hands and feet, head, shoulders, elbows and knees—and to find out the extent of movement possible within this range. Working with the elastic draws attention to your own shape and to the strange shapes it's possible to form with your body.

The elastic forces you to reach outward, away from yourself, and to really stretch. In a group make shapes in relation to shapes formed by others, in a kind of moving sculpture. There is grace and beauty to these forms, which you'd rarely achieve were you merely to strike a pose.

Joy of Movement

As a child, long before you had words, you communicated how you felt through your body. Movement was your language. Your smiling was total and delighted; your crying was total and despairing; your anger was total and explosive. When you said a nonverbal yes, everything in you said "Yes!" When you gave forth a no, everything in you said "No!" You were undivided.

Gradually you learned to buy and sell with your behavior, hoping for love, avoiding disapproval. You curbed instant reactions and unconsciously imitated the movements around you. You picked up the set of your parents' bodies, absorbing, without knowing it, their attitudes toward the body.

You succumbed to the requirements of teachers, acquiring restrictions and limitations. You were put at a desk for hours at a time and told to keep still. The expression of feeling was relegated to sketchy instruction in the arts; the experience of movement was assigned to required gym or athletics.

Almost completely by the time you were in your teens, you moved only for a reason, isolating your actions. When you were younger, you bent over to look at a bug and your whole body bent. But now you looked only with your eyes and a restricted movement of your neck. Your smiling came from the mouth only. Your crying got kept down. Your anger turned into tension. You became physically inexpressive, your gestures mere shadows of feeling.

Thus, you lost the wonderful joy in movement that children have. Movement among adults is intellectualized: a means to an end, taking place in response to mental images of going someplace, doing something. Dr. Marvin Solit, an osteopath in Boston, has found many people he has helped at first startled by the realization that they treat the body like a slave under the command of the mind. "It does not even occur to the mind that the body has an integrity and needs of its own—needs [that, if] not satisfied, may lead to degeneration of the slave or to an outright revolt and refusal to work." Jane Stembridge has expressed this idea in a poem entitled "About Certain Jobs and the Way Bodies Bend":

> if
> the body's buckled up,
> the mind is
> buckled,
> too.

Life and feeling are expressed in movement. Movement is natural to you. It is the closing off of feeling, the stilling of activity, that is unnatural and numbing. Through movement you can increase your capacity to feel. You can explore sensations you didn't know you had. You can extend the range of your physical gestures. By learning to trust and express your spontaneous reactions, you can allow yourself to be more creative.

Dance therapist Mary Whitehouse has reported that very frequently in her workshops people moving about for the first time find themselves emotionally stirred in a way that surprises them. "It is a feeling of wanting to cry, or suddenly feeling sad, and both men and women experience it. I believe it is a spontaneous nostalgia for an earlier time when walking about, skipping, stretching the arms up to the sky, or bending over were all natural impulses freely allowed. Something has come alive, and no matter how one disapproves, or says, 'Isn't that *silly*,' one has been touched, one is moved from within, not only physically. The body has become *real*; it is ourselves feeling."

SPONTANEOUS DEVELOPMENT

Ideally, when experiencing movement, you have the sensation at once of moving and being moved, a coming together of what you are doing and what is happening to you. It is as if you were a boat both propelled by its own motor and at the same time swept along by the current.

Mary Whitehouse has said, "Movement, to be experienced, has to be *found* in the body, not put on like a dress or a coat." In one workshop Mary suggested that the group rise in the simplest, most direct way they could. A woman in the group recalled, "I had absolutely no muscle control or technical ability, but I rose in one complete spiral movement, my legs unwinding me upwards like a corkscrew. Physically, if I had been asked to do it, I could not have. It moved me; I did nothing."

Again and again, Miss Whitehouse has noted, physical action takes a form that would not be possible at will or that would take a long time to learn by conscious intention. Despite their normal rigidity, people balance incredibly well without knowing how to balance, twist or turn, and jump or run when they have long since forgotten how. "There is nothing magical about this. Shrunk to the size of the ego, movement appears as inhibition, self-consciousness, poverty of gesture, deadness. The openness of attitude allows the . . . body to function freely, producing much more of the natural range of physical action, which is the birthright of the human being."

In order to achieve this freedom of movement, you need to develop your kinesthetic sense, the awareness that accompanies or informs you of bodily movement. You were born with a natural timing and coordination in motion. But if your kinesthetic sense is seldom used, it is lost to your consciousness, and you live instead as something of a marionette, ruled by your head and moving with distortions, short circuits, strains and mannerisms.

Dr. Marvin Solit has observed: "Most people have no concept of their body moving without directions or specific purpose. Almost all of an individual's activities in an average day, except perhaps eating, urinating and moving his bowels, are motivated and to a large extent directed by the mind—and may I add that many people have managed to control and direct these functions, too."

▶ Experiments in spontaneous movement can help you restore your kinesthetic sense. Sit with your legs crossed and eyes closed. Assume an attitude of open waiting, a way of listening to your body. Wait until you feel a change—perhaps your body will begin to tilt, your head to lower slowly to one side. Follow wherever this inclination leads, as if it were a pathway opening up before you.

You may find yourself falling. Gravity is a word you've often used. Have you experienced it before?

You may wish to rise. Your body can tell you when and in what way. Let your body find its own rhythm, and let it move in that rhythm.

BABY ROLL

The baby roll was designed by Sally McClure to help you connect with your inner momentum, letting it flow from inside and propel your body wherever and however it wants to go.

▶ Lie on your side. Lift your knees close to your chest, and open them wide. Let the momentum pull you over, rolling across the floor, opening, closing, opening. Let your arms go. Find out how fast or slow you want to go. Try not to think about your body or how you look. Just do what your body tells you, and be aware of how you feel.

The Baby Roll

Float, tumble, rock like a baby. Open wide like a child. Wherever the motion goes. You may feel the relationship between bodily movement and your open and closed inner feelings. Some comments of people who've tried it: "Groovy." "Weird." "Good."

▶ Another way to move out of your accustomed types of motion is to keep long colored crepe-paper streamers flying through the air. It looks easy, but you really have to work hard even to get them off the ground. Unless you fling the streamers upward, then follow through instantaneously with running and with wide arm sweeps, the streamers will fall limp at your feet.

JOINT EFFORTS

Do you avoid reaching out to people because you're afraid of being impeded by them in some way? Your body can help you learn how you react to close contact, how to handle limitations that you may feel others impose on you. These experiments translate such restrictions into physical terms. See how enjoyable your contact with another person can be if you hang loose and move free and easy.

▶ *Balance your efforts.* When working with others, do you tend to carry too much of the burden or too little? Experience what it's like to balance your efforts with your partner's.

Stand toe to toe, clasp hands, and pull back. Two people of different weights, sizes and statures can get into balance. But it requires cooperation in tension and relaxation.

If you pull too much, you can overpower your partner; too little, and you become dead weight.

When you're in balance, though, motion between you seems to flow, and you may be inspired to try swinging in new ways.

▶ *Move in tandem.* If you find it hard to move in conjunction with someone else, here's an effective experience in cooperation: Try getting across the floor with your partner, using any form of physical contact that occurs to you. No need to conventionally walk hand in hand or arm in arm. You can also tug, pull, push, dance, bounce and run three-legged or wheelbarrow style.

React to the initiative or lack of it in the other. Let your body decide how close or how distant you want to be, how resistant, how giving.

BODY ENGLISH

Movement is nonverbal and yet is communicated. Impressions of people are gathered as much from physical attitudes and gestures as from words and clothes. Nervousness often shows itself in little extra movements of hands, feet and face; tension, in raised shoulders as well as in voice; depression, in downward-drooping lines of the whole body; fear, in limited and carefully controlled movement.

Indeed, the body rarely lies. Though your lips may whisper "No, no," your body will show a "Yes, yes," in your heart or at least will feel the strain of falsehood. Though you may say "Yes" with vehemence, if you don't mean it, there will be a part of you that holds back—a tension, a half-heartedness (the expressiveness of figures of speech!)—that may be evident to everyone else. Think how often you have sat down to a relaxed conversation only to have your presumably attentive listener say with every gesture of his body, "Hurry up! Get on with it!"

Awareness of how your body feels can help you become more aware of what it is trying to communicate. You may discover that this is different from what you *think* you are saying or how you think you appear.

In the following experiment you and a partner can tap feelings about each other through movement. These feelings may be in conflict and can change from moment to moment. A conversation in movement can help you explore these feelings and become aware of how you express them in motions only, without talking.

► Crawl toward your partner, moving as close or as distant as you want to. How much do you wish to say? Do you want to touch or not? Feel what the other person is saying to you, and react with your own body in response. Stop whenever you feel your conversation has come to an end.

Your movements may indicate that you and your partner are sparring, testing each other, reaching out in tenderness, pleading for attention, repulsing the other's advance. You can express apology, seduction, impasse, defeat, acceptance—a myriad of subtleties in relation to another person.

The body has a voice of its own. Listen to what it is saying and what your partner's statement makes you do in response. Don't look for meanings. Merely let yourself react in physical terms.

"Each couple has its own distinct and unique kind of body talk, according to their feelings about each other," Sally McClure reported after conducting one such encounter. "Nothing could be predicted. It just happened in interaction."

Postscript: Male and Female

Trainers in body awareness cite, very broadly, differences in how men and women experience their bodies and space.

For example, women, in general, feel as if movement proceeds from something interior that pushes outward. Men tend to express it as something that magnetizes the body, drawing it forward. A woman might perceive movement as a surge of energy from within, as from the engine of a locomotive. A man is likelier to perceive movement as a pull from without, which the body feels or follows.

Women are generally most comfortable on or near the floor. They find the passivity and the sinking of their weight pleasant. Men have a tendency to feel restrained, therefore restless, on the floor.

For the woman open space is often frightening. For the man it represents action and freedom.

Not a whit of this may hold true for you, and it makes you no more or less masculine or feminine. But as yet another way of tuning in to yourself, see to what extent these tendencies describe you.

6

Games for Letting Yourself Go

Your body is your personality made visible.

Your personal qualities are not wholly accidental. Your emotions lead you to adopt special body attitudes. Every expression of your body—whether it is strong or weak, tight or loose, straight or bent—has a meaning and a history: the quality of your handshake, your posture, the look in your eyes, the tone of your voice, your way of moving.

These expressions reflect your emotional biography. A Harvard philosopher, William Ernest Hocking, once remarked that you're born with the body God gave you, but by the time you're forty you have the body you've created for yourself. The distortions, tensions and restrictions within your body are often the same as those within your personality. If your body is heavy and sluggish, there is that within you that is heavy and sluggish. If your body is still and unyielding, so somehow are you. If it is tight and prim, you are as well.

Form follows function in body development. If you're on a track team, your legs will become thickly muscled from running. Muscles can also become developed from isometric exercises, in which you tense muscles while you yourself are stationary. In the reverse way, if you're bedridden and don't exercise, your legs will become scrawny and weak.

Not so widely realized is the fact that emotional factors can promote similar development or atrophy. Harry, a commodities broker, has such bulging calf muscles that people often ask him,

"Were you a track star?" Harry, in fact, was never athletic and now rarely moves from his telephone. Psychologically, however, he's running all the time. Though his legs aren't racing literally, they're always getting ready to run. The constant stretching and pushing, though done unconsciously and in a sitting position, are like isometric exercises and have given Harry the legs of a long-distance runner.

Conversely, Emil is the inheritor of a large family business. But personally he is weak and insecure. Feeling menaced since childhood, he's stepped through life gingerly, sensing little support. Now, at fifty, despite his large head and solid body, his legs are flimsy and poorly developed.

Again, figures of speech and the language of the body coincide: Emil is weak-kneed. He is poorly balanced. His feet are not well planted; his legs have often been knocked from under him.

In large part your body is sculpted by childhood pressures. Marlene learned when very young that it could be hurtful to her to say what she felt. Her wishes would be ignored, her opinions ridiculed, her soft side torn into. Now she watches carefully lest a spontaneous, unrehearsed expression slip out. Her physical being, too, has been enlisted to guard against her speaking out. From early in life she kept her jaws clenched. Now they are strong and overdeveloped. Behind her back friends remark on her resemblance to a piranha.

Likewise, your body is shaped by how you wish to see yourself and be seen by others. You enlist your body to help you play your roles. Fran is a big girl who wishes she were petite. She's acquired stooped shoulders from years of trying to be small. Joe's a little guy who'd like to be big. His ideal is the movie cowboy. He swaggers when he walks and has broad shoulders and narrow hips that make him look like Hopalong Cassidy in miniature.

Such physical formations are generally the result of chronic muscular tension. Character traits cause you to inhibit your movement, twisting and tensing muscles in areas of your body. The muscles become permanently contracted. You may be surprised that you cannot relax them voluntarily.

Fred was frightened and afraid of betraying his fear. He covered up by an exaggerated expression of courage. His shoulders were squared off, his chest inflated, his belly sucked in. Despite the camouflage the fear never left him. He entered therapy and in an early session was astonished to find that he could not ease his shoulders, deflate his chest or relax his belly. He locked in epic combat with his body, seeking to loosen it. Sweating on the floor, he yelled, "I feel like I need a crowbar!"

Most chronic muscular tension results from unresolved early conflicts. Under stress you may hunch your shoulders, tighten up, curl inside, freeze. Persistence of the tension can create a spiraling of emotional difficulties. Any physical rigidity you suffer can interfere with your coordination and impede your responses to problems, which may then make your tension worse.

In addition, anxiety in childhood may have disturbed your natural breathing. You may have abnormally sucked in air, or you may have been afraid to breathe deeply. If anxiety persists, the disturbance of respiration can become structured in tenseness in your chest and abdomen. Thereafter your inability to breathe freely under emotional stress intensifies the anxiety you experience in stressful situations.

Your personality traits not only shape your body. Your abnormally contracted muscles and your impaired breathing also serve to limit your emotional expression. If your muscles are rigid, if your breathing is tight, so, too, will be your responses. Only as you physically loosen up and as you breathe more freely can you be liberated emotionally as well. The armor—as in the terms "body armor" or "character armor," which describe this phenomenon—is thus not only a barrier against perceived attack but also an imprisonment of feeling.

To sum up, then, about armor: Emotional stress causes physical tensions, and vice versa. By relieving emotional tension, you can relieve physical rigidity. Conversely, by reducing physical tension, you can help resolve an emotional problem.

As your tensions are released and as your breathing eases, you are likely to release the feelings lying behind the tension. Depression, for instance, is literally an attempt to press down—in the sense of sit on—painful feelings. If unblocked, the seeming lethargy of depression will be replaced by the emotions held in check, and the depression is likely to dissolve in the expression of these feelings: most often in raging or sobbing.

Dr. Alexander Lowen told of a young woman, an unsuccessful

actress, who had great difficulty in crying and making any loud sounds like screaming or yelling. When an urge to cry rose in her, her throat became tight, her jaw became hard and set, and the urge disappeared. When this happened, her thought was, "What's the use?"

How did this come about? The actress was one of ten children. She always felt that she could not assert her needs in the face of the huge demands already made on her mother by the other children. She learned to hold back her crying and suppress her desire for more attention and affection.

The result was a grim-faced, unexpressive young woman, whose throat was constricted, whose jaw was chronically set and immobile and who tended to hold her breath. In the course of therapy it became apparent that her early impulse to suck had been severely inhibited. She had considerable difficulty making sucking movements.

On one occasion when she put her knuckle into her mouth and tried to suck on it, she burst into deep sobs. She spent much time learning to relax the muscles of her jaw, throat and chest. Her grimness and inability to express her feelings were responsible in part for her failure as an actress.

One of the main objectives in this work is to unify the individual, so that when he feels angry, for instance, he is aware of his anger in his gestures and body attitudes, as well as in his words.

Jerry came to a group, seeking emotional release. He was able to bring himself to the point of tears, but his feelings never erupted. While his eyes were sad, his jaw stayed clenched. Each time tears would begin to surface, his jaw tension would increase and block the flow. A physical approach, as is presented in this chapter, made him aware of what was going on in his face and relieved the tension blocks that prevented his expression of feeling.

The experiments in this chapter are recommended to you with a word of caution: They can release unexpected feelings, including anxiety. Also, you may feel pain in parts of your body that were previously immobilized, especially your lower back.

Experience shows that neither the released feelings nor the pain is ordinarily cause for alarm. Each passes and is supplanted by a feeling of well-being.

At the same time, don't do the experiments compulsively or

push them to an extreme. They are of little value if you become bored with them. Indeed, in these activities seek a growing awareness of the meaning of the act, of its particular role in your own situation. At whom do you want to scream? Whom or what do you want to pound? Sense that it is you who are doing it and are responsible for it.

Without such deep involvement the action is a bluff and a mere forcing. If you bully yourself into doing something on the grounds that it is what you are "supposed" to do to fulfill the experiment, you will rasp your throat and strain your muscles but will not achieve the integration you are seeking.

Beware, too, of intellectualizing. When fears or social pressures remain so great that expression cannot break through, you may fall into the wholly inadequate motions of thinking, "What does this mean?" "What am I supposed to do?" "Why bother?"

The powerful freeing movements that could help release a block are often in a clinch with self-controlling tensions in the diaphragm, throat and head. The only way to release the energy is to express it. If an impulse fails to find an appropriate outlet, the cramped muscles give rise to psychosomatic pains. Such may be part of the price of your unrelenting self-control. This chapter is designed to help you start letting yourself go.

EXPAND AND CONTRACT

If you watch an amoeba under a microscope, you'll notice that this one-celled organism constantly pulsates with waves of energy originating in its nucleus. Normally, the amoeba is free to expand, as it does when reaching out for food. But when the amoeba is attacked by its environment—if, for instance, it's stuck by a pin—it contracts.

You react in essentially the same way. Life is a process of opening and closing. This is not just a metaphor—the rhythm has a physiological basis. You open up a little more each time you grow. When threatened, you literally retreat into yourself, draw in much like the amoeba.

The process is rooted in the autonomic nervous system. If you diagrammed your entire network of nerve fibers as an electrician might chart the circuits of a building, you'd find two major branches. One—the one you're most aware of—is the cerebrospinal system. It carries sensory impulses to your brain and, from your brain, transmits impulses regulating the voluntary movement of your muscles.

The other system—the autonomic—works below your conscious level (it's autonomous, hence its name) and is far more important to sustaining life. Within its realm is the regulating of your circulation and digestion, accomplished through two opposing subsystems: the parasympathetic and the sympathetic. The parasympathetic produces expansion or dilation of the blood vessels (thus a feeling of warmth) and increased activity of the glands and of the digestive and reproductive organs, all generally accompanied by feelings of well-being. The sympathetic system causes contraction, tightening, chilling, often with a sense of malaise.

Popular speech recognizes the contraction of the sympathetic system. People have "cold feet" and are "frozen with terror." Conversely, "bursting with enthusiasm" or "swollen with pride" refers to parasympathetic expansion.

You are somewhat like a charged battery in that the food and oxygen you take in create a considerable repository of energy. Biophysicists are fond of drawing up tables telling how many ergs you expend brushing your teeth. Broadly speaking, you convert the energy into complex chemicals that can be used by your body. In this form energy is carried throughout your body chiefly by your circulatory system. Extra charges can be supplied to any specific part of your body at need. Your autonomic nervous system directs the flow of energy by opening some blood channels and closing others. You may perceive a wave effect in these flows of energy. In expansion you may sense the impulse moving down from your head to your genitals, both areas being parasympathetic nerve centers. In contraction you may feel the excitation spreading up and down from the solar plexus, a focal point of the sympathetic nervous system.

In sexual excitement the normal expansion of the parasympathetic system markedly increases. Your skin becomes warm and dry. Your pulse is full and slow. Breathing is deep. Vision is sharp. Your genitals fill with blood and become acutely sensitive.

Note that in anxiety states your normal contraction is exaggerated. Your skin becomes cold and moist. The blood leaves the surface of your body. Your pulse is rapid and shallow. Vision is blurred, with dilated pupils. Your genitals are contracted and devoid of sensation.

The chronic muscular tension that constitutes body armor is a state of permanent contraction. The armor originates to reduce anxiety, to hold back painful feelings, to keep you from surrendering to emotion that may expose you to further hurt.

Unarmored contact is simple, spontaneous, direct. When unarmored, you have full contact with others and with yourself. Energy flows throughout your body. You are a warm, freely moving person.

Armor, on the other hand, restricts your emotional range. The tension literally blocks your energy flow. People markedly enclosed with armor are often cold people—they are emotionally chilly and also sensitive to drops in temperature. The tight, tense person who says, "I wish I were warmer," usually means it both ways.

▶ To explore the body's processes of expansion and contraction, go over a partner's body with the back of your hand. Detect the areas that are warmer than your hand. They are charged up with parasympathetic expansion. If they are cooler than the back of your hand, they are in a state of contraction. Most people have blocks in the back of the neck and the back of the pelvis. The buttocks are often cold, because they are held tightly. Try this with several partners to experience the differences among them.

Breath of Life

If you breathe better, you'll feel better.

The Greeks were aware that breathing is directly involved with one's emotional state. The term "psyche" is derived from a Greek word that came to mean "soul" after it had originally meant "the vital breath."

By controlling your breathing, you seek to control your feelings. Children do this as one of their first defenses. Watch a small child being yelled at by his parents or harassed by companions. Though he shows virtually no other response, his breathing will almost certainly become shallow and labored. At the end of his ordeal he may instinctively take a deep breath to restore his respiration.

Or he may not. And after a number of such stressful situations his breathing may be permanently impaired, thus reducing or deadening feelings. Limited breathing is one aspect of body armor.

As a child, you held your breath to stop crying. You drew back your shoulders and tightened your chest to contain your anger. You constricted your throat to prevent screaming. Each of these maneuvers reduces respiration. As an adult, you may have continued to inhibit your breathing to keep these feelings in check.

Thus you may have been caught in a vicious circle. You cut down your breathing to suppress painful emotions. But the very reduction of breathing makes you more vulnerable to emotional pain, and a limitation of breathing can be a major obstacle to emotional health.

You cannot have a maximum orgasm if you are not panting. You cannot fully discharge anger unless you breathe deeply and synchronize your breathing with your angry gestures. You cannot really cry or sob unless you breathe deeply.

Inadequate breathing reduces your vitality, increasing tiredness and exhaustion. Depression and fatigue are often direct results of depressed respiration. Dr. Alexander Lowen has noted: "The metabolic fires burn low in the absence of sufficient oxygen like a fire with a poor draft. Instead of glowing with life, the poor breather is cold, dull and lifeless. He lacks warmth and energy." Lack of oxygen can directly injure your circulation. In chronic cases of poor breathing the red blood count drops, and the small arteries become constricted, reducing blood supply.

If you're like most people, you're a poor breather. Your breathing is shallow, and you have a strong tendency to hold your breath in any situation of stress. Even in such simple stress situations as driving a car, writing a letter or awaiting an interview, you may limit your breathing. As a result, you increase your tension. Moreover, as if you were in a stuffy room, you are restless and unable to concentrate.

Some severely disturbed people have the so-called reversed-breathing pattern, which reduces the breath to a minimum. The abdomen is pulled in. Since there is no exhalation, no breath can enter. The bottle is filled with consumed air, and the person chokes his way through a strangulated life.

Conversely, deep breathing charges your body and literally

makes you come alive. You look and feel better. Your eyes sparkle.
Your muscle tone is good. Your skin has a bright color. Your body
is warm. You are better able to express emotion. You become more
relaxed.

Servicemen taking rifle practice are often advised to take three
deep breaths before pressing the trigger. Almost always the arm
steadies and the shooting improves. If you sit in the dentist's chair
barely breathing and in a state of tension, you increase your fear
and also intensify the pain. Concentrate on deepening your breathing instead. Not only will you be less afraid, but the procedure will
hurt less.

► As a curative, when you are in a state of distress of any kind, put
aside every thought for a moment. Take three slow deep breaths.
Begin by exhaling every bit of air in your lungs. Then inhale long
and deeply through your nose. Hold the breath. Exhale. After the
third such breath, you'll ordinarily be much better able to deal
with your problem.

In long, deep breathing you may develop tingling sensations in
your feet, hands and face. Occasionally the tingle may extend over
the whole body. On the whole the effect is pleasant. But if the
tingling sensations become intense, dizziness and feelings of
numbness and paralysis may intrude.

These sensations may be symptoms of hyperventilation, an unaccustomed intake of air that can injure people with heart and lung
conditions. Relax your breathing if this occurs. When your breathing returns to normal, these symptoms ordinarily disappear. As
your capacity to tolerate deeper breathing increases, you're likely to
be less and less troubled by symptoms of hyperventilation.

The tingling, however, is a superficial excitation that tends to
intensify specific feelings as you continue work on breathing. Sadness, longing and crying may emerge and, in turn, may give way to
anger. If you again block these feelings, you may suffer renewed
numbness and paralysis, indications of contraction and withdrawal.
But if you give vent to the emotions that surface, you're almost
certain to end the experiment feeling great.

Note: If you suffer from a cardiovascular or respiratory disease,
ask your physician before doing any experiments designed to
deepen your breathing. Similarly beware if you suffer from epi-
lepsy; hyperventilation has been known to cause seizures.

ORGASM REFLEX

Healthy breathing involves your whole body. Inhaling begins with an outward movement of your abdomen as your diaphragm contracts and your abdominal muscles relax. The wave of expansion then spreads upward to your chest. It is not cut off in the middle, as it is in disturbed people.

Exhaling starts as a relaxing in your chest and proceeds as a wave of contraction to your pelvis. It produces a sensation of flow along your front, ending in your genitals.

In healthy breathing the front of the body moves in a wavelike motion. If you lay down and exhaled completely, at the end of the exhalation your pelvis would tilt forward of its own accord, your shoulders would drop and your head would fall backward. You can see this "orgasm reflex" at work in a sleeping baby.

The orgasm reflex is the most enduring and widely accepted discovery of the controversial psychologist Wilhelm Reich. The reflex resembles the orgasm of sexual intercourse in both the pattern of its movement and the feeling of release, in the complete surrender to the natural contraction and the expansion it affords. Most adults are too full of tensions to be capable of complete orgastic movement, either in breathing or in intercourse. For example, the pattern is disrupted if the pelvis is too rigid to move backward in inhalation and forward in exhalation.

How capable of the orgasm reflex are you?

► Begin to notice your breathing by observing the breathing of others: the rate, irregularity, stoppages, sighs, coughs, chokes, sniffs, wheezes. Then, in your own breathing, see if you can examine the parts of this process.

Can you feel the air going into your nose, down your throat, into your bronchi? As you inhale, can you feel your ribs spread apart, your back stretch, the amount of space you occupy increase? Is your exhalation the normal effortless return of elastic ribs and muscles?

See what tensions you find. Is your chest expanded even when no air is coming in? Do you hold in your stomach during inhalation? Is there tautness in your throat and jaws? Concentrate especially on any tightness of your diaphragm, located in your midriff.

► During the day—when working, when near someone sexually

desirable, when confronted by a problem—notice how you tend to hold your breath instead of breathing more deeply, as the situation biologically requires. Sense what impulse you're restraining by holding back your breath. Do you want to cry? Run away? Punch someone or something?

Physiotherapist Magda Proskauer tells of a young dancer who suffered from severe anxiety attacks. She was an intellectualizer who relied exclusively on her reasoning capacity. "When I asked her to exhale gently, then wait and observe how the next breath came in, she became extremely anxious. She realized through this experience that she could not trust anything to happen of its own accord, not even respiration. Only what she controlled could occur."

This insight brought the dancer great relief. It led her to remembering her childhood—dominated by an overburdened, domineering mother, who knew no natural tenderness—and to understanding how these painful early experiences had made her mistrustful.

LUNGS ALIVE

Chances are you're a half-breather, breathing shallowly and keeping residual air in your lower lungs. You may find it a strain to take a full deep breath. To breathe lower into your lungs, you need to exhale more deeply.

► Yelling helps get the old air out, along with held-in feelings. Slap your entire chest, vigorously but not painfully. As you slap, yell "Ahhhhhh" as loudly as possible. After half a minute or so let the yelling and slapping subside. Experience the effects.

Next, take an enormous breath. Keep your lungs filled as long as possible, until you're desperate to breathe. Now slowly expel the air. Empty your lungs until you can't force out another puff of air. Stay completely empty, to the limit of your endurance.

Not yet! Not yet! When you're absolutely sure you can no longer bear it, let the air rush in. You will almost surely feel exhilarated, more vigorous, a renewal of life flowing into you.

PILLOW FIGHT

► A good way to stimulate breathing in a group activity is to have a pillow fight. The pillows should be a good handful but small enough to be throwable. For five or ten minutes hurl pillows at anyone in sight.

► Another group game combines breathing with other expressions of warmth. Dr. Charles R. Kelley, a psychologist in human-factors research, suggests this group activity: Stand in a circle, holding hands. Keep eye contact with the person next to you, and belly-pant sixteen times—draw in sharp, rapid breaths as deeply as you can. Squeeze hands, and sense the feeling of life.

Do a cycle of sixteen deep sighs, and squeeze hands again. Then do a cycle of chest gasps. Look at your partner, mouth open wide, and in a surprised way gasp, "Oh!" This freeing of your chest and mouth can be especially powerful in releasing feelings near the surface.

BEND OVER BACKWARD

► For an extremely effective stimulant to deeper and fuller breathing, arch backward over a stool two feet high. Stretching backward compresses your chest, spurring you to exert efforts to breathe. For a cushion use a rolled-up blanket, secured to the stool with string. Place the stool next to a bed to support your head and arms. Relax your pelvis, and keep your feet flat on the floor, about twelve inches apart.

Arch Backward over a Stool

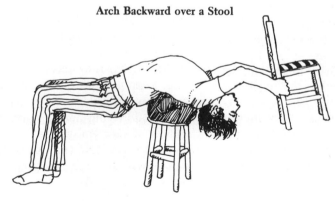

First, stretch back, with the blanket roll supporting your shoulder blades. Keep your mouth open, and allow your breathing to flow freely and easily. Breathing will generally get deeper and fuller without forcing. You may tend to hold your breath in this position as you do in most stress situations. Consciously counter this tendency.

Start slowly, and don't hold a stress position like this for more than two minutes. You're seeking to promote your breathing, not test your endurance.

Pain in the lower back indicates tension in that area. It will ordinarily disappear as you relax into the position. Don't hold the position if it becomes too uncomfortable or if you feel choked.

To mobilize other areas of your back, lean backward so that the stool rests midway between your waist and neck. Also rest on the stool at your waist and at your buttocks.

These positions stretch the muscles of your back and release tensions in your diaphragm. Try doing this every morning on arising for a good setter-up.

This exercise sometimes surfaces powerful feelings. Lowen recalls a patient who developed panic in her first experience with the stool. She took several deep breaths, then suddenly was on her feet, gasping for air. After a moment she burst into sobs, and her panic disappeared. The deep breathing had opened a feeling of sadness that welled up in her throat. Unconsciously, she tried to choke off the feeling. Her throat closed, and she could not breathe.

FORCED AIR

Breathing forcibly, like a bellows, is often effective in releasing tension.

▶ Suck in air through tightly pursed lips, as though you were breathing through a straw. Then push the air out, as though you were squeezing water from a sponge. Put your consciousness in parts of your body where there is blocking. Your concentration of thought will stimulate these parts and open them up to more feeling. Grunt, gasp, yell, as you breathe—the sounds are stimulating.

Bellowslike breathing can be invigorating in any position, at any time; it can be especially effective while you arch back over a two-foot-high stool. Forcible breathing over a stool is especially good for freeing your pelvis. Combine the breathing and stretching with a rocking back and forth, similar to what a driver does to free a tire stuck in snow.

►A related experiment is employed by psychologist Charles R. Kelley. He has developed methods for mobilizing body energy to induce feelings. Here is an edited transcript from a Kelley workshop, in which a participant named Bob experienced a surge of energy:

KELLEY: Gravity helps you breathe from the belly if you take an animal position.

[*Bob gets on his hands and knees with his head hanging. One person kneads each foot.*]

Dizzy? Breathe softly. Don't force. Breathe loudly out of your mouth. Now intensively take seven or eight breaths through your belly. Let everything loose. Now get on your back.

[*Bob lies on his back and bends his knees up, so his feet are flat on the floor. A helper moves Bob's knees back and forth, because there is a tendency for his pelvis to lock.*]

Without breathing faster emphasize the exhalation. Open your eyes, and check with each of us so that you know we are here. Keep your eyes open. Make deep sighs.

BOB: Fantastic! There are currents in my arms.

KELLEY: Give in to anything you feel. You're doing well.

BOB: If I let go, I'm going to feel stupid.

KELLEY: Gasp with your chest. Try to make just your chest move. Slower. Give in to that sound. Open your eyes.

[*He reaches under Bob's head and kneads the back of his neck.*]

BOB: My arms are falling asleep.

KELLEY: So much current numbs them. Soften. It could be pleasurable.

[*He directs some helpers to knead Bob's arms.*]

BOB: My nose feels like electricity. I can't control it. I'm a believer now. . . . It's like a mild electric shock. It affects the way you talk.

Test Your Tensions

A man once described how he spends his days: "Well, I get up in the morning and I vomit. Then I have breakfast and I vomit. Then I go to my office and vomit."

"Hold on," his friend said. "You vomit all the time?"

"Sure," the man said, puzzled. "Doesn't everybody?"

So it goes with chronic muscular tension. In the absence of specific symptoms, such as headaches or lower back pains, you probably aren't aware of the tensions in your body. Abnormal stiffness or flaccidity can become so much a part of you that you take it for granted. A first step in relief is to gain contact with areas of tension.

People are often afraid to feel their bodies. You may be aware that your body is a repository for repressed feelings but disinclined to encounter them in the flesh. Inevitably, you need to accept the relationship between your physical condition and your mental functioning.

For example, if chronic muscular tension makes you a rigid person, you move mechanically and you act unfeelingly. You are literally afraid to let go, afraid to let feelings come through in spontaneous movement, afraid to let your real, physical self take over. Muscular flaccidity suggests you're weak: emotionally as well as physically underdeveloped, possibly lacking in backbone.

However you may intellectualize, your body may reveal your emotional state. In one of Alexander Lowen's group sessions a participant raised repeated objections to every proposition Lowen advanced, trying to modify their import by introducing side issues. "His attitude could not be countered logically, since it would entail an endless discussion that would play into this person's defensive position," Lowen recalled. "This defense became clear when he began to work physically."

In every position, as the stress increased, he would wriggle and squirm. Biologically, he could not tolerate the stress, because of the tension in his body. Though he denied it at first, he at last realized that he habitually squirmed out of every stressful situation confronting him—sometimes verbally, but now physically.

To overcome any remaining doubts you may have about the reality of the mind-body unity, you may need to experience how your physical tension limits your personality, and how a release of this tension is also an emotional liberation. You're likely to find hope in discovering that your body has a wisdom of its own and the capacity to heal itself, and this realization may inspire in you a new respect for the instinctive forces of life.

Physical stress can work on you just as emotional stress does. You may experience strong feelings of inadequacy in the following positions. Be prepared for sudden urges to break out in rage, cry, vomit, behave sexually, both under the stress and when the tension is relieved. Urges you experience at the start will usually come from near your surface of awareness and can be coped with. If you fear possible embarrassment, by all means try these muscular experiments in solitude at first. If you are subject to anxiety attacks, familiarize yourself with what you are going to do by first describing it to yourself.

THE BOW

► Stand with your feet about thirty inches apart, toes turned inward, hands upon hips. Maintain your normal breathing, and arch yourself backward, with your knees bent as much as possible. If your body is integrated and coordinated, you can assume a position easily in which the line of your body from your heels to the back of your head forms a perfect arc.

The Bow

If your body is too rigid, you cannot arch properly. Bending your knees pulls your pelvis backward, and the upper part of your body leans forward. At the opposite extreme, if your body lacks muscle tone, you may show an exaggerated break in the arch of your back. In either case breathing is strained.

If you have tension in your lower back, you may feel pain in that region. Heels turning inward often indicates tenseness in the muscles of the buttocks. A sense of imbalance suggests that your feet are not properly grounded and thus support you poorly. The normal body is in a state of gentle oscillation. If your legs tremble violently, most likely their muscles are too tense. If you are tight as a drum, you may not vibrate at all.

The bow is a natural position for the body to take in gaining momentum for a strong forward movement, as in throwing a ball or swinging an ax. The bow has its greatest importance in sexual intercourse, for tensions that hinder your thrust will decrease your ability to achieve a full orgasm.

► As a follow-up to the bow, bend forward until your fingertips touch the ground, with your feet about twelve inches apart, toes turned inward, knees slightly bent. This may produce an involuntary vibration in your legs. Fine vibratory movements are a good sign. If you lack proper muscle tone, you may experience violent, erratic shaking. You literally can't hold your ground.

Oscillation will not occur if your legs are so tense that no feeling develops in them. A doctor participating in a group session had thickly muscled legs, which he assumed were strong and sturdy. They would not vibrate, and he realized that something was amiss. Ultimately he con-

**Bend Forward until
Your Fingertips Barely
Touch the Ground**

cluded that his severe leg tension was an expression of his unconscious fear of collapsing if he let the uncontrolled part of his being develop.

FINE TUNING

How much of your body can you let go into involuntary movement?

► Lie on a bed on your back, with your knees up. Breathe deep into your pelvis. Slowly, deliberately, move your knees together, then sideways toward the bed.

As you continue to do this, you will find a point in the arc where the vibrations in your legs and pelvis are most intense. Play around this point, and focus your deep breathing on it. If the area is alive and flexible, the vibrations will ordinarily get stronger and free of your control. Ideally, the vibrations will produce a fine tingling, extending into the upper half of your body, an internal stimulant to your breathing.

SPECIES STANCE

A cornerstone of Albert Pesso's psychomotor training is the "species stance," a drooping cavemanlike position, in which you relax all your muscles short of falling to the ground. Try to drop your defenses and inhibitions. Allow your mind to go blank.

Attaining the stance may make you look like the village idiot. If so, you're on the right track, for you're seeking to be an empty vessel, oscillating between gravity and your body-righting reflexes.

▶ Let your arms fall to your side and your head drop, so that your chin sinks to your chest. Let your stomach muscles loosen, and allow your belly to protrude.

You may be surprised how hard it is to let go of your body—until now you may not have let your body go, except when falling asleep. Are your controls insistent and persistent? Is your mind a whir of activity?

If you're an intellectualizer, you may feel that there is no control over your body except what you consciously exercise, that you'd fly apart if you eased your watch. Learn to let go, and perhaps, to your delight, you'll find that even when your conscious control is off, all is not gone. There is self-protection besides your conscious control—your automatic body-righting reflexes, your unconscious protection against falling.

The following experiments employ the species-stance position:

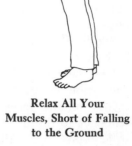

Relax All Your Muscles, Short of Falling to the Ground

▶ *Hand Flop.* This exercise is a good measure of how tense you are. Let a partner raise your wrist, so that your elbow bends to about 90 degrees while your upper arm hangs loose. Without warning your partner now drops your arm. A relaxed hand will fall smoothly, with a bouncing motion at the end. A tensed hand will go down slowly if it is controlled; or too forcefully if you are trying to help it along. Some especially tense people leave the hand in mid-air.

See if you give your partner total use of your arm. You may get tense when your partner touches you. Are you trying to force yourself to relax or to "help" your partner raise your arm? Such supposed help is often a form of compliance without trust.

When your arm is raised parallel to the floor, your hand, if relaxed, hangs loose from the wrist. A gentle shaking by your partner produces a flopping, with no resistance or control from you.

► *Torso Twist.* When you feel limp in the species stance, twist your torso—your mid-body from shoulders to hips—to the left or the right with a sudden jerk. If you're relaxed, centrifugal force will fling your arms and head to the side. Your torso will then have a pendulum motion, because of the elasticity of the muscles surrounding the spine, and will swing left and right until it settles back into the center.

See what tensions restrict you. You may be too rigid to turn the torso alone or to swing with enough force to fling out your arms. Are your arms relaxed enough so that they can fly up of their own accord? Does your trunk swing back and forth of its own volition?

► *Free Fall.* If you trip and start to fall, a series of reflexes will activate your legs and shift your body weight to restore your balance. You can easily inhibit these reflexes and let yourself fall—forward, until you catch yourself on your hands; backward, if there is someone behind to catch you. Just before you go all the way over, there is one final reflex—the fall catch—which is a lightning-swift lurch that can retrieve you, though you're practically on the floor.

Now become sensitive to the reflexes of falling, and practice dampening the earliest reflexes so that you can experience the fall catch. From the species stance lose your balance slightly. Note your tendency to rise up on your toes or rock back on your heels and stiffen your knees. Allow yourself to fall slightly forward, tipping over, unbent at the waist. Repress your early righting reflexes more and more until—at the lowest point of your tilt—you take a sudden lurching step forward, followed by shorter steps, which will end in a normal posture.

One lesson to learn is that you're safer than you may have thought in the hands of your natural processes. At first you're unlikely to be able to relax enough to let yourself fall free. Though you know you are holding back, you may feel you cannot help yourself.

Do you also sense that you can't let yourself go emotionally? The fall catch can be a rough measure of your spontaneity of emotional expression. It requires that you remove voluntary controls and let your natural reflexes take over. The action is violent. It may remind you of a strong emotional reaction and thus may frighten you. Can you give in to your impulses? Can you reduce your controls, permitting your instincts to act? You are safter than you realized in the hands of your natural body processes.

Squeeze and Stretch

Here's an experiment that gives instant relaxation so effectively that it's hard to believe. Try it before going on.

▶ Sit on the floor, and see how small a space your body can occupy. Bend your knees, and encircle your arms around them, pressing your heels into your buttocks. Bury your face in your thighs.

Then contract. Clench your fists, forearms, biceps. Bring your shoulders forward, and contract your belly. Scrunch up your face, so that it is as small as you can make it. Squeeze closed your toes, feet, calves, thighs, buttocks, eyes.

Hold this position until it becomes absolutely unbearable, a minute at least. Keep tightening up muscles that ease loose.

See How Small
a Space Your Body
Can Occupy

Now release—and instantly do the reverse exercise: Stretch; re-al-ly stretch, so that you occupy as much space as possible. Arch your back. Spread your toes and fingers. Pull apart your wrists, elbows, shoulders, your ankles, knees and pelvic joints. Stretch your face. Open your eyes and mouth wide. Stick out your tongue.

Hold for a minute or two. Release, and breathe deeply and

slowly. A great wave of peace is almost certain to come over you.

What's happened? Your body has gone from stress to strain to natural equilibrium. When you tense part of your body voluntarily and consciously, you can become aware of the tension and voluntarily let it go. Voluntary tensing, like the kind you've just done, can raise your unconscious tensions to a level of awareness. Thus, they may be relieved.

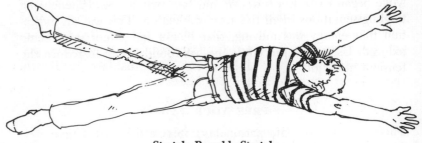

Stretch, Re-eal-ly Stretch

Some people, when asked to tense their muscles, protest, "Why? I'm too tense already." There is a difference between the voluntary tension you are aware of and the involuntary, unconscious tension that can cripple you.

You can deepen the tensing and relaxing experience by slowly contracting and releasing one muscle area at a time. Dorothy L. Nolte, a physical therapist in Laguna Beach, California, has devised an experiment to help you unwind, an adaptation of which goes as follows:

▶ Make a fist as hard as you can. Let the vibrations take over. As you breathe, visualize this area—this "directing your breath" can have the effect of channeling energy into a particular part of your body. Now tighten your wrist and lower arm, then the upper arm and shoulder. Hold on. Let it all go at once. Melt into relaxation.

▶ Repeat the tightening procedure—but instead of releasing the whole arm at once, let go in reverse order, from shoulder to fist, and experience how you can control your state of tension and relaxation. Now do this with your other arm. Go on to every muscle in your feet, legs and buttocks. Then your belly, chest and head.

"I make good money. But my boss is driving me nuts," said Mike, a young machinist. He had trouble sleeping because of his tension. When he was criticized at work, he would go over the incident again and again in his mind. Now he sat in his chair stiffly. His hands trembled. His mouth was drawn. He had a crick in his neck.

Using the principle of tightening up in order to relax, the therapist suggested that he do the preceding experiment, with special attention to obviously tight areas, like his mouth and his neck. Mike began to look less drawn and said that he was experiencing tingling sensations in all the areas worked on. This was an indication that energy was moving, that blocks and armor were being reduced. Using this procedure, he has found a way to reduce the tensions of his job.

FREE YOUR JAW

There is a type of rigid personality often revealed by a tight jaw. The individual has tension lines around his mouth, sometimes giving him a canine look. His jaw muscles are overdeveloped from clamping, bulging his face where his jaws meet and often pulling his jawline into a triangle. He usually is tight-lipped and has an indistinct voice.

His personality matches his physiognomy—understandable, since the formative tensions are the same. He holds things in: emotions, ideas, words. Getting him to talk is literally like pulling teeth. He gives little away and is frequently stingy. He hangs on to exhausted relationships and holds on to outworn customs, to memories, to grudges. When there is risk, he visualizes only the possible losses, rarely the compensating gains.

Mark was such a person. He showed a clear split in his face. While his eyes seemed alert, his jaw area looked tight and pale.

"Let's use the stool to deepen your breathing," his therapist suggested.

While arched backward over a two-foot-high stool, Mark worked his mouth and lips, stretching them, grimacing. He pinched his upper lip. He stuck his lower jaw out until it trembled by itself.

He sucked in air as if through a straw and exhaled as though he were squeezing every drop of water out of a sponge. He distended his chest as much as possible and then emptied his lungs as completely as possible. After this work Mark said he detected increased feeling in his face. For the first time his face looked all of one piece. There was color in the lower part, and the pinched look was gone.

▶ An enjoyable way to loosen chronic tension in your jaws and neck is for you and a partner to have a tug of war with a towel. Put the end of a towel in your mouth, and clamp down tight with your teeth. Your partner does the same with the other end. Then struggle with each other, the way a pair of puppies might play tug of war with a rag. Pull steadily—jerking your head may wrench a neck or loosen a tooth. Growling and snarling as you pull may enhance the experience.

▶ As another technique for mobilizing a fixed jaw, make your lower and upper teeth touch each other lightly. Concentrate, and your teeth may soon begin to chatter, as if from cold. Allow this to spread into a general shivering excitement through your muscles. Try to let yourself go until you are shaking all over, and meanwhile try to give up all your rigidity, even to the point where you're dizzy. You're likely to feel refreshed and possibly permanently more relaxed when you stop.

▶ In yet another experiment, which can be performed while you are shivering with release of tension, touch your teeth together in various positions by rotating your jaw. In the meantime, press your fingers against the sides of your head where the jaws meet. Concentrate on any painful spots of tension. They may be noticeably lumpy. Try massaging them for relief.

Now clamp your teeth hard. This will create a painful tension in your jaws that will spread to your gums, mouth, throat and eyes. Concentrate on the pattern of tension. Suddenly release your jaws, and feel the tension ease.

EXTEND YOURSELF

Some ball parks have the fans stand up and stretch in the seventh inning. The seventh-inning stretch is often the most enjoyable part of the game.

Stretching restores muscle tone. Your urge to stretch and yawn is your body's spontaneous effort to break loose from the constrictions of being held in.

▶ Take a seventh-inning stretch right now. Use as your model a cat that has just awakened from a nap. Luxuriously it arches its back, extends its legs, feet and toes as far as they'll go; spreads its jaws as if they will fall off—and all the while balloons itself up with air. Once it has swelled to its maximum of space, it permits itself slowly to collapse—and then is ready for new business.

LET YOUR BODY UNWIND

▶ Close your eyes, and let your body tell you where it would like to stretch. Don't forget to push your shoulders way back—it may relieve tension at the base of your neck. Also twist and kick and punch the air—oft-neglected forms of stretching cramped muscles. Sigh. Moan. Yawn. Afterward, experience the effects of being loosened.

Make it a habit to yawn and stretch frequently, especially on awakening. For a really good stretch get four friends to grab hold of your arms and legs and pull at once. Encourage them to have a four-way tug of war on you, since they're likelier to understretch than overstretch.

A final experiment is effective in stretching the muscles of your front thighs, which are often cramped but, under normal circumstances, hard to extend.

▶ Lie flat on a bed. Raise your belly, and inch your hands toward your feet. You'll form an arch grounded by the top of your head, the bottoms of your feet, and your forearms and hands. Breathe deeply, and you're likely to feel invigorated along your front and pelvis.

Since the pelvis is freely suspended in this position, it may develop a spontaneous movement if you're relaxed. These involuntary movements can give your body a feeling of aliveness.

You'll Form an Arch

Laying On of Hands

Bernard Gunther of Esalen offers a plan for world peace in which each person in the world would massage and be massaged by a new person every day. This means that every human being would spend at least two hours a day in giving and receiving warmth, comfort and well-being.

Body massage is a means of conveying friendship, sympathy, tenderness. Many physicians recognize that in this age of wonder drugs and medical technology, their laying on of hands is an important part of therapy. Touching the patient's body provides feelings of support, help, reassurance and acceptance that transcend words. In giving massage, you can experience the pleasure of feeling the contours and muscles of the body, the yielding of tension under your hands, the satisfaction of helping and caring for another. When receiving a massage, you can indulge in the luxury of letting go, of trusting and of being cared for.

Physiologically, massage stimulates the flow of blood and improves muscle tone. Reducing chronic muscular tensions generally requires considerable physical manipulation, especially for the muscles of the jaw, the base of the neck, the shoulders, the spine and the pelvis. While some procedures of massage entail a knowledge of anatomy and physiology, much can be done by the average person if his touch is sensitive. Learning to massage is a bit like learning to swim and ride a bike—almost anyone can do it adequately with a little practice.

TIPS ON MASSAGE

▶ A massage out-of-doors in the sun is ideal. Next best place is a quiet room at a comfortable temperature. Soft music or the sounds of nature make a soothing background. Keep talking to a minimum.

For added relaxation take a hot shower or bath before beginning. Because rubbing dry human skin can cause friction, use some form of oil. A good home formula is 1 part baby oil to 2 parts vegetable oil or mineral oil, with a few drops of oil of cloves. Or try commercial oils or creams.

If you're not sure how much pressure to use, ask your partner. In general, a gentle, firm touch is best—but a particular area of tension may call for a different kind of pressure. Too much will hurt; too little can strain your partner's patience.

A rule of thumb is to stroke and press toward the heart—upward on the arms and legs, downward from the neck and shoulders, inward from the chest and back. Keep at least one hand on your partner. Breaking contact can cause a subtle disturbance.

You need not always massage the whole body. Concentrating on one area often provides great release. This is especially true of the hands, feet and back of the neck. You could spend an hour on the feet alone, and the whole body would benefit.

When you're being massaged, try to keep your mind on what is happening. Feel the experience. Without trying to hinder or help, allow whatever impulses that develop within your body—surges of emotion, urges to stretch or quiver, impulses to yawn or groan—to be expressed.

In giving a massage, seek to locate and release your partner's tensions. Concentrate on his muscles, breathing and movements, and sense from his reactions what he is experiencing. Is he peaceful? Angry? Does he want kneading, slapping, pounding? Or soothing and stroking?

You and your partner can so tune in to each other that you will instinctively do the right things, although neither of you may be able to express in words what the needs and responses are.

Massage need not entail only a duet. In a group of three or four decide which of you is feeling the most tightness. The others then work together to relieve his tension.

► Methods of massage are practically limitless. Experiment with a variety of ways of massaging your partner. Here are some basic ones: *Corkscrew* up and down fingers and toes, as if you were undoing a bottle top. *Press* thumbs into hands, wrists, feet, ankles, upper and lower back. *Knead* the big muscles of the arms, legs, buttocks, as if they were dough. *Wring* arms and legs, as if you were wringing a washcloth. *Draw* circles with your index finger on the neck, back and sides.

"JUST THROUGH TOUCH"

Hal Streitfeld's wife, Virginia, was introduced to massage techniques in a workshop conducted by Ned Hoke, who gave massage at Esalen. When she came back, she sat down at her typewriter and recorded her impressions about what had happened:

"Some of the people wanted to talk about what we were doing, but I didn't. What really struck me was how much communication there was just through touch. One girl who hadn't talked at all came over and massaged my back, and I felt so much with her. I didn't want to hear her hangups or problems—the typical encounter-group stuff—I just wanted to know her through sensual touch.
► "Ned demonstrated on somebody. He starts very slowly, making contact with the person by a laying on of his hands. It is not an intellectual process but an instinctual, feeling one. There are no express techniques or rules, but it is done as communication with feeling.

"Ned starts by laying his hands on the upper chest. He said that at Esalen he has just laid on his hands and sat there with the person for two or three hours—with someone whom, he felt, needed just that.

"Oh, yes! The oil! At first the idea of using oil seemed somewhat repellent to me—so greasy. But it was wonderful. It sort of soaked in and at the same time allowed your hands to move more easily over the body. A much more sensual way than just rubbing over bare skin. There was a great association with the phrase 'all the oils of India'—a very rich, caring, sensual feeling. The whole thing comes to have ritual dimensions. Massage and meditation just go together in a way I had never envisioned.

"Later in the demonstration Ned was massaging his co-leader, and she started to give directions from her prone position. Ned got very angry, and he tried to explain the essence of this kind of massage—that it is nonverbal communication: The person receiving it must let go of his own ideas and be open to what comes; the person doing the massaging does not follow rules but responds to the body as he experiences it. Even something like your feet have so much to say!

"Ned explained the great and usually overlooked importance of the feet—our sole contact with the ground, the base of support for our whole body—and how much we abuse them from too-tight shoes, high heels, constantly enclosing them, etc. We don't think of the feet as being a center of great feeling—except when they hurt—but remember children and how much pleasure they receive out of tickling the feet.

"One thing Ned emphasized is to use much more pressure than beginners tend to. The order in which the body is massaged is not that important—different people use a different order. The main thing is to communicate with warmth of feeling.

"Another guideline is, if you do one foot, do the other; one side, also the other. Don't leave the body out of balance or unfinished. Another tip: Don't get up right after being massaged. Stay with the feelings, and extend them. If two friends are trading massages, don't interrupt the reverie with 'Now it's my turn.' Wait until your partner is ready. This isn't so hard to do, for the giving of a massage is as sensually rewarding as the receiving.

"The whole give-and-take of massage is wonderful for couples—a learning to give and take without talking, a real putting of yourself in the other's hands. A real trust thing. One part of massage that shows this clearly is the head lift and massage in the neck. You don't realize how much you hold your head until someone else tries to lift it and you can't let him do it. You can't give up the control. I think it would be very hard to fake a head lift.

"Massage provides a natural climate for nudity—you have a specific reason for it: How can you massage with clothes on? And hiding behind towels—the traditional massage way—does seem pretty silly. When Ned started massaging someone's face to show us how, she was clothed. Then, when he started reaching to the muscles at the base of the neck, the clothes started to interfere. He stated that fact and said, 'I guess it's time we took our clothes off.' And he took his off. We all found ourselves following suit, with such ease that you'd have thought we were nude workshop professionals. Through massage you can get to know another's body and to feel your own without it becoming sexual, unless you chose to go on to that."

Let It Out

Pete was at loose ends. He had just come back from two years in the Peace Corps and didn't know what kind of work he wanted to do. He was unhappy living in his parents' house. Yet, he was draft bait and hesitated to make long-term plans. He had no friends, felt in no position to make any and was lonely. "Everything and everybody bugs me," he complained.

Talking got him nowhere. Then, in an encounter group, he tried a nonverbal representation of his conflicts. He and Jack, the leader, gripped each other's shoulders and pushed and pulled. The struggle grew titanic, but Pete didn't utter a sound. "Yell," Jack urged.

"I can't," Pete replied. "It's hard to have different ends of my body going at once."

"Get on the floor," Jack suggested. He pulled at one of Pete's arms—a loose end. Ben, another group member, pulled on the other arm. Pete struggled and began to yell. Other members grabbed his legs. Pete was stretched, yelling and writhing.

The people pulling at him were like the forces in his life, tearing at him but keeping him on dead center. "Okay," Jack said. "Struggle with all your strength against these forces." Pete mobilized his strength, concentrating it first on one pressure, then on another. Thereby he experienced the most effective way of responding to a multiplicity of life's pressing problems. The physical activity alone helped him release tension.

"I feel great," he said at the end of the session. "I feel really great."

"Real good, huh?" someone said.

"No. Great," Pete replied. "Like Alexander the Great."

Like Pete, you can confront your emotions through simulations that are largely physical. You feel essentially the same whether you are "pulled apart" figuratively by conflicting demands, or literally by four people tugging at your limbs. What exactly do you feel when you are "pushed around" by a boss, spouse, parent? You can find out in a game situation by having some person literally push you around. The beauty of such games is that you can not only explore your emotional response but also grow by experimenting with new ways of responding.

Judy was a college instructor in her late twenties. She was troubled by loneliness and explained her lack of contact with people: "Everyone I know is blah." Talking provided little insight for her. She created a barbed wall of wit, carrying on about the blahness of her dates ("Alfred's so dull he doesn't have dreams"), her friends ("They live in *Better Homes and Gardens*"), her parents ("I fell asleep during one of their postcards").

She said she came to an encounter group to "meet people." She added, "I thought I might learn something about human relations. I'm not getting through to my students."

"They don't like you," a group member interjected. "Is that what you're trying to infer?"

"Also, I'm not too crazy about them," Judy replied. "And it's not 'infer.' It's 'imply,' dumbbell."

Phil, the leader, spoke up. "Judy, I get the feeling you can talk the arm off a brass monkey. Care to see what happens without the words?"

Judy nodded.

"You and Larry"—Phil pointed to a man in the group—"go to opposite corners of the room. Walk toward each other, and act out anything you feel."

Judy approached Larry with visible hesitancy. When he got close to her, she suddenly pushed him away. He came back. This time she lashed out at him with her fingernails.

Phil interrupted. "Now act out what you'd *like* to feel."

After a moment Judy turned to Larry, put her arms around him and held him close.

The subsequent discussion expanded little on the pantomime. Judy saw through some of her defenses and summed up: "I want to keep people away. When they come close, I feel crowded. It's not that they're such boobs. It's that I'm afraid of intimacy. Which I dearly crave. And which, if Larry's typical, probably won't kill me."

Only when Judy found herself lashing out with her fingernails did she realize the feeling that lay behind her sharp words. As you let go in the following experiments, welcome the irrational side of

your nature. Your muscular coordination is likely to increase spontaneously as your movements—kicking, striking, reaching—gain
emotional meaning. Follow the example of children at play.
Though on one level a child knows he's in a game, he takes it seriously and responds with authentic emotion. Thereby, in a relatively risk-free setting, he develops strengths that will serve him in
real life.

TEARS FOR JOY

The rule for this game is simply: Cry.

► Think of the worst episodes of your life. The incidents of grief
and sadness. The moments you've been betrayed. The times you've
been shit on. And let yourself cry.

Convulsive crying is a primary mechanism for releasing tension
and expressing loss and disappointment. You feel better after a
good cry. Psychotherapists observe that after crying, a patient's
body is less rigid, his breathing easier and deeper, his eyes brighter
and his skin color better.

Biologically, crying is a rebound from a state of contraction. But
in our culture crying is frowned upon. A junior-high-school coach
told his despondent team after a near win, "Crying's for fags."
Women who cry "too much" are termed weak sisters. Youngsters
who weep are taunted with the worst epithet of childhood: "Cry-
baby!"

Conversely, the culture applauds keeping a stiff upper lip (another painfully apt figure of speech). After the assassination of
President Kennedy and then of Robert Kennedy, the press was full
of praise for their widows. Jacqueline and Ethel Kennedy were un-
doubtedly brave. But for what explicitly did they get credit? For
not breaking down and crying. If they had, they presumably would
have discomforted the nation.

When you were a child, your parents were most likely perturbed
by your crying and took measures to make you stop. Some parents
reward the child every day he doesn't cry. Others punish or humiliate him for crying. Either way, the effect is approximately the
same: The child learns to inhibit his crying, thereby denying himself an important outlet for tension and thus becoming more rigid.

It is unjust to force a child to stop crying, even when his crying stems from tiredness, crankiness or unreasonable demands. If you can't reasonably comfort a child, you have a right not to be disturbed by his crying. You act in fairness and compassion if you tell him, "Cry if you wish. But please go into another room."

If you are afraid to cry, you almost certainly are also afraid to smile. You hold yourself together rigidly so that you won't cry. Pleasure challenges this rigidity, causing you to become anxious lest, as your tensions relax, you lose control and break down in tears. Your anxiety reflects the conflict you suffer between your need to let go and your fear of letting go.

Thus, a fear of crying may severely limit your capacity for pleasure. So cry. You'll have more fun.

NO TRESPASSING

You have a large area of your personality that says, NO TRESPASSING. Here is your privacy: the traits and preferences that you instinctively hold to, to define yourself as an individual being. Anyone intruding on this precious preserve of yours will trigger a charged wire: your anger.

Anger is a healthy emotion. It is your personality's first line of defense against assault and exploitation. But in order for anger to stay healthy, it must be expressed. Just as a trapped surge of electricity can burn out a motor, so anger, if not discharged in actions or words, is likely to turn into resentment.

Anger is vibrant, active and can be quickly gone. Resentment is passive and eats away at you, like a cancer. Anger flashes. Resentment seethes and smolders and can explode in destructive rage.

Our rigid, conforming culture is intolerant of vehement expressions of individuality. As a child, you may have been punished for letting off steam. (A savvy parent lets a tantrum run its course, even gives a child safe things to throw.) Or made ashamed of it. "You're too sensitive," you may have been told. Translation: "Anger shows you're weak." Thus, you may fear normal, inescapable anger and thereby be plagued with undischarged resentments. If your childhood was further upset by your parents' raging at each other, or if you were much smacked around by an angry parent, anger in your mind may equal destruction: of relationships, of life itself.

Anxiety over anger, the desperate need to hold in anger, can cause rigidity. You cannot let go for a moment, for fear you'll expose the anger welling up inside you. Since rigidity dulls all emotions, neither can you unself-consciously cry, enjoy yourself or express most other feelings. When the pressure of your anger becomes unbearable, you explode—possibly confirming the notion that originally inhibited you: that anger destroys.

Respect, then, your moment-to-moment anger. It's an essential safety valve. Follow the practice of Dr. Sam Ableman, the hero of Gerald Green's *The Last Angry Man*. Cross Dr. Ableman, and he gets his back up and tells you you're a galoot. In one episode he's summoned to a police station to treat a prisoner. Before seeing the patient, he stops to settle accounts with an officer who was rude to him over the phone. In a society strained by its efforts to hold in anger, Dr. Ableman is also the last happy man. And, free of resentments, probably a better doctor.

If your anger is justified and you express it, you may be surprised at how quickly you get an apology. The very fact that you can express anger gives you a tactical advantage, useful in dealing with aggravations like rude clerks and incompetent plumbers.

Also, far from destroying a meaningful relationship, expressing anger can strengthen it. By being open, you say to the other person that you care enough about him to let him know what you're feeling, and enough about your friendship to save it from reserve, sarcasm and other masks of resentment.

Anger exists on four levels, according to psychiatrist Daniel Casriel. The first level is intellectual anger. Superficially, you're aware in your head that you are angry. This is the deepest level many people feel. It is rarely satisfying emotionally.

You feel the second level, riddance anger, in your throat. It is directed toward people who are important in your life and involves the feeling, "I'm angry. Get away from me." Saying as much usually discharges a spurt of anger with, say, a member of your family.

The third level, felt in your chest, is deeper and characterized by murderous rage—"I hate you and want to kill you!" Expressing it gets the feeling out, leaving no further need for action or expression. Expelling the rage can often bring about an amicable end to even the most savage argument.

The deepest level of anger is called identity anger, because it involves your whole being. It is an emotion that your whole body feels. It is expressed by the statement "Don't you ever do that to me again!" When felt and declared, it allows you finally to be free of those who have hurt you.

Though expressing your anger to the person who offended you is ideal, it's often impractical (a boss; a teacher); injudicious (the episode is long over; the person is emotionally incapable of responding well to your anger); or impossible (you don't see the person any more; he's dead). You can, however, express your anger physically and may thereby relieve the feeling you hold against him. Having gotten over your rage, you can give a careful, controlled response. In an appropriate way you can declare where you stand.

► Possibly the most effective technique for physically releasing anger is to pound a bed murderously with your fists and forearms and to kick it viciously. Be out to kill.

► Other ways that work: Punch and strangle a pillow. Whack a bed with a tennis racket—the reverberations zooming up the handle are invigorating. Ditto if you hit a tree with a stick.

Psychologist Charles Kelley has suggested that you add an element of triumph to your expression of anger in a simulated killing of a rattlesnake:

► Get on your knees on the floor, and grasp one end of a towel with both hands, as if you were clutching the tail of a rattlesnake. From the pit of your stomach work up a paroxysm of fear, loathing and anger. Remember that if you ease up, the snake can whip around and bite you. Close your eyes, breathe deeply—and smash it down as hard as you can; keep thrashing until you kill it. You are likely to experience a great feeling of relief and expansion.

If you can't express anger verbally, release the emotion through physical means. To discharge your anger, you need not confront your antagonist in the flesh.

► Shout as you perform the movements. Cursing and screaming are part of your physical expression and will help relieve tension in your throat. As you strike, bring to mind the person you're angry at—parent, spouse, business associate—and direct your shouts and curses at him. If you're into the emotion, you'll get nearly the relief of actually saying this to the person.

At first, in working off anger, you are likely to be fragmented and uncoordinated. The tone of your voice may fall short of expressing the venom you feel. In striking from a standing position, you may flail your arms without involving your back and legs. In kicking a bed while lying on it, you may use your legs aggressively but hold your head and the upper part of your body rigid.

Your lack of coordination is a sign that you haven't committed yourself fully to the activity. You may be resisting it for the same reasons you have trouble showing anger in the first place. If your movements don't involve your whole body, they will be less than wholly satisfying. As your coordination develops, your expression of anger will become more of an emotional experience. Anger you've long suppressed is likely to rise to your consciousness to be released.

► When the occasion arises, you can invite an antagonist to an innocuous form of physical combat. Shoulder pushing and arm wrestling are often used in encounter groups to let adversaries vent their hostility. Almost always, the opponents feel better toward each other afterward.

The struggle can bring you insight into the cause of your hostility. Dr. Elizabeth E. Mintz, a psychotherapist in Manhattan, suggests that an encounter-group member who expresses hostility or competitiveness select an opponent and engage in arm wrestling. This is often a symbolic struggle—you're fighting not so much the other person as you're fighting part of yourself.

"You son of a bitch," one participant said afterward. "I really hated you . . . then suddenly I realized it wasn't you; it was my brother!" He went on to close his eyes and imagine himself talking to his older and stronger brother, expressing the rage and competitiveness that he had never worked through in years of more conventional therapy.

A physical struggle may also reflect how you generally handle conflicts. One young woman said she could never express her opinions clearly to her boss, a woman. Dr. Mintz invited the girl to arm-wrestle and quickly pulled her over, though the girl was much stronger.

"I went down like a cream puff," the girl reflected. "I couldn't use my strength at all."

Almost at once the girl became aware of how she was unable to express herself with anyone who reminded her of her mother. This awareness led to a useful exploration of her feelings of guilt, helplessness and submissiveness toward her mother.

A man who thought himself afraid of losing found himself top-pling over. "I thought I wanted to win, thought I was winning," he remarked. "Suddenly I was down. My God, I do the same thing at tennis!"

He soon realized that he was actually afraid of winning. This was a carry-over from clashes with his father, in which he feared victory and consequent punishment. The arm wrestling shed light on why he tended to lose not only at tennis but in life.

THE WORM TURNS

In San Francisco dancer A. A. Leath has held weekly classes in using movement creatively. During one class eight of his students executed a "pile-up" on a husky young man, who had a hard time asserting himself. They held him flat on his back until he so strug-gled and screamed obscenities at them that they let him up. Since then, he's found it easier to assert himself against people who hold him down.

"No" is the operative word in asserting yourself. If you let your-self get pushed around, it's likely that you're afraid you'll be re-jected or punished, even destroyed, if you say no. Possibly you think of yourself as being "nice," "good-natured," "easygoing." But almost certainly you build up resentment at being used. And since users can pick out patsies the way owls spot mice, you in-crease your own burdens by attracting precisely the kind of people who are likely to take advantage of you.

The ability to say no protects you from being overwhelmed by outside pressures and allows you to discriminate among the de-mands and inducements to which you are constantly subjected. Al-exander Lowen has argued that if you can't say no, neither can you say a meaningful yes: "In the absence of the ability to say No, an assent is merely a form of submission and is not the expression of an individual who has a freedom of choice. The person who cannot say Yes is afraid of commitment, because he is unsure of his own mind. To know your mind is to mind your No."

"No" is an expression of opposition that is the cornerstone of individuality, Lowen adds. The child who opposes his parents is saying, "I am me. I am different. I have a mind of my own." Such a child will learn to think for himself, whereas the "good," obedi-

ent child—the kind whom authoritarian school systems beam upon
—sacrifices his individuality and loses his ability to think for himself.

If your negative and hostile feelings were severely inhibited early
in life, in adulthood they may find expression indirectly and de-
structively. Negativism—as expressed by stubbornness, spite, sarcasm, chronic dissatisfaction, the inclination to be a put-down—is
often the product of suppressing your no. (If you're negativistic,
you may benefit from Chapter 9, "Games for Building Warmth
and Trust.")

► This experiment will help you assert yourself, with your whole
body. First concentrate on the feelings of resentment you have
that stem from feeling put upon. Now lie down on the floor—and
throw a tantrum. Rhythmically kick and punch the floor, with the
hand and foot of the right side, then the left. Do this as hard as
you can. At the same time, yell the words you're ordinarily afraid
to say: "No! Get away from me! Leave me alone! Don't bother
me!"

Abandon yourself freely to the movement. Let go of your head,
so that it moves together with the rest of your body. In a tantrum
your head rotates to the side that's kicking and punching. At first
you may be frightened by a feeling of being carried away by the
movement. There is no danger. You have plenty to kick about, so
give in to the feeling, and enjoy the release.

One person for whom this experiment worked was Sally, a divorcee and part-time employee of a publicity firm. She was a helpful,
giving person—but felt obligated to be nice all the time. Neighbors
sent their children to her house with the message "Can you watch
me while Mommy's at the store?" Single friends dropped in
around dinnertime, and she invited them to stay, with only a rare
added word of sarcasm. When she finally did get fed up and ex-
ploded, it was usually some innocent—often her own children—
who got burned.

A TV producer wanted one of Sally's clients on a talk show.
Sally made the necessary arrangements with the client, normally
the limit of her responsibilities. Then the producer called. "Do me
a favor," he said. "It would make a better show if a couple of other
people appeared with your man." He gave Sally three names, and

she agreed to make arrangements with them, although she had great misgivings.

The producer called again. "Gotta reschedule, sweetie. Get things right with your people, will ya?" Sally then got in touch with her client again, as well as with the three extras. The arrangements became complicated, as one or another of the guests couldn't make it, and well over a dozen calls were needed until a new date was set. Meanwhile, Sally began hating herself.

The producer called once more. "Just get everybody to the studio an hour earlier," he said. Sally noticed that his tone was becoming ever more abrupt. Lips pursed, she complied. But she at last became aware that the problem lay within her.

She talked the problem over with a clinical psychologist. One of the most helpful of his recommendations was that she practice the "tantrum" exercise for physical self-assertion. She did so. A few days before the broadcast the producer called her up and barked, "Listen, I need news releases and pictures of those people right away."

"I'll cover my client," Sally told him. She went on to inform him in no uncertain terms precisely what she thought of him and his highhanded ways.

After a pause the producer replied, "I'm sorry. I'll do it myself."

IV

←————————————————————————————————→

INSIDE
YOUR SELF

You have within you a self. This stable core of strength and growth is the essential you—who you really are, what you really want. If you deny your self, you are doomed to a life of pain and dissatisfaction. But if you find your self and act in accord with it, you will be self-accepting and at peace.

7

Games for Being Yourself

You are a battlefield between impulses that are distinctly yours, indeed that define *you*, and pressures from the outside.

On one hand, you have at the core of your personality a stable center of strength and growth. In Western psychology this wellspring of your being is most often termed the self. It has been perceived and reflected on in other fields of study, of which Christianity and Zen are the most influential. In various writings it has been termed the soul, the spirit, the essence, the inner being.

Empirically, your self exists. It is the essential you—who you really are, what you at root want—over and beyond the expectations and behavior patterns forced on you by others. Your self is the unique, autonomous you, the you that theoretically would continue to function even if everyone and everything else on earth were to disappear.

Like an armature in sculpture, your self is the central strand of your personality. It underlies all your thoughts and words, all your actions and emotions. If you act in accord with your self, you will be self-accepting and at peace. Your life will be rich, productive and happy.

But if you deny your self, if you lead not your own life but somebody else's, you will suffer emotional distress. At the least, you are likely to be lonely, for no one is relating to the real you. You may often be bored, since you are not really interested in what you are doing.

Attempting to disregard your self is much like trying to ignore a full bladder. Though you may continue to function, you will suffer recurrent discomfort.

Outward success is not necessarily a criterion of whether you are fulfilling your self. What you do must feel right for you—otherwise beneath it all you may feel like a failure. A business giant comes to a psychiatrist after his latest coup and complains, "I just made a million bucks. When do I stop being miserable?" A physician groans after his latest professional triumph and asks his therapist, "Why don't I feel real?" A suburban housewife ticks off her achievements as a mother and homemaker, then wants to know, "Where am I in all this?"

Each is a success by everybody's standards but his own. Each has manipulated himself into excelling according to the general standard of achievement. The very success is a kind of trap, since the smiles of fortune make it that much harder to break away. But each senses that the success is phony and hears the inescapable self whispering relentlessly, "Liar. Cheat. Traitor. Fake."

The purpose of this chapter and the next is to help you be a success on your own terms, to express your self despite the opposition of much of the world, and to thereby behave in a way that is authentic—truly expressive of you.

Self-Study

A milestone in the study of the self occurred after a young man named Abraham H. Maslow came to New York from Wisconsin. Maslow was excited by the city's being the center of the psychological universe of the late 1930's. He seized the chance to take courses with the near-legendary anthropologist Ruth Benedict and psychologist Max Wertheimer.

"They were the most remarkable human beings," Maslow recalled in "Self-Actualization and Beyond" (*Challenges of Humanistic Psychology*, edited by James F. T. Bugental). "My training in psychology equipped me not at all for understanding them. It was as if they were not quite people but something more than people."

In an effort to fathom them, Maslow took notes on them and later wrote: "I realized in one wonderful moment that their two patterns could be generalized. I was talking about a kind of person." Maslow tried to see if their pattern could be found elsewhere. "I did find it . . . in one person after another."

In that moment of insight Maslow saw that Wertheimer and Benedict were "self-actualizing" people. They and others like them were Olympic gold-medal champions of health and growth and could be understood only by an exploration of questions new to psychology: What is the best that people are capable of? What are they like when they achieve it? What are the strengths of human nature?

Maslow embarked on landmark studies of the "supernormal" person, the individual who departs from the norm, not by being sick but by being exceptionally healthy. This approach was a marked departure from conventional psychological research, which had focused on the pathological, and broke ground for other investigators venturing into the study of the normal. Since Maslow wrote about the self-actualizing person, Carl Rogers has spoken of the "fully functioning person," Sidney Jourard of the "disclosed self," Marie Jahoda of the "mentally healthy," Charles Morris of the "open self," and Theodore Landsman of the "beautiful and noble person."

Together they have pioneered a psychology of optimism, an empirically based view holding forth great hope for human potential. Maslow's investigations, substantiated by virtually all who have followed him, indicate, in essence, that you have a biologically based inner nature that is good or at least neutral. "A human being is not a *tabula rasa*, not a lump of clay or plasticine," Maslow has observed. "He is something which is already there." This "something," the self, is a well-developed structure representing, at minimum, your inborn temperament and proprioceptive biochemical balances.

Moreover, Maslow has reported, what you can be, you *must* be. You have a hierarchy of basic needs that you almost automatically direct your life to gratify. After the gratification of hunger, the most basic need, you seek to gratify your need for feelings of safety, belongingness, love and self-esteem, more or less in that order.

The need to be self-actualizing—to let your self guide your life— ranks just after these, Maslow found. At the peril of a stunted emotional life, you thus have not only a desire but also a pressing urgency to fulfill what you are potentially.

STEPS TOWARD SELF-ACTUALIZATION

The self-actualizing person has risen to his full height emotionally. He often looks as he *is*: brilliantly alive. Adjectives commonly describing him are "alert" and "radiant."

He is more in touch with reality, more perceptive and accepting of himself, others and the world. He is unconventional and spontaneous, without calling attention to his differences. So much is he his own man that just as he rarely conforms for conformity's sake, he seldom nonconforms for nonconformity's sake. This highly unusual individual dresses and outwardly acts much like everyone else. His general attitude seems to be that as long as one set of traffic rules works as well as another, he might as well follow the one in mode. But if a rule goes against his grain, he is likely to disregard it.

He receives his satisfactions from inside himself, thus enjoys solitude more than other people do. While ordinarily cordial in his relations with others, he is self-directed. He is largely free of a need to impress other people or to be liked by them. Though sometimes labeled "distant" and "selfish," for the most part he has a generous view of his fellow man. His sense of humor is gentle and self-aware, rarely hostile.

The self-actualizing person has a great ability to love and to enjoy sex. He is spontaneous, open and giving in love relationships. He is a creative person, less constricted in his thought processes. He has a deep empathy with people and can have profound relationships with others. He has the capacity for continuing wonder about life, the ability to see a rainbow fresh and whole each time.

How can you start on the path to self-actualization? What does expressing your inner being mean in terms of actual behavior, actual procedure? Here, paraphrased from a talk before a group of guidance counselors, are eight modest beginnings that Maslow has set forth:

▶ Devote yourself totally to experiencing one moment. Try to feel it fully and unself-consciously, the way a child would. Become totally absorbed in it, to the exclusion of everything else. You probably have such moments of intense concentration occasionally; you can make them happen more frequently. "At this moment of experiencing," noted Maslow, "the person is wholly and fully human. . . . This is a moment when the self is actualizing itself."

► Think of life as a "process of choices, one after another." You have to make dozens of choices a day. Each time, you decide either to progress or to regress; to move on in development or to fall back on habit or fear. Try to make the growth choice more and more. "Self-actualization," according to Maslow, "is an ongoing process." If you make the growth choice instead of the fear choice a dozen times a day, you thus "move a dozen times a day toward self-actualization."

► Listen to the "impulse voices" inside your self. Look within your self for your tastes and decisions. "Most of us," Maslow pointed out, "listen not to ourselves but to Mommy's introjected voice or Daddy's voice or to the voice of the Establishment, of the Elders, of authority, or of tradition." Concentrate instead on how you actually feel about something, not how you think you are expected to feel.

► "When in doubt, be honest rather than not." Most of us opt for diplomacy and discretion, rather than for honesty when we're in doubt about what to say. But if you are honest, you are looking to your self for answers, and you are taking responsibility for what you find in yourself. And each time you take responsibility for your self, you are taking a step toward actualizing your self.

► Be courageous. Dare to be different. Risk making unpopular statements if they reflect what you feel. In the avant-garde art world, Maslow feels, a conformity of taste is demanded. Most people try to make sophisticated-sounding remarks about the art they don't understand. Instead, be prepared to say, "I don't know what to make of that dance program. I'll have to think about it." Or, "That painting puzzles me."

► Find out what you want to do, and work hard to do it well. Be as first-rate as you can. This may mean, says Maslow, going through an arduous period of preparation to realize your possibilities.

► Leave yourself open to peak experiences, those "little moments of ecstasy"—for they are fleeting moments of self-actualization. Try to set up conditions in which peak experiences are more likely to occur, and accept them when they do. According to Maslow, almost everyone has peak experiences, but "some people wave these small mystical experiences aside" and deny them. Instead, look for them, and savor them. (Peak experiences are discussed in Chapter 4, "Games For Expanding Your Consciousness.")

▶ As much as possible, identify your defenses—behavior patterns you have seized on to protect you from emotional pain—and find the courage to give them up. This is painful but necessary, for repressing a problem won't solve it.

If you work at following these steps, you are on the path toward self-actualization—toward finding out who you are, what you like, what is good or bad for you; toward exploring your self and acting on what you find in your self.

Sensing Your Self

The concept of the self may elude you at first. Professor Martha Crampton of Sir George Williams University in Montreal has noted: "Most of us who are working with the concept of the self in therapy have had repeatedly the experience of a patient who simply cannot grasp the idea—who looks upon it as a logical construct or an abstraction, something unrelated to experience or reality."

You may have cut your eyeteeth in psychology with a purely logical construct: The id-ego-superego troika postulated by Freud does not describe any flesh-and-blood phenomena. These concepts are convenient abstractions for summing up emotional processes. By contrast, the self is not an abstraction, but an actuality. It is there and can be perceived.

Another reason you may find it hard to believe the self exists is that you may never have glimpsed it. Professor Crampton pointed out: "Although the awareness of the self seems so self-evident to one who has analyzed his consciousness or had a spontaneous experience of this kind, most persons . . .—including highly intelligent and sophisticated people—have no spontaneous awareness of the self."

One reason that your self may be under wraps is that respecting it is often frowned on by our culture. The concept of original sin and the influence of Puritanism have given forth the feeling that man is inherently evil. If you are like most people, you feel worthless if you are doing little more than living from day to day. You feel you must *do* something to justify your existence. "To like one-self just for being human and alive is simply un-American," Dr. Stephan A. Tobin, a psychologist in Encino, California, has re-marked.

At one workshop the participants experimented with acting to-tally on impulse. The hilarity was tremendous as the members recaptured some of the freedom and joy of childhood. Yet, in the discussion afterward, several people complained, "We had a great time, but we didn't accomplish anything."

Furthermore, the culture decrees that though *you* are satisfied with what you are doing, you can never rest on your "laurels." You are expected to continue proving yourself, striving to conquer new goals constantly. If you ever stop, you are likely to fall in everyone's estimation, especially your own.

Another aspect of this culture's belief that man is evil is found in its harping on self-control, which generally means curbing your im-pulses to conform to social norms. Possibly one of the earliest con-nections you had with "self" was when your parents admonished you, "Control yourself." While very young, you may have gotten the feeling that if you'd let go of yourself, you'd do beastly things.

Inner controls are, of course, necessary for social living and also for the constructive channeling of your energies. Having restric-tions imposed on you prematurely or excessively, however, can re-sult in a destructive imbalance: In some ways you become overcon-trolled—rigid and unable to express your self. In other ways you become undercontrolled: You lack self-discipline; your tolerance of frustration is low; you require immediate gratification. If you are awry in the realm of control, you can suffer both these seemingly opposite extremes.

To help you control yourself, this culture has an assortment of authoritarian institutions: the family, the school, the armed forces, the athletic team, the factory, etc. In the main, they are run on the premise that if you were not somehow kept in line, you would run berserk.

In addition to punishing, our institutional dictators also mete out rewards. It is thus largely parents, team coaches, teachers and employers who validate your worth as a human being. To be loved or approved, you must accomplish according to their standards.

What is more, these dictators match you against everyone else.

From the time you were a small child, you were constantly placed on scales of comparison: You were "smarter" than Tom, but Alice could count better than you. It is hard to maintain a good feeling about your self when important people are always implying that you, on your own merits, don't measure up. A child can conclude for himself that he's worthless if, in this enforced competition, someone is constantly preferred to him.

The self is tough, but not sturdy. It is akin to a sapling, which yields and bends but is elastic enough to resist breaking up, even while straining against the pressure. Maslow called the self "cartilaginous." Like your nose and ears, which have a framework of the resilient tissue cartilage, your self is strong only in a passive way.

The late psychiatrist Fabian Rouke of New York used this onionlike model to show how the self can get submerged when you seek to shield yourself from hurt:

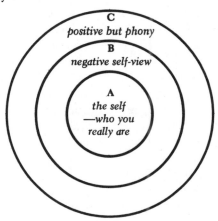

In the center (A) of your personality is your self, which Rouke described as a source of dignity and humility—"the essential worth of you, because you are a human being . . . the finest thing in creation!" Ideally, you would express your self in behavior and thereby be self-actualizing. But B intrudes—a wholly negative view of yourself, arising from criticism in childhood, parents you couldn't please, other monstrous threats of early life. This view of yourself as an inadequate and rejectable nonperson is impossible to live with. Furthermore, a child is like a little animal in a jungle—he feels terribly vulnerable. Therefore, he accommodates by throwing up C, a façade of protective behavior. "This defense is superficially positive," noted Rouke. At least for the time being, it serves to allay the threat. "But it is *phony.*"

In opposition to your inner nature you may thus adopt a repertory of phony roles. Although the term "role" smacks of play-acting, a role is not necessarily artificial. Almost any consistent pattern of behavior can technically be described as a role. You unavoidably play the role of son or daughter, student, citizen, reader and so on for thousands of diverse positions you occupy in everyday life. These are social roles. You run into trouble when a role you play is so limiting that it does not give your self free rein— or when the role does not reflect your self, in which case it is phony.

"Phony" is a particularly appropriate word to use to describe a role you assume in denial of your inner nature. It comes from "phone" and originated in the early days of the telephone, when transmission was so bad that a voice sounded tinny, or "phone-y." How fitting! In a phony role your voice and gestures are mechanical. A role opposed to your self can make you act robotlike and feel like a fake human, a machine.

Consider two men, each playing the role of physician. For Mark the role is genuine. He entered medicine because he enjoyed science and wished to help people in a profound way. Intellectually, he welcomed the challenge of a fast-moving, ever-changing field. He chose private practice rather than research, because he has a practical bent and prefers application to experimentation. The high prestige and good income were secondary to Mark; they merely helped fit medicine in with his material expectations.

Frank, by contrast, entered medicine mainly because he was a good boy who wanted to please his parents. They expected him to be a professional man. He was in moderate rebellion against them by the time he entered medical school, but he had absorbed enough of their values to stick his medical training out. He chose private practice chiefly because it pays better than research. Also, researchers need to stay abreast of the field, which Frank finds only dimly interesting.

Mark loves being a doctor. He shrugs off the long hours and hard work and wouldn't quit medicine for the world. It is a true expression of his self. His only regret is that it leaves him too little time for other important parts of his life, especially being with his family and also developing his long-neglected talent as a sculptor. To gain more free hours, he is considering selling his practice and taking a salaried job with a medical group.

If Frank had it to do all over again, he would have taken up another career, although he doesn't know which one. He's bored and depressed much of the time. He resents the long hours and feels dimly betrayed that he has garnered neither the acclaim nor the riches he envisioned.

Mark and Frank have privileges at the same hospital. The staff notes that Mark, who is by far the more skilled physician, is relaxed and informal, while Frank insists on receiving every bit of deference due him. A basic difference between them, of course, is that Frank has only the shell of being a physician, while Mark has the substance.

The following experiments aim to help you distinguish between the shadowy roles you play and the reality of your self.

ALIAS WHO?

Debbie, age seven, felt that her older sister, Marjorie, got all her parents' attention. To win her mother and father from Marjorie, she tried a number of maneuvers—being smarter, funnier, louder —but none worked. Then, one day in the second grade, Debbie, who was ordinarily a good pupil, forgot to study for a spelling test. She got a low mark and came home wailing.

To her astonishment her mother said soothingly, "That's all right, dear. Marjorie's our clever daughter. You're our lovely one." Her father played jacks with her before she went to bed. Though no one put it into words, Debbie got the message: It paid to be stupid.

From then on Debbie was cute and anything but bright. She was spared being in competition with Marjorie and got more than her share of attention from her mother and father.

A crisis, however, was brewing. Debbie was by no means as dumb as she acted, or as "lovely." She had a sharp intellect and a strong personality, which yearned to come out, but at home she dared not express either.

At eighteen she went off to college. In her first trimester she scored nearly a straight-A average. This was unsettling to her, and her parents received the news coolly—they were not welcoming changes in their daughter.

In her second trimester Debbie's average declined to just over a B. By the middle of her third trimester she panicked and dropped out of school. A therapist helped Debbie see that she had been playing a role to gain her parents' favor, and that she could henceforth function as the competent individual she really was.

Most roles you play can be summed up in an apt word or phrase, and this description can help illuminate the nature of the role. Debbie and the therapist agreed that the name of her role was Dumb Bunny. "Birdbrain" did not quite capture the adorable quality that Debbie had affected. "Deadhead" was much too cold and vacant.

Once the role was defined as Dumb Bunny, Debbie could examine it at a distance and see how playing a role limited her. Being a Dumb Bunny was like wearing a suit of armor. It protected her— but was terribly confining.

A role may have nothing to do with your own background. Ira, a middle-class Jewish college student from the Bronx, had unconsciously assumed the stern, superior air of an English army officer, a role evidently picked up from the movies. He recalls trying on the role at around age ten, during a period when he was at odds with other boys in his neighborhood. It fit nicely. Not only did it allow him to dismiss the boys as beneath contempt—it also accommodated him to his father, a rigid moralist, and gave him the upper hand over his weak, fluttery mother.

At no point was Ira aware that he was playing a part. But he was cast into it—"cast" like a statue, as well as like an actor. The stiff, unyielding officer pervaded his life. Self-discipline that would do the royal Guards proud got him high marks in school. Lofty ideals kept him aloof from people his age, while a stiff upper lip helped him bear up with his generation's inadequacies.

Outwardly he was functioning well, and he was only mildly troubled by his anger and coldness. Then, one evening, he stopped by an acquaintance's apartment. "This fat sloppy girl was there," Ira remembers. "My first reaction was to look away from her in disgust, and be sorry I was near her."

The conversation took a turn he'd rarely experienced: The

others in the room began talking about their feelings, and the fat girl candidly told how bad she felt about herself. "Suddenly she seemed beautiful to me," Ira says. This exposure to open emotion left him shaken. "All sorts of feelings started rising up inside me. I didn't know what they were or how to account for them."

As his emotions came alive, he lost confidence in his façade. He became ever more aware of the emotional side of life he'd suppressed. A few hours with a therapist helped him realize the nature of the role he'd been playing, that this mythical martinet had been dictating his every move. The insights helped free him to be a warm, enthusiastic young man.

► What phony roles are you conscious of playing? Good Mother? Stud? Nice Guy? Big Success? Clinging Vine? Examine each role in turn, and decide on its most appropriate name.

Now talk to this phony part of you. If you are in a group, have others speak to you while you are in this role. What does this part of you have to say? What are you like when in this role? How do you want to be seen?

The answers to these questions will often reveal what gave rise to the assumed identity. Eddie, a long-haired college student, revealed his primary role as Hip Eddie.

"What do you have to say about yourself, Hip Eddie?" he was asked.

"I'm cool. I smoke pot. I don't give a shit."

"What are you afraid of?"

"That people will get to me."

"How do you mean?"

"That they'll find out about me."

"Find out what?"

"That I'm not what I seem."

"How do you mean?"

"That I've never been laid."

UNMASKING

Some people are so aware of the masks they wear that there is a widely shared fantasy: The person imagines he is actually holding a cardboard mask in front of himself.

► You can often spot a person wearing a mask, because his face may have a masklike quality: a fixed expression, with little emotion getting in or out. You can observe this readily on your television screen. Watch the dead faces of talk-show personalities who, by profession, are trying to be charming.

► How is your own face? Next time you're with company, sense the expression you're wearing. Glimpse yourself in a mirror. Are you wearing a mask to impress others with your interest in them? Your free-spiritedness? Your sophistication?

One businessman noticed that when visiting, he kept his eyes opened wide and his eyebrows raised high, as if he were in a perpetual state of astonishment. He explored what he was feeling and concluded that he was afraid people wouldn't like him if he displayed his natural aggressiveness. His wide-eyed look was an attempt to appear ingenuous.

► Another tip-off for telling if you're wearing a mask: When people ask you ordinary, interested questions, do you feel they're prying? Granted that your privacy sets limits, an emotionally open person welcomes questions and gives answers in a free-flowing give-and-take. Prying suggests closedness. Are you afraid of being opened up, of having your mask pried off, and thereby being exposed?

A closed person can likewise make you feel you're prying even when your questions are sincere and in good taste. He may sense his pose is threatened and, therefore, may seek to evade your scrutiny by closing up and making you feel guilty for "intruding."

One college English professor has his colleagues thoroughly intimidated over the seeming delicateness of his sensibilities. He declines to take part in scuttlebutt over grants and promotions ("I can't be bothered with things like that"), rarely goes to the movies ("I saw the Olivier *Hamlet,* and it disturbed me for a week"), and discusses his students in ways that other experienced teachers never imagine ("Goldfarb has a certain primitivism in his admiration of Faulkner"). The pose keeps people at a distance, and no one has yet dared to say, "Oh, come off it."

► Engaging in feedback may result in others' pointing out to you roles you may not be aware of (see the discussion of feedback in Chapter 2, "Ground Rules"). Dr. James F. T. Bugental of Los Angeles has devised a game employing feedback principles. Go around a circle, telling each member, "The way I see you is. . . ."

Do this rapidly, to keep your impressions as spontaneous as possible. After impressions are discussed in feedback, the next person goes, and so on.

Dr. James V. Clark, a behavioral scientist, tells of a nurse in her middle forties, who became aware of a phony role as a result of feedback. Joanne, a plain woman who wore no make-up, saw herself as motherly. In her group was Henry, a retiring young man in his early twenties. Several times when he started to participate, Joanne interrupted, saying, "Isn't it *nice* that Henry is talking finally?"

At last one member told her, "You're trying to dominate Henry."

"I'm trying to be supportive," she defended herself.

"You're not at all supportive," he replied. "You're hateful."

She made yet another remark at Henry's expense. Someone else present groaned and doubled up as if he'd been hit in the stomach.

Joanne looked shocked and for the next two sessions said absolutely nothing. She was asked about her silence and refused to answer. Commented one participant, "If I were you, I'd keep quiet, too. So I wouldn't appear to be a hateful person."

The next day she sought out the leader of the group. Almost bubbling over with enthusiasm she said, "After all those remarks, I suddenly saw that, being tall all my life, I'd simply hated short and unassertive men, which was how I saw Henry."

She'd never realized her hatred before and felt exhilarated at this insight. Trying to be motherly and nursely, she recognized, was a cover-up for much anger and hostility she felt in her home life and at work. She got a fresh hair style and started wearing make-up and younger and more feminine clothes. She no longer "mothered" Henry.

IMITATION OF LIFE

You may have mannerisms, possibly whole ways of life, which you take for granted, though they are not truly expressive of your self. While they are relatively painless, they are not satisfying—and often they impede your assuming more satisfactory substitute behavior.

See how you incorporate attitudes and ideas into your personality. Once you are aware that a trait is not necessarily part of you, you can affirm it or else modify or discard it.

To begin with, you constantly imitate other people. It is no surprise that children do this all the time—but adults do it to only a slightly lesser degree, generally confining their unconscious mimickry to those with whom they identify: members of the same family and the same socioeconomic group, for example. Such mutual imitation is an important element of group solidarity; it helps explain how a new attitude or life style can snowball through a community.

▶ To become aware of your tendency to imitate others, copy a partner's gestures as he talks to you or acts out different roles, giving forth expressions and gestures that come to him. Deliberately copy what you see him doing. Imitate his words, voice inflection, facial expressions. Do you get a sense of merging with him? You may find that you meld into him and his responses much more readily than you'd have expected.

▶ Sense how easily you assume roles, by transforming yourself into a road, a car, a baby, the baby's mother. Be two years old.

▶ Once you've gotten the feel of yourself as an imitator, consider as many of your traits as you can—your speech, preferences, general behavior—and determine from whom you acquired them by imitation. Are you being yourself or some other person? Whose life are you living? Are you acting a part written by someone else?

One man, on reflection, realized that he was imitating his father in always being the "sage," the solver of other people's problems. "I'm uneasy about this," he said. "While I get true pleasure from helping close friends where I can—and so does my father—I don't feel grateful to him for teaching me to be the center of the troubles of all and sundry."

▶ Family Sayings is a related game devised by Drs. Daniel I. Malamud and Solomon Machover, authors of *Toward Self-Understanding: Group Techniques in Self-confrontation*. Every family has its own favorite expressions, proverbs, slogans, warnings. List all the repetitive expressions you recall from your childhood.

What is their underlying message? What values do they represent? For example, Mother Knows Best can be translated as "You have no mind of you own." Charity Begins at Home may be another way of saying, "Don't give anything away." How many of these messages have stuck with you until today?

WHO ARE YOU?

Dis-identification is the process of filtering out the parts of you that are not essentials of your self. You consider a role or an attitude, then exclude it. What you seek is the irreducible minimum that is your self.

▶ Perhaps you really don't believe that you exist apart from your activities and titles. If so, experiments in dis-identification can be especially helpful to you. This one, developed by Dr. Stanley Krippner of the Maimonides Medical Center in Brooklyn, New York, may be an eye opener:

Take nine small pieces of paper. Ask yourself "Who am I?" nine times, and write your answer each time on one of the sheets. Your reply may be anything that comes to mind that you feel may identify you: your age, sex, profession, a symbol, an image.

After you've finished, go through your answers, and number them in order of importance. Number 1 is most central to you; number 9, least. Place them face down on a table.

Turn up number 9, and look at it. Think about it and what it represents. Then consider what life would be like without number 9.

Repeat for number 8. If you are concentrating, by the time you reach numbers 3, 2, or 1, you may come to an awareness of an existence beyond these externals. The responses of Elise, a woman lawyer, were as follows:

9. An attorney.
8. A partner in [name of her firm].
7. A human being.
6. Elise.
5. A woman.
4. Joan of Arc. [Elise saw herself as a martyr.]
3. A glint in my father's eye.
2. The world.
1. A breath.

▶ Dr. Claudio Naranjo, a psychiatrist, has devised a related technique for use with two or more people. Have a partner ask you only the question "Who are you?" using many different inflections and tones of voice. "*Who* are you?" "Who *are* you?" and "Who are *you?*" are three different questions. With each answer make an effort to go deeper into your personality, beyond the roles and into the depths of your being. A third member is helpful in refereeing to see that your partner stays with the question and that you probe deeper into your identity.

Often there comes a point at which your answer to "Who are you?" can't be articulated with labels. In one experiment, the young woman replying to the question started out describing herself as a Negro, a singer, a lover of plants and animals. Before long she replied, "I'm me."

"Who are you?" her partner went on.

"I'm *me!*" she said insistently.

"Who are you?"

In response, she spread out her arms in a loving, enveloping gesture. Afterward she recalled what insights had come to her: "Suddenly I saw that all these other things—Negro, singer and so on—were dancing around a central point, and that's when I said, 'I'm me.' But then I realized my me is all by itself, different from everybody else's me. Here's this me sitting there, and I'm it: 'I'm *me!*' And with that I realized I've had it with words—there are some things you just can't express with words—and what I wanted to say was that my me feels so big and good it wants to hug the whole world."

▶ Dr. Graham C. Taylor, a professor of psychiatry at McGill University, has asked patients to write him a short essay once or twice a week in response to the question "Who am I?" One of Dr. Taylor's patients was an engineer in his early thirties, a rigid person who tended to treat people as though they were mechanical problems. He was mechanistic, too, in his thinking—perceiving things only in terms of black or white, good or bad, yes or no, with little tolerance for reality's ambiguous, uncertain shades of gray.

His first response to "Who am I?" was typically cold and mechanical: "I am an engineer who has worked through the design ranks to the position of engineering manager. . . . People have a tendency to become tools or a means to accomplish the task as-signed."

In trying to write the foregoing, he became acutely depressed. His distress seemed to be related to the realization that his efficiency and self-assurance were a façade. He really didn't know who he was. This, in his words, was a "shattering thought."

Gradually he came to accept that the ability to tolerate ambiguity—live with the real world's paradoxes and contradictions—is a characteristic of maturity. Uncertainty, he saw, was not a sign of weakness, as he'd believed, but a necessary first step in seeking the truth.

After six weeks his "Who am I?" response revealed him to be a more sensitive person, who could live with a degree of uncertainty: "I seem to feel the emotions and feelings of others I am with and can be affected by them. Basically I like people and am liked by them but can be shy or hesitant in moving into a situation where the human element is unknown. Possibly there are elements of insecurity in my make-up."

8

Games from Your Unconscious

► Shut one eye, and squint the other one until it is practically closed. Glance around the room. You will see something, of course —but you will also be missing out on a wealth of sensation, detail, richness, color.

The limitations of your normal waking consciousness are similar to those imposed by your squinted eye. Many people think they know all that is important about themselves. They are deluded. A great proportion of significant human experience lies outside the conscious sphere. To limit your perception to the conscious is to view yourself and life through a peephole.

"Beneath man's thin veneer of consciousness," wrote Dr. Arnold M. Ludwig in *Archives of General Psychiatry*, "lies a relatively uncharted realm of mental activity, the nature and function of which have been neither systematically explored nor adequately conceptualized."

Within your unconscious lies your self, and through unconscious processes it can burst forth into your conscious awareness. Much like a prisoner yelling desperately for help, your self may struggle to make you realize what you really want.

It is a commonplace that your unconscious may reveal itself through symbolic representation. "Deep down," observed Maslow, "we look at the world through the eyes of wishes and fears and gratifications. . . . Think of the way in which a really young child looks at the world, looks at itself and at other people. . . . It has nothing to do with time and space or with sequence, causality, order, or with the laws of the physical world. This is a world quite other than the physical world."

A word, then, in a fantasy or dream may have little to do with its literal, dictionary meaning. Rather, it may reflect an emotional state. "Hawaii. Hawaii. Hawaii," a voice said insistently in a woman editor's dream. Throughout the week that followed, she repeatedly heard her inner voice saying, "Hawaii." She stopped off at a travel agency to pick up some brochures about the islands. "Gee," she told the clerk, "I'd like to escape there."

At once she saw that her "Hawaii" was only tangentially related to the actual place bearing that name. She had a great sense of duty but was bored with her husband and job. "Hawaii" symbolized her unexpressed wish to get far, far away from her supposed obligations. It occurred to her that she might have chosen an *island* retreat because her husband was afraid of water. Realizing that she didn't have to subjugate herself to her husband, that she didn't have to control every detail of her job, helped her enjoy her life more.

The great emphasis that symbolism has received in psychological writing makes it worth pointing out that messages from your unconscious can also be extremely explicit. Indeed, to get its message across, your self is capable of being as subtle as a sledgehammer—signaling you not only in words but using physical force as well.

Trevor, a young English immigrant to America, was about to marry a girl he wasn't sure he loved. "Brenda's family had been very nice to me since I got here," Trevor recalled, "and I was going along with it mainly because I didn't want to hurt their feelings." As the wedding drew nearer, he developed a recurrent stiffness in his legs and arms. Doctors could find no physical cause.

Three days before the wedding, he was having dinner with Brenda and her parents. "Suddenly, while I was sipping coffee, I distinctly heard my voice roar 'NO!' In fact my whole body went 'NO!' as if pulling on the brakes of a bike speeding downhill. 'My God,' I thought, 'my symptoms.' "

He turned to Brenda and told her he was sorry, but he couldn't marry her. "So right was this decision that I remained blissfully peaceful through the uproar that followed. I even managed to smile when Brenda's bastard father threatened to get me deported.

I was *self*-assured, I decided later. And those symptoms haven't bothered me since."

WHAT'S IN A NAME?

Some primitive tribesmen have secret names. They believe that to know a person's name is to have power over him. In some tribes bestowing a name is the greatest gift you can give a friend.

Similar tribal customs are found in modern societies. Many people have secret names, or at least names they don't use publicly, as exemplified by the thousands of people with stage names, pen names and names legally changed from the ones they were born with. Great significance is attached to wives taking their husbands' names, or a man acknowledging an illegitimate child and "giving him his name."

Chances are you have strong associations with your name. It's been with you throughout your life. It was probably the first word you were able to spell and read. You identify closely with it. For example, how do you feel if someone forgets it or mispronounces it? As if *you* were forgotten or abused?

This constant companion of yours, your name, can help you become aware of many feelings now locked below your consciousness. Try this game for a start:

▶ Write your name very slowly with your left hand (or your right hand if you're a lefty). Form the letters as slowly and carefully as possible. Many people find that they drift back in time as they reenact the painful effort of first learning to write. Dr. William C. Schutz of Esalen has observed that women often get so involved that they write out their maiden names.

▶ A related game can be played by a group. Each person is asked to give his first name and give a memory, association or feeling in connection with his name. At the same time, he can choose another name he would prefer to be called in the group. Frequently a person who has chosen another name will suddenly become aware of his reasons for choosing that particular name; associations with a given name and with a chosen name can be quite revealing.

In one group session, for example, a severely dressed, whispering librarian was asked what associations she had with her name, Agnes. "Straight-necked, prim, colorless," were words she volunteered. When asked if she would prefer to be called by another name, she got a gleam in her eye and shyly said, "Zsa-Zsa." Subsequently, she was noticeably brighter.

▶ Dr. Daniel I. Malamud and Solomon Machover have devised a game in which you spell out your first name in reverse. Eric would thus become Cire. Pretend that this is a word in the Martian language, and define it as it would appear in the Martian dictionary. In one case a woman named Bernice defined Ecinreb as "a small household receptacle that is used for spitting in." This message reaffirmed her suspicion that she hated being a housewife and ought to re-evaluate her plans for herself.

▶ You can get a message from your name by pretending that each letter in your name, spelled backward, is the beginning of a word. Together these words will form a sentence or group of words that will have significance for you. Concentrate on each letter, and see what it wants to say to you. Don't discard anything because it seems irrelevant or foolish.

Though many such messages may be cryptic, some can be extraordinarily clear. Malamud reported that in one case a Richard (Drahcir) received this message: "Don't regret anything. Have careless intercourse, regardless." Richard expanded on this, saying, "This means live a little; don't always anticipate what is going to happen and what the consequences are going to be. I am always bogged down in that. I lose precious moments by being concerned about the weeks and months and years."

▶ Here is another way your name can give rise to feelings. Have a partner or all the other members of a group say your name in a variety of different ways: angrily, pleadingly, whiningly, and so on. The manner in which your name is spoken may make you aware of feelings you've long buried.

Ted, who was generally withdrawn, got no results at all from this game. Then another member of his group realized Ted's real name must be Theodore. When some called out, in a singsong voice, "The-o-dawr," Ted flushed. This was how he was teased in elementary school by boys who thought him a sissy.

"They also called me The Odor, holding their noses while all the girls giggled," Ted recalled. He had tried to shrug it off, by smiling and being a "good sport." Now, twenty years later, he at last vented his rage.

Picture This

A young poet-patient of psychoanalyst Emanuel F. Hammer has written:

> Extend to me a picture of almost things
> Of things not quite expressed . . .
> Abide with me awhile
> To unlearn words.

A picture is worth considerably more than a thousand words. Pictures are closer to the concrete, the actual, than are words. Words are restricted in meaning to conventional definitions. To be understood, they must be set forth in a logical, grammatical order. Pictures are unfettered by convention or logic. They can express an infinity of meanings and can flash forth complete, in an instant.

Pictures constitute much of the language of the unconscious. They are the natural way to express the nonverbal, nonlogical phenomenon of emotion. Freud found that patients could frequently express themselves more easily through graphic means of communication than through verbal ones. In trying to describe dreams, patients would often tell him, "I don't know how to say it, but I could draw it." August Strindberg, dramatist and master wordsmith, made use of drawings when he felt unable to express himself adequately with words. He tried to "say" his otherwise inaccessible mental experiences in pictorial ways.

Dr. Robert S. De Ropp, a psychiatrist, talks of the "inner theater," the practice of projecting the self pictorially and watching its behavior. You intentionally create visualizations, sensations, forms, situations, experiences, within the theater of your mind.

Every creative artist, be he novelist, playwright, painter or sculptor, makes use of the inner theater to some extent, notes Dr. De Ropp. The poet William Blake was almost continuously immersed in this inner performance, which went on more or less independently of his conscious will. The process may generate visions that can add an extra dimension to your existence. Blake, for instance, regarded this new dimension as one of his most precious possessions.

IMAGE OF YOURSELF

► One way of pointedly expressing how you see yourself is through imagery. How do you visualize yourself?

Use any metaphor that comes to mind, in any category you choose. In one group, members reported and amplified their self-images as: spaghetti with a lot of garlic ("interesting, spicy, but people avoid me"); Petunia Pig ("the fat virginal girl friend of a fat virginal stutterer"); a volcano about to blow its top; John the Baptist ("I keep losing my head because of some broad").

► A related method is to choose a great person, living or dead, that you admire, and to be that person. Think about the qualities that you admire in that person, and try to express them. Don't talk about what "you" did historically, but be that person as he would be. You may become aware of role-playing qualities that you affect in daily life.

One man chose Dwight Eisenhower as his great person. He realized that he constantly strove for a fatherly blandness that he hoped would make people like him. A woman college professor identified with Dag Hammarskjöld, the late Secretary-General of the United Nations, a distant mystical figure. Young people frequently assume the roles of Bob Dylan and of Mick Jagger of the Rolling Stones ("freaks who made it").

Your image may be discernible to outsiders. At one group session the leader got a clear vision of one member and told him, "You look like a mole sticking his head out of the ground." Later on the member described himself as a turtle, and other members said this was about the picture they were getting of him.

► What metaphors would you use to describe friends and members of your family? Imagery hits the nail on the head. It clarifies how you feel about a person, with elements that can be seen and heard.

When telling others your reaction to them, use imagery. "Images are more *experienceable* than other forms of communication," notes Dr. Emanuel Hammer. They move a person closer to his feelings—to, in Dr. Hammer's words, "*think-feel* an interpretation."

Dr. Hammer was treating a thirty-six-year-old man, who pretended boyishness to feel safe. The patient showed no real grasp of his behavior until Hammer told him, "I hear a 'gee whiz' and a 'golly gee' in between the lines whenever you talk." Then the patient got the point.

Another therapist told a woman, "You seem to comfort yourself by hugging your misery like a Teddy bear"—thereby getting across both her childishness and her exploiting of her woe.

Hammer once observed to a masochist, "How nice to get a wound you can lick."

"Wham!" the patient replied. "That connected."

Once you discover your image, you may find it freed to change and grow. One girl saw herself as a "newly hatched bird that has been crushed." Not long afterward she looked at herself again and said, "I feel I can fly."

Recalls Doris W. Davis, an editor of the *Bulletin of Structural Integration*: "One of my particular idiosyncrasies was a lower body which felt stronger and better defined than the upper half. I had seen myself as a tree with strong, well-developed roots, but with an underdeveloped top half—no foliage, no fruit, no shade, incomplete. This image has been changed to a more symmetrical one, top half balancing bottom half, and right and left halves gaining a well-differentiated equivalence."

Professor Martha Crampton has used mental-imagery techniques in helping the patient to see in a vivid manner what his problems are and what kind of growth he may expect. One patient described her problem as having a dominating husband. She was asked to visualize the way she felt about this relationship and saw herself as a little bird being tightly held in a clenched hand. The bird was frightened, helpless and could not get away. "Imagine the hand opening," Miss Crampton suggested.

The woman saw the bird fly away to a nearby branch. She was surprised to note, however, that the bird would not venture far from the hand. It was a "sugar bird" that fed on sugar provided by humans. It had forgotten how to get food for itself in the natural way and thus had to depend upon people to live.

Through this visualization the woman was able to see that she had allowed her husband to dominate her, because she felt more secure being taken care of, like a child.

"Try to see the bird eating the kind of food that wild birds normally eat," suggested Miss Crampton.

"The bird would have to move to another island where there's more vegetation," the woman said.

She imagined riding a fishing boat, since the other island was too far away to reach by flying. The bird was happy to find that there were plenty of seeds to eat there and that it could also enjoy eating sugar from time to time for a treat.

This session alone led to a marked improvement in her relationship with her husband. As it turned out, he was delighted to have her assume more independence.

DEPICT YOUR FEELINGS

Here are some games that can show you in a tangible form how you feel about yourself and what your self is like.

► Find an object that you respond to, that seems to describe or express you uniquely. Think about why this object represents you. One middle-aged man found a thistle with a blooming blossom at the tip. He didn't know why he had chosen it. But he accepted the interpretation of the thistle as his past life, the blossom as the life he was trying to grow into.

► You may be able to get a fuller impression of how you see your self by building a representation of yourself in three dimensions. To do this, raid a utility drawer or junk closet or garage. Dump out a collection of heterogeneous materials, such as papers, pictures, blocks, string, marbles, scraps of wood, pieces of cloth and any other odds and ends. Gather some of these things from the pile, and build a portrait of yourself out of them. You can use objects in the room as part of your portrait. One participant, for example, attached his materials to a lamp base that suggested a figure. A hammer handle became his penis.

► Doodles can be valid representations of your state of mind. Try to find out something about yourself through your doodles. Doodle aimlessly until you feel that your doodle has expressed something meaningful to you. Save your doodles, and see if you can find evidence of change over a period of time.

While talking with his wife, one beleaguered husband always drew circles. These, he realized, reminded him both of the links of a chain and of a hangman's noose. After his relationship with his wife improved, these images disappeared from his doodles.

▶ See now if you can draw a picture that answers the question "Who am I?" See if you can make progressively more meaningful pictures each time you ask yourself the question. After you've finished a picture, write yourself a description of it.

More than likely, the description will restate your feelings about the picture. In some cases, however, the discrepancy can be revealing. One aging woman drew herself as a rather pretty valley. But when she started describing it, she found herself writing about "old breasts that no longer give milk."

One of Martha Crampton's patients made a free drawing of a crowded city, saying that this was where he felt most at home.

"What feelings are aroused in you?" Miss Crampton asked.

"Feelings of being constricted and caged in," he replied.

He was asked to visualize this caged-in feeling and saw himself imprisoned as a spy in a small cell somewhere in a foreign country. His jailers gave him no opportunity to defend his point of view and were attempting to brainwash him into a confession of guilt. He felt that the only possibility of escape was to "con" his way out by some lie.

At this point Miss Crampton explained to him that the various figures in the visualization represented parts of himself and asked him to visualize how he played each role in his daily life. This gave him insight into his needs for power and his use of manipulation.

"As a child," he recalled, "I would con my parents by pretending to agree with them just to keep them quiet."

Fantasy Trips

Your "inner theater" can show movies more exciting and spectacular, and certainly more meaningful to you, than any ever filmed by Hollywood. Without drugs you can experience a trip much like those reported by users of LSD.

Deliberately add movement to your visualizations. With your eyes closed, let your images travel from one association to the next. One of these four techniques may spur fantasy trips as long or as short as you wish.

▶ *Hum.* Merely going "M-m-m-m" may stimulate your mind to take off from the present moment. As the vibrations tingle your head, then the rest of your body, you may be transported from one emotionally significant scene to the next.

► *Study a coin* (the shinier the better), reading over one side again and again. After a minute or so, look away. One image may seem to leap from the coin—from an association with, say, part of Washington's face on the quarter, or the word "LIBERTY"—and may flow into another image, then another.

► *Gaze at a bright spot* against a white surface: a dot cut out of colored paper or one made with a blue or red pen. Hold it only a few inches from your face, and stare at it, without blinking, for a minute or so. When you shut your eyes, you'll see a spot of the reverse color (green for a red dot, yellow for a blue one). Concentrate on this, and you're likely to start a train of fantasies.

► *Rub your forehead* with your eyes closed. You're likely to see flickering lights. If you rub several fingers vigorously up and down against your forehead, you'll have even more vivid sensations. To really see what an explosion of images is like, experiment with placing your forehead next to a stroboscopic light.

► For the following exercises relax completely. Lie down on the floor. Let your body sink into the floor, with no support from you. Just let go, so that your muscles go limp and your body feels as if it's falling of its own weight.

CRUISE TO PARADISE

► Imagine that you are floating on your back down a river. To get there, it may help if you breathe deeply and feel yourself sinking. Visualize the sinking feeling, as if you were in a whirlpool, and watch yourself going down down down into the vortex.

Come out on a gentle little river that is winding its way through a beautiful forest. It's a sunny day, and the sun is warming your skin. You pass trees and great fields of beautiful flowers.

There's a meadow. Smell the grass and flowers. Hear the birds. Gaze up at the sky.

What do you see now? Where do you wish to go? This uncharted part of your trip is up to you.

► Dr. George I. Brown of the University of California at Santa Barbara suggests that you float down a river to a mountain. Float into a cave, and see what happens. Spend above five minutes there, and take about five minutes for your return trip.

▶ Dr. Jean Houston, director of the Foundation for Mind Research, suggests that you leave the river and walk across the meadow. Enjoy the grass on your ankles, the lightness in your step. Come to a large tree. It has a door in it. Behind that door is your personal paradise.

Open the door, and enter.

One woman found herself on a beach, suffused in pearly light, the stars visible in a golden heaven. She sat down at a piano and composed a piece so majestic that tears came to her eyes. Her husband appeared, playing a violin in perfect duet. With the music swelling over them, they went swimming, then made love.

"Bodies. Women's bodies," is one man's recollection of his paradise. "Unclothed. It was like a whole sea of them, and then I went from there to the starry heavens like a rocket moving very strong through the heavens. As if I reigned throughout the entire universe."

▶ For a different kind of expedition, take yourself on a trip around the world. Set a kitchen timer for two minutes. See how far you can go—how many different experiences and images you can have in that short period of time.

When your time is up, come out of your fantasy, and remember your adventure. How did it differ from your real world? Did you act in a way you would like to act every day? Do you feel freer and happier?

A *group* fantasy can be enjoyable and illuminating. Lie face up with your heads as close together as possible, like the spokes of a wheel. One person begins by relating a picture that comes into his mind. The others enter the visualization, and contribute what they in turn are fantasizing.

"I see a beach," was how one group fantasy began. Someone fantasized a house. Others helped build it, adding fanciful details like gazebos and cupolas. In fantasy the group went down to the sea and saw beautiful colored fish. Next they went to a cabin in the mountains.

The cabin disturbed one girl, and she withdrew from the fantasy to explore her feelings. She concluded that the cabin's exposure to the elements made her feel vulnerable and inadequate, sensations that in real life (she saw) limited her range of experience.

SHUTTLE HERE AND THERE

► When you are bored or lonely or faced with difficult problems, close your eyes and withdraw on a fantasy trip. In Gestalt therapy the natural inclination toward withdrawal that you experience from time to time is not dealt with as a resistance to be overcome, but as a rhythmic response to be respected. Consequently, when you wish to withdraw, shut your eyes and travel in fantasy to any place or situation in which you feel secure. Note what you see and feel.

Withdrawal is a healthy, self-protective device. Like sleep, it can replenish your energy. Through the visualization of fantasy you can be put in touch with your self. Your unconscious can express what you really want to do, where you'd really rather be.

► Fritz Perls, the founder of Gestalt therapy, invented a game in which he asked participants to "shuttle between *here* and *there*"— between reality and fantasy: Close your eyes, and go away in your imagination to a place where you feel secure and happy.

Come back to the here and now. Compare the two situations. You may be more aware of this world and have your goals more clearly in mind.

Most likely the "there" situation was preferable to the "here" situation. How was it preferable? *What* is it you want?

Close your eyes, and go away again, wherever you'd like to go. Notice any change since your last fantasy.

Come back to the here and now, and again compare the two situations. Has any change taken place?

Continue to shuttle between here and there until you feel comfortable in your present situation.

Do this in any boring, tense or uncomfortable situation. "Very often the *there* situation," Perls pointed out in *Gestalt Therapy Verbatim*, "gives you a cue for what's missing in the now." The difference between your "there" and "here" can show you the directions you want to move in. As a long-range goal, try making your real life more like your fantasy life.

A woman in one of Perls's groups withdrew to a desert island

and reveled in the freedom she found there. She swam nude in very clear water. At the same time, she found that she needed people more than she had been aware of.

Next, in fantasy, she went on a hike with her husband. She reflected on the fantasy: "He loved me more than he does now, and there was a great euphoria about our relationship."

To recapture this euphoria, she shut her eyes and returned to the hike. "Then," she recalled later, "I began to appreciate the fact . . . that he was carrying part . . . of me in the relationship, and I think I bring back . . . to the present situation both the joy and the realization that I have to carry myself."

SIGHT AND SOUND

Dialogue in fantasy experiments can help elicit answers from your unconscious.

► Have a partner ask you questions, which you answer in terms of images you see. Psychotherapist Martha Crampton has used such a visualization technique and has often gotten answers that are almost totally in metaphor.

One man came to Miss Crampton, complaining of anxiety over trying new experiences, over getting his feet wet. She suggested that he close his eyes and answer her questions in terms of what he saw on his mind screen.

"What disturbs your serenity?" she asked.

"I see black crows of doubt," the patient replied.

"What do they represent?"

"They are agents of the forces of destruction."

"What are they doing in the field?"

"There has been seed recently planted. They are trying to interfere with the growth of the crop."

"What do they represent?" Miss Crampton asked.

"If a child makes mistakes, you can either praise it or criticize it, have faith and promote its growth or make destructive criticism. I see myself trying to write a speech, but the ideas are strangled by the critical forces within me."

"What is the source of this?"

"I see an image of my mother getting angry one day when I was a small boy and came home with my feet wet. She said that an

aunt of mine had died from pneumonia from getting her feet wet."
▶ If you can't get such answers from your unconscious directly,
you may be helped by imagining a go-between, through whom you
can communicate with yourself. A wise old man is a common in-
termediary.

One of the authors of this book (Hal) was going through a period in which he was unsettled as to which direction his career
should take. He had a fantasy in which he was on a boat but had
somehow let go and wasn't steering.

A wise man appeared, and Hal asked him, "What should I do?
Where should I go?"

The wise man replied, "Go on TV. Go on TV."

The light was tremendous. Hal thereafter embarked with renewed energy on promoting and developing (through TV) a
growth center he directed.

▶ Your go-between need not be human. Answers can as well be
elicited from a bird or a fountain.

You can also write your answers on a blackboard. One patient
told Martha Crampton that he could see no significance in a dream
in which he and his cats were being beaten in a battle with some
rats. Miss Crampton asked him to imagine himself writing the
meaning of this dream.

"I see the word 'protection,' " the patient reported.

"From what?" Miss Crampton asked.

"From the world and people."

"What do the rats represent?"

"People. Tax people."

"Why are you afraid of them?"

"They represent authority," the patient replied, and became
aware of his habit of impotently provoking authority figures.

▶ What if a fantasy turns frightening? If you develop unpleasant
imagery—a demon, a wild animal—confront it as completely as
possible. Examine it in careful detail. You will thereby be facing an
unpleasant aspect of your own personality as it has been symbolized by your imagery. If you conquer your fear of the image, you
will also be overcoming a negative part of your personality.

Dr. Hanscarl Leuner, a German psychiatrist who has developed
a method of psychotherapy called "guided affective imagery" or
"guided daydream," has found that an effective way of overcoming

a frightening animal image is to *feed* it. A young woman seen by Leuner was asked to imagine she was standing on the edge of a forest, waiting for a creature to emerge from it. A large black-brown bear came out, with "a mean, dumb, but crafty animal look in his small eyes." Dr. Leuner suggested the woman feed the bear with two large jars of honey.

She poured the honey out on the ground and stepped aside. "The bear immediately dropped to all fours and attacked the honey. He wallowed in it, rolled in it, and scooped it up in great handfuls."

The psychiatrist suggested that the woman tell the bear it was she who had fed it. She did so. "I was surprised to see that he had changed into a panda . . . much less fierce. . . . He continued to shrink . . . until he had metamorphosed into a lovely large collie dog," the woman reported.

She romped with the playful dog, still slightly wary but largely unafraid. For, in confronting the frightening image of the bear, she had overcome it; it had gotten smaller and more manageable.

"In retrospect," the woman reported, "I found that the most impressive and enduring aspect of the experience was my surprise at discovering how hungry the bear was, *i.e.*, how badly the bear needed to be fed by me! This led me to wonder whether my father, a man who finds it difficult to express and give affection, needed my love, needed me to give to him. The next time I saw my father, I felt as if I possessed a precious secret, one that I would never reveal, because I would not want to embarrass him. This new secret knowledge made me feel strong and tender toward him. It was almost as if I had become the parent and he the child!"

Dream World

Mme. Émilienne Delacroix was a fifty-five-year-old housewife who has become famous as the Grandma Moses of the French Riviera. She never took an art lesson in her life. In a dream one night she saw herself as a great painter. Next morning she decided to try her hand at art, and today her fame is worldwide.

In Gestalt therapy Fritz Perls introduced an emphasis on the organism's seeking emotional balance, a point of equilibrium from which it can respond not out of past anxiety, but realistically and appropriately to the present situation. You reveal disturbances— "holes" or "unfinished business," Perls termed them—with *all* of you: not only with your words but with your gestures, manner of carriage, thoughts, fantasies and dreams.

Dreams are the principal way in which you reveal unfinished business. If you dream that you are being chased across the field by a man with a knife and you come to a cliff, in Perls's view you are not only you but you are also the field, your pursuer, his knife and the cliff. All these images originate in you and represent aspects of your personality.

By experiencing your dreams as parts of yourself, you may be able to finish the business the dream represents.

DREAM DIARY

► To help you remember dreams, Dr. Stanley Krippner, director of the Maimonides Medical Center's Dream Laboratory, has recommended that before you go to sleep, you lie in bed and repeat aloud, "Tomorrow morning I will remember my dreams." Say it slowly at least ten times, like a chant. The rhythm of the words will help guide you off to sleep.

► Keep a pad and pencil next to your bed. As soon as you wake up, write down the dream in the greatest possible detail. Relax, and try to bring back the whole dream.

If you don't remember anything, lie quietly and see what comes to you. "The first word or picture that pops into your mind is most likely related to your last dream of the night," Dr. Krippner has pointed out. "Start to free-associate on it, and it will usually take you to your dream."

► When you have accumulated several weeks of notes on dreams, look through them. See what kinds of situations and which people occur most often. Notice sounds, colors, tastes and smells that show up in your dreams. Roughly sort your dreams in any way that seems meaningful to you.

Try summing up your dreams in headlines: "AFRAID TO TRY"; "UNDER ATTACK"; and so on. What messages are repeated? What are your dreams trying to tell you?

RELIVE A DREAM

Gestalt therapy provides a method for working in depth on a single dream. "We don't interpret a dream," Fritz Perls wrote. "We bring it back to life."

Relive your dream, as if it were happening now. Instead of telling the dream as if it were a story in the past, act it out in the present.

▶ Say the dream aloud, using the present tense. Be aware of what you are feeling when you say it.

▶ List all the elements of your dream: the people, animals, objects, colors, moods. Be particularly aware of any situations, such as dying or falling, which you *avoided* in the dream by running away or waking up.

▶ Act out each of the elements. What does each part have to say? What do you have to say to it? What do the parts say to each other? "Ham it up," Perls suggested, "and really transform yourself into each of the different items. . . . Use your magic. Turn into that ugly frog . . . the dead thing . . . the demon. . . ."

If, in your dream, there were situations you avoided, try to finish the dream by acting through the frightening situations in fantasy. Thus, if you avoided opening a door in your dream, see if you can open the door in fantasy.

In so acting out the parts of your dream, you turn into a dreamer again and become one with your dreaming self. You may give words to characters whose emotions were unspoken in the dream, so that now they engage in a dialogue.

In "Contributions of Gestalt Therapy" (*Ways of Growth*, edited by Herbert Otto and John Mann) psychiatrist Claudio Naranjo tells of a man who dreamt of himself in a corridor full of lockers. He was looking for some books in one of them, but he couldn't remember which locker. An attendant tried in vain to help him.

Naranjo asked the man if he could sense this dream as an image of his existence. Yes, he felt that his life was like a corridor full of lockers—gray, enclosed, impoverished, boring and unsatisfactory. And he was searching for something with no success.

The patient began to act out the dream:

PATIENT: Here comes the attendant. He takes the key and wants to help me. I know better than he where I left my books.

NARANJO: Tell him.

PATIENT: *You* can't help me. I know better than you and can do best when undisturbed. Leave me alone.

NARANJO: What does he answer?

PATIENT: I am sorry, sir. I only wanted to help you.

NARANJO: Be the locker now.

PATIENT: Here I am, a gray locker. I have a number on me. People come and use me. They open me and close me. They put things in and take things out of me. I am pretty tired of this. I am sick and tired of it! How I would like to disappear, not to be found again! . . . I know now . . . I know I can play a trick on this fellow. I can have him be deceived so he doesn't find me! Yes, I will have the attendant "help" him, so he is misled and does not find me.

NARANJO: Now be yourself opening the locker.

PATIENT [*opening the locker*]: So it was you! *You,* trying to deceive me!

NARANJO: What does the locker answer?

[*The patient lets out a laugh of triumphant mockery and does a slow, powerful dance at the center of the room.*]
Do you still feel gray and like a number?

PATIENT: Not any more.

Observed Naranjo: "The patient came to experience himself as the one playing hide-and-seek with himself, and not merely the searching victim. When his self-defeating wish was enacted and channeled into the dance, he was not at an impasse any more but creatively expressing himself and feeling himself as a living being."

WINDOWS TO EMOTION

Dreams are windows to your unconscious. What you dare not face, what you dare not admit to yourself, often comes through in dreams.

▶ If you can stay with the essence of your dreams, you may be able to become aware of and work through "holes" in your personality. A dream may start off a chain of emotional associations. Stay with these feelings. Pursue them until you have defined the emotion and come to grips with it.

In a workshop conducted by Dr. Marilyn Rosanes-Berrett of New York, a member named Pete told of a dream: "This dream is in two parts. In the first one I was on a rooftop, and I was wresting a gun from a man; and in the other part I was about to enter this woman who was lying before me, but there was another woman, and she interfered or interrupted the proceeding, and I could not go through with it. I was absolutely furious."

Immediately after reporting the dream, Pete felt acutely embarrassed. Dr. Rosanes-Berrett encouraged him to stay with the feeling of embarrassment and see what it could tell him about his dream.

Pete said he felt the group was "an amorphous mass" sitting in judgment on him. "I don't have difficulty . . . if it is a one-to-one relationship," Pete said, "but only when it is in a group situation."

Dr. Rosanes-Berrett referred back to Pete's dream:

ROSANES-BERRETT: But when you had two women there—in your dream—you had a group, too!

PETE: Um! It's the presence of a third party that disturbs me. I don't like it. I am all right on a one-to-one basis.

ROSANES-BERRETT: Are you the third party in your dream?

PETE: Oh! I see! The third party is really the interrupter. It's the one who really interrupts the proceedings . . . oh, boy! Now I am . . . okay! I am staying with the embarrassment! Oh . . . it is really my interrupting my parents having intercourse. *That's* the embarrassment. . . . I could not see any connection between the two parts of my dream and now I can. . . . I am fine. I really am!

The Climactic Voyage

Some therapists have been experimenting with a method of having a patient take a fantasy trip through the layers of his personality and arrive at a visualization of his self. In what is surely one of the most exciting moments in the entire realm of psychology, a person actually sees and experiences his inner being.

Some people fantasize physically entering into their bodies and going deeper and deeper until they can go no farther. One woman had the image of going into her grin and traveling to her nose, then into her body.

Others may see images of different places that more closely personify them. For example, a young man had adventures at a forest, a muddy hill, a waterfall and a field—before finding that his self resided at a vast, sunny beach.

Still others may find their images in past events. Scenes from childhood, recent episodes, scenes from movies, actual people and those from dreams and books—all may combine in a sequence of fantasies.

Whatever the content or path of the trip, the self is likely to be experienced either as a beautiful place where you feel at perfect peace, or as a bright, white light, like the sun. One patient reported: "I started to see sunshine—the sun—then I got a feeling of rays of light coming from beyond my field of vision above."

A person in touch with his inner self feels self-accepting, joyful, often exalted. Thus in contact with his real self, he can know the full range of his emotions and desires—can understand who he is and how he wants to lead his life. If he is asked questions, he generally responds from his inner being—what *he* really wants, free of phony roles. Once found, the self can be revisited and consulted.

Martha Crampton, one of the therapists who has pioneered in the use of this method, has asked patients to start the experience by trying to visualize the outermost layer of the personality. She then urges them not to reason or censor themselves, but just to look for a picture. Once the patient starts on the trip, she might ask him how he feels about a certain layer of himself, or have him describe some image in more detail, or she might urge him to go on to the next level. She rarely interrupts with an interpretation.

As if drawn by a self that *wants* to be discovered, the traveler follows his images to the center of his being. Here, from Miss Crampton's records, is a description of a man's climactic voyage to his inner core:

Layer 1: A circular path leading to the center—a spiral form. At first I saw a set of concentric brass rings. Now I see myself walking on a path through the woods. The sunlight is streaming through the trees. It seems to be an exploratory path—not too well marked, but I seem to feel I'm on the right track.

Layer 2: I'm in the garden . . . seated there with a large drafting board. I seem to be working on an architect's general plan of the universe—trying to demonstrate the place of man in the total scheme of things.

Layer 3: A cloud, grayish-blue. Now it becomes a pearly or silvery color. All of this seems to have emerged from a volcano that appeared for just a moment. The cloud is all there is; it is not a discrete object. The feeling is one of wonderment. The cloud seems to be flashing or flickering, as though there are dots of light in the center of it. It may represent the whole universe either prior to creation or at the first stage of creation; or then again, it seems to be a sort of warning or indication of something to happen—a kind of riddle.

Layer 4: An eagle with wings outstretched as though ready to take off in flight.

Layer 5: The same bird in flight—climbing as though into the sun. The bird is black, with the golden light of the sun reflected on its wings. The sun is a deep gold or orange-red color.

Layer 6: This one is hard to understand. It's as though I'm looking down from a mountain on a vast expanse of sunny plain. On the plain is an array of geometric figures that seem to be made out of silvery metal. There is a triangle, a double helix—as though the two helices were intertwined like two snakes standing upright—and a sphere. They are grouped in a triad at the bottom left corner. In the top right corner is a purplish background with a white swan or egret—some bird with long legs, which is standing up. The bird represents peace or serenity. The triangle seems to represent truth —it rings true when struck. The sphere represents beauty to me, and the serpents or spirals might represent love or goodness—I should say wisdom, which would combine both of these. The helices seem to preside over the other geometric symbols. It is the dominant theme. If these three symbols remain there, the bird of harmony or serenity will remain ever-present against this regal background.

Layer 7: A colleague and . . . I are meeting for the last time on the shores of a sea. Above us is a huge V sign spreading out like two arms of a rainbow. . . . The two arms of the rainbow indicate that our work is to radiate upwards and outwards.

Layer 8: A golden plain or surface. This time there is only the helix or dual serpent of shining silver. At the end of the plain there is a sun—more golden now—casting its light upon the helix, which in turn is casting a shadow. The scene is motionless and has an eternal aspect.

Layer 9: A boundless ocean—the sun sparkling on the waves. The sun with different helices like silver coils coming out of it as a corona. Just then the silver cloud came back, and the glitter of the ocean left. The cloud and sun seem to have merged. The cloud is brighter than it was—like a throbbing mass of light, with pinpoints of additional light. It is somewhere between gold and silver—with the warmth of gold and the light of silver—a pearly gold. This pearly cloud is all there is—a warmer feeling now—a feeling of joy.

PERSON
TO PERSON

By engaging in growth experiences with others, you can build
warmth, closeness and trust. You can also break through blocks
caused by negative feelings, such as resentment and fear of rejection. Other games have special value in improving family relationships. You can invent your own games to meet new situations.

9

Games for Building Warmth and Trust

A Jewish tradition, *shivah,* follows the death of a loved one. *Shivah* in Hebrew means "seven" and stands for the seven days during which the immediate family stays home and is visited by relatives and friends.

After the first day or so in a household sitting *shivah,* tears of grief are usually punctuated by laughter and easy-flowing conversation. One moment a distraught widow will be sobbing her heart out; the next, she'll be exchanging gossip with a neighbor. For, over and beyond its religious purposes, *shivah* is personally beneficial. The sheer presence of sympathetic people provides a warm, supportive setting in which the bereaved can make a difficult emotional transition.

This 2,000-year-old custom is one of the oldest forms of group therapy.

Concerning his experience with groups Dr. Clark E. Moustakas, of the Merrill-Palmer Institute of Human Development and Family Growth in Detroit, noted in *Individuality and Encounter:* "I have discovered that people learn to listen and care for one another. They learn to help one another grow. They become more sensitive, more alive, responsive, aware, understanding of self and others, more honest, and more gentle and loving."

Dr. Carl R. Rogers, a pioneer in the development of the encounter group, has summarized the effects of the intensive group experience which features much freedom and little structure:

• The individual will gradually feel safe enough to drop some of his defenses and façades.

• He will relate more directly on a feeling basis with other members of the group.

• He will come to understand himself and his relationships with others more accurately.

• He will change in his personal attitudes and behavior.

• He will subsequently relate more effectively to others in his everyday-life situations.

This chapter and the next deal largely with such intensive group experiences: short-term interactions involving you and others. This chapter treats the heightening of positive feelings, such as warmth, closeness, trust, joy. Chapter 10 has to do with reducing negative ones—resentment, rejection, anxiety and other painful emotions.

You can play many of these interpersonal games with just one other person, a friend or your spouse. But these games are derived from *group* experiences and for greatest benefit are best played by three or more. With a number of participants you can build on a broader foundation of perspective, ability and sensitivity and, therefore, can have a richer experience. The foundation is also likely to be more stable—the group setting tends to have a maturing influence on its members, often a welcome safeguard.

On the other hand, the more is not necessarily the merrier. The maximum size for an effective group ranges around a dozen members. For a good rule of thumb, if you have more than fourteen participants present, break up into two groups.

What Makes Groups Tick?

Professional leaders are constantly surprised at the unpredictability of the chemical reactions that take place in groups. A group can seem to be sinking into a thrall of boredom; then, in an instant, can explode into life. Two members who appear to be dwelling on different emotional planets suddenly interact—and the flame of their encounter ignites relationships across the room. An activity supremely successful with one group may lay an egg with another group almost identical in make-up. Then this same game, tried later with the same group, may open up feelings that will keep the members going for hours.

While no one knows exactly why groups work, certain catalysts are almost always found in successful group reactions. Possibly the most significant of these is the willingness to share yourself with others—your doubts, conflicts, pain and joy, your immediate feelings and perceptions. By opening up, you can help a group—and you—thrive. "To share," Dr. Clark Moustakas has observed, "is to touch others with oneself."

In sharing you create a climate in which you recognize yourself as you really are and in which you really notice the others you encounter. "That which we know we come to trust," notes Moustakas. "As each person shares himself in the personal, private world in which he lives, real knowledge is generated; a clarity of self and others is emerging. As each person finds a way to be with others, while growing both in his concern for himself and for others, a bridge of meaning is created."

There is at least one other ingredient essential to a rewarding group experience: You need to provide a conducive setting. Thus, in bringing together an encounter group, what preparations should you make? Emily Coleman, a lecturer and writer on behavioral sciences, has sponsored parties centered on growth games and offers these tips:

▶ 1. *Do ahead of time* whatever you can do to keep things flowing smoothly, without interruptions. Make any snacks beforehand. Put the cat out. Take the phone off the hook. Then relax. "Your mood can't guarantee the success of a party. But if it is bad, others will pick it up, and the whole thing will flop."

▶ 2. *Don't invite people who work together* or who are in the same line of business or who know each other really well. "If you do, it will be like fighting City Hall, you against an entrenched organization determined to maintain the status quo. They will talk shop or tell stories or exchange miseries or one-up or do whatever they usually do."

Do invite people in relatively the same socioeconomic level, people you think have something in common, such as interests, goals and values, people who are relatively open-minded and people who do not have sandpaper personalities. Keep your guest list small for your maiden effort.

▶ 3. *Prepare your guests for a different kind of evening.* Encourage them to ask questions of one another. Give them specific permission to refuse to answer questions that they don't want to answer. Tell them what your plans are for later.

▶ 4. *Avoid alcohol if possible.* Otherwise serve only wine or punch. "Be very stingy with liquor if you want these games to be taken seriously and not to be laughed away as nonsense by those persons who are most in need of getting close to people. The persons most alienated from others, most desperately in need of personal contact, may be convinced that they can't function in public without alcohol."

▶ One other pointer: *Keep your first games simple* and devoted to breaking the ice. An excellent way of beginning is to have everyone let out a mighty roar and bang and stamp the floor. People bring a lot of tensions and frustrations to a group, and this is a good way to get them out.

Here is an assortment of other introductory activities:

GETTING ACQUAINTED

▶ *My Name Is.* Perhaps the method most often used to get a group acquainted is to have each member give the name he wishes to be known by and tell what he wants to get out of his experience with the group: resolve an inhibition; get rid of feelings of guilt or resentment; experience closeness.

▶ *Now I Feel.* Tell the others how you feel sitting here *now*. If you have a special feeling toward any other members—favorable or unfavorable—express it.

Stay in the present moment—"Now I feel tense"; "Now I feel happy." Don't say, "Now I feel that I am tense"; "Now I feel that I am happy." "I feel," as used in this verbal construction, means "I am of the opinion." It is a thought—a conclusion about your observing yourself—and not a genuine tuning-in to your emotions. What do you *feel?*

▶ *Values.* To break a group into subgroups for quick getting-to-know-you interactions, Dr. Daniel I. Malamud has tried reading off a set of three statements reflecting values of one kind or another. Each member decides which one of the statements he considers most important. The participants are then divided into smaller groups according to their choices.

For example, the items might be: "To be generous toward other people." "To be my own boss." "To have understanding friends." All those who choose "To be generous toward other people" as most important gather together in one subgroup to talk over their choices for five minutes. Another set Malamud has used is: "To have a good meal with a friend." "To get a good night's sleep." "To have a good orgasm."

► *Birth Order* is another Malamud game for getting acquainted. He groups members according to who were the oldest children in their families, who were the youngest, who were the middles. These subgroups go on to explore the various experiences they had by virtue of their birth-order positions.

CONVERSATIONS

► *Gibberish*. Break up into pairs, and have a nonsense conversation, using only gibberish. As your conversation proceeds, you are likely to find that you can convey a great deal of emotional content without needing words. Can you express affection? Anger? Fear? Joy?

► Gibberish can serve another purpose as an icebreaker: It is impossible to be uptight when you and others around you are being absurd. Ergo, to break the ice, engage in an absurd conversation. One suggestion: Stick your tongue out, and try to talk seriously. You can't be very formal with someone after you've stuck your tongue out at him.

► Also fun: Roar. Squeak. Gurgle. Burble. Make other noises. Let your partner imitate yours, then you imitate his. You'll find conversations like this taking place:

"Grnggzblltt."

"Grngbllzt?"

(Insistently) "Grnggzblltt!"

"Ah! Grnggzblltt."

► *Baffling Conversation* can give you an insight into the frustrations of trying to communicate with an unresponsive person. Talk to a partner about something important to you. As you speak, your partner is silent, averts his eyes, slowly moves away. Notice what your impulse is toward the person who doesn't listen. Do you feel like pushing him? Buttonholing him? Rejecting him?

Change roles and be aware of how you feel when you don't permit yourself to respond to someone. Do you resent him? Want to run away? Get closer to him? Do you have feelings of power over the other person, who must keep talking to fill the gap you've created?

Now play the game through a second time. This time touch the other person as he is speaking, and respond to what he is saying. *Vive la différence!*

▶ *Mutual Interview.* Learn as much as you can about your partner in ten minutes. Ask him questions to find out the really important things abut him. Then switch and have your partner interview you.

A variation of this is to interview each other in a single fifteen-minute period. Be aware of what is happening between you as the dual interview takes place: Who takes the initiative and how? Who talks more? Are you angry, resigned? What if the interview doesn't go the way you think it should?

Next, introduce your partner to the group, relating what you've learned about him. After all introductions have been made, have the group discuss whether the introductions contained really important information about each person. Note what you deem important to know about a person and how much about someone else you remember. Tell how the group could get to know and understand you better.

TOUCHING EXPERIENCES

Touching is a normal expression of interest and affection and can help you know someone in ways that words can't convey.

The importance of touch is conveyed in this moving account by Althea Horner, a psychotherapist:

"I was born to a mother who could be tender and demonstrative towards the helpless baby, but who withdrew love when the child's developing will led to the first 'no. . . .' I do not remember the last time I was held affectionately in my mother's arms. I grew up convinced that she did not love me, and questioned my lovability. Then I married a kind but undemonstrative man, who grew up in a home where open affection was not shown. My need for touch, for stroking, for contact comfort, was once again thwarted. My self-image became more and more one of being an 'untouchable.'

"As a graduate student, I went into psychotherapy, where, from time to time, I would express my longing to have the therapist hold me. Each time I was told that my problem was that I wanted gratification instead of therapy. Now I had learned something new about myself. Not only was I untouchable, but my wish for contact comfort was 'bad.' "

Then Mrs. Horner attended a workshop at Esalen led by Dr. Herbert A. Otto. Part of Dr. Otto's technique is the issuing of lapel buttons that indicate the individual's willingness to be touched. "Suddenly I found myself in a situation in which touch was neither bad nor feared, but valued and encouraged."

Later that week Mrs. Horner attended a workshop conducted by Virginia Satir, a specialist in family therapy. "Once more . . . I found myself being held like a child by its mother when, sensing my anguish, Mrs. Satir sat down on the floor beside me and gently held me in her arms. Men, women—it made no difference. The need for the kind of contact that says you are not untouchable, bad or dangerous has no sex."

Here are some games for getting acquainted through touch.

▶ *Rump Bump.* With your eyes closed, slowly back in toward the center of the room. As you make contact with other backs, gently bump hello, and move on. After about a minute, stop next to one back, and get to know this back with your own. Have a back conversation: Try an argument; then be playful, tender. Do a back dance, exploring all kinds of motion. After five minutes, stop and be aware of each other; then gradually move apart. Experience how your back feels. Open your eyes, and look at your partner.

▶ *Slap Rap.* Have a conversation by slapping your partner's arms and shoulders. Start the conversation by slapping with both hands simultaneously. Your partner answers. This goes back and forth like ordinary conversation.

▶ *Blind Milling.* Walk about the room, with your eyes closed. When you find someone, explore him with your hands—touch his shoulders, face, hands, hair. Communicate with him just by touch. See if you can convey a message about how you feel about him; let him communicate back. Now find a way to say good-bye. Continue

milling until you bump into someone else, and touch-talk with
him, too.

To get some perspective on the freedom offered by blind milling,
try milling with your eyes open. Are you self-conscious? Distracted?
Closed in? What accounts for the difference?

▶ *Hand Conversation*. Here's a clear way of experiencing the two
opposite extremes of conversations: normal cocktail-type chatter
and the deeper talk of touch.

First, sit back to back with a partner, and talk about yourself.
Very likely you'll find it hard to make gut contact. Most such talks,
in which not even the eyes are in contact, stay on a superficial
level: "How come you're here?" "What do you do for a living?"

After five minutes or so, take an opposite tack. Face each other,
with your knees touching. Keeping your eyes closed, see how much
you can express merely through touching each other's hands.
Through touch alone you're likely to find an exchange consisting of
warmth, interest, possibly anger and frustration, but nonetheless a
great deal of feeling. One participant observed: "I never dreamt a
conversation without words could be so intimate. Exploring a person's fingers can be like feeling between his legs."

Because of such lightning intimacy, and because of general pro-
scriptions equating touch with sexuality, men sometimes find it
difficult to have hand conversations with another man. If men are
afraid of the homosexual overtones, it often helps to get started
with aggressive rather than delicate emotions, and then gradually
build up to more tender expressions. A variation on a hand conversation calls for a third person to suggest the emotions to be
expressed: "Now express anger. . . . Now, pleading. . . . Now,
irritation. . . . Now, concern." The idea is to point up the enormous range of feelings that can be expressed nonverbally.

▶ *I and Thou*. Here is a touch exercise that may give you yet another dimension of experience with another person: a sense of oneness, of merging with the other.

Find a partner, with your eyes closed. With your left hand touch
your own face; with your right hand touch your partner's face.
Try to touch the same features of your face and your partner's at
the same time. Do this for about five minutes. You're likely to get
the sensation that two faces—indeed, two beings—have become

one. Conversely, you may become more sensitive to the other as you become aware of the contrasts between you.

As a variation on this game, again close your eyes, and explore a partner's face with your fingers, as a blind man would. See if you can tell not only what he might look like, but also something of what he might be feeling. When you've explored each other's face, slowly open your eyes at the same time, and gaze into each other's eyes.

Getting Closer

Dr. Sidney M. Jourard of the University of Florida has described two kinds of encounters: the encounter that mystifies, and the encounter that reveals.

The encounter that mystifies is illustrated by the young man on the make. His real intent is: "I want her to tumble for me," but he does not express it. Instead, he tries to mislead the girl as to his real intentions. Observes Dr. Jourard: "He will show aspects of himself that aim at persuading or influencing the other. The other person has been reduced from the status of a person to the status of an object, a manipulandum, something to be used if it is useful and neutralized or changed if it is not."

An encounter that mystifies invariably results in the maintaining of emotional distance. No genuine feeling is exchanged.

By contrast, the encounter that reveals brings you and another closer. "In genuine dialogue, each experiences the other as a person," noted Jourard. "Transparency, not mystification, is one of the goals. . . . The aim is to show oneself in willful honesty. . . . Dialogue is like mutual unveiling."

Whenever open and direct feeling is expressed and responded to in a relationship, a heightened feeling of closeness results. Realness is the soil out of which flower warmth and trust.

The following games will help you learn to be more open and direct in expressing your feelings.

FIRST IMPRESSIONS

▶ Stand in front of another group member, and look him in the eye. Touch him if you'd like, and tell him as honestly and openly as you can what your first impression of him is.

Give your first impression of each group member in this fashion. Repeat until all group members have given their first impressions of each other. Ann was somewhat surprised when the impression of her was of a nice New England type, a good sister, bright, well organized. She thought of herself as a New York girl, artistic and somewhat nonconforming. But this image didn't come through.

After thinking about it, she realized she gave a stiff impression, that it was a part of herself that she often wanted to forget about. Yet her dress was a crisp classic shirtwaist, her eyes had a wide-open, innocent bright look, her talk was schoolmarmish. Who was she? This game of First Impressions brought the question up with new immediacy.

▶ How do the first impressions you have of a person compare with those that others in the group have of him? What do your impressions of others reveal about *you?* Simon's first impression of Myra was: "I see you as a dominating female, a real PTA-type, middle-aged authority figure."

Actually, Myra was a shy woman, only five years older than Simon and still in her thirties. Simon realized later that he felt threatened by her seeming competence—and that "with women who remind me of my mother I act like a little boy."

▶ Deliberately seek out a person whom you *don't* like. Tell him in detail what you find dislikable in him.

Then reflect: What is there in him that you don't like about yourself?

"You're fat. You're ugly. You're disgusting." Alan's voice was thick with loathing toward Don, a shambling, overweight figure with thick eyeglasses and an inadequate air.

"Come on," a member of the group said. "Don's no beauty. But he's not that bad. What's bugging *you?* How does he make you feel?"

Alan thought a while.

"Embarrassed," he said at last.

"Embarrassed?"

"He reminds me of Milo Berryman."

"Who the hell is Milo Berryman?"

"The class creep when I was in elementary school," Alan explained. "I used to dread being associated with him, because I was embarrassed that people would think I was his friend. Don, it's not your problem. It's mine."

SILENT LANGUAGE

▶ *Accepting feeling.* Fred's wife had just recently left him. He came to the group to get some feeling of closeness and to hear about the hurts of other people. Dr. Clark Moustakas in *Individuality and Encounter* noted that as Fred talked on and analyzed various people, he revealed himself to be defensive and sarcastic. Several participants told him that he was not able to take anything from the group.

"Go into the center, Fred," Moustakas told him. "Stop shielding yourself with words, and simply make yourself open to what each member of the group might feel like coming up to give you."

One person came up and massaged his shoulders. Someone else shook his hand. Someone else kissed him. One fellow had him lie down on his back and simply lay on top of him for a couple of minutes.

When they were through, Fred began to talk in a different tone as he recalled his loneliness as a child, and tears began to roll down his cheeks. For the first time this experience allowed him to open up his painful feelings to the group. He brought forth affectionate and caring responses from people who previously had been hostile to him.

▶ *Eyeballing.* Sit facing a partner, and stare directly into each other's eyes for five minutes. Tell him something important with your eyes. See what he has to say to you.

Afterward, spend a few minutes talking about your experience. Typically, the talk will be more open and animated after the nonverbal encounter. The eyeball-to-eyeball meeting frees emotions by forcing you to *look* and make genuine contact with your partner. You'll find new truth in the old adage, The eyes are the windows of the soul.

Psychologist Paul Bindrim often asks participants in his workshops to spend five minutes talking with a partner, learning as much as possible about him, then five minutes gazing wordlessly into his eyes. Most participants report feeling they've learned much more about the other from the nonspeaking eye contact.

► *Hugging.* An important part of group experiences is hugging. It can help a group feel closer and can physically express the warmth and affection the members feel toward one another. At the same time, hugging can develop into a ritual in which it becomes almost mandatory for every person to hug every other person. To keep the hug from becoming a cop-out, make sure you really feel like hugging. When you feel the urge to hug someone, express it. Sometimes a whole group wants to express its closeness by hugging. All members get as close as possible and put their arms around each other. Spontaneous swaying often develops.

**Sometimes a Whole Group
Wants to Express Its Closeness by Hugging**

One participant described his feelings about a group hug: "Six of us standing close in a circle with arms around each other, talking, caring. I have never known this much acceptance. It overwhelms me. They see—draw closer."

► *Pantomimes* provide another nonverbal way of communicating with your partner. Pantomime your impressions of him. Do you like him? Are you put off by him? Show your feelings, with gestures and facial expressions.

Then pantomime how you feel your partner feels toward you. Afterward ask yourself: "Is this how I really feel toward myself?" These pantomimes often permit people to express feelings toward themselves and others that they would not ordinarily verbalize.

Alice, a retired schoolteacher, liked her partner, a housewife named Joanie, and sought to tell Joanie, "I'm very fond of you," in pantomime. In the discussion afterward Joanie said, "I disgust you, don't I?" As the woman talked, Alice realized that she had a lot of difficulty expressing warmth persuasively. Moreover, it occurred to her that she was often oblivious of other people's feelings: She had not noticed the look of hurt on Joanie's face.

Joanie, on the other hand, also found a lot to think about, since she had interpreted Alice's positive expression as being one of disgust. She concluded that she was frequently suspicious of other people's claiming they liked her, since she had a fairly low opinion of herself.

Joanie and Alice continued on to the next step, in which you express how you think your partner sees you. Joanie puffed up her cheeks and expanded her arms in front of her belly pantomiming fatness. In reality, she was reasonably trim. But she had been a fat child and teen-ager—and now, though in her early forties, she carried around a corpulent afterimage of herself that she loathed.

STRAIGHT TALK

The object of these games is to help you verbalize your feelings, expectations, fears, hopes, problems—to help you talk to people about things that really matter to you.

▶ *What Do You Want?* Keep asking your partner one and only one question: "What do you want?" Say this with many different inflections and gestures as your partner keeps trying to answer the question. Then switch roles. Answer with respect to what you want at *this* moment.

This experiment can help you sharpen your perception of the ever-changing flow of wants and desires that exist in you. It can also help you express these wants to another person.

One man's list of responses to "What do you want?" was as follows:

"I want to take a deep breath."

"I want you to leave me alone."

"I want to love my wife more."

"I want to go to bed with Muriel [a girl in the group]."

"I want to laugh."

"I want to cry."

"I want you to turn around."

"I want to walk in the country."

► *When I Grow Up.* Share your fantasies of what you would like to do and be. Such fantasies are not always as impractical as they seem. One young accountant said that his boyhood wish had always been to become a deep-sea diver. He expected derision, since his parents had always laughed. But instead he got encouragement. "You have only one life," said a group member, "so you really ought to do what you want." The young man thereafter began training for a career as a diver.

► *Major Event.* All members of a group share with one another the most significant moments of their lives, happy and sad.

In one group an elderly man talked about having his face destroyed in an automobile accident and then surgically reconstructed.

This was the first time he'd ever exposed how he felt about living a life disfigured by scar tissue. When he finished, several members who previously could not bear to look at him now found they could gaze at him with genuine warmth.

► *Current Problem.* One member relates a problem that represents a pervasive threat in his life. Other members listen carefully, asking questions and offering suggestions.

► *Sharing Games.* Share with the group:

► . . . an incident from your childhood that was deeply formative.

► . . . your happiest moment.

► . . . your most embarrassing moment.

► . . . a personal secret.

► . . . your feelings about the part of your body that you like the most, that you like the least.

▶ . . . how you feel about your work—its satisfactions and frustrations.

▶ . . . how you feel about your financial situation, income, savings, debts.

▶ . . . your love life, past and present.

▶ . . . your problems in marriage, its daily annoyances, you and your partner's basic differences.

▶ . . . your feelings about other members of the group.

Building Trust

Emily Lynn Lewis, eleven months old, loves to be thrown in the air and caught on the way down. She squeals with delight when she's swung by her feet. She often initiates a game in which she falls backward into her mother's lap.

It doesn't occur to her that she might be dropped. She feels completely trusting of her parents, loved by them and close to them. So far they haven't let her down.

Most relationships between people are characterized in their early stages by uncertainty, which often includes fear and distrust. To reduce your uncertainty toward people you newly meet, you may attempt to fit them into categories that you feel you can understand, believing, "If I know she is a teacher [Catholic, Southerner, divorcee, etc.], then I know what she is like and what she will do." This assumption is often erroneous and at best superficial—you see not a person but a type, not what she is but what you expect her to be.

Another way you may seek to reduce your uncertainty toward people is to be a stickler for formalities. Not only Victorians stand on ceremony. Codes of behavior—"the way things are done around here"—exist everywhere and are often enforced to make people more predictable and, therefore, less threatening. Rigid politeness can be a similar out. It can keep people at a safe distance, prevent negative comments and, in general, serve the unrealized needs of a fearful person.

In some groups, the members begin things by drawing up rules and regulations to "rule in" order and "rule out" chaos. A group may assign a timekeeper so that one person won't monopolize the session. It may appoint a chairman or decide in what order people will speak. All are attempts to keep people "within bounds."

"The group in its early stages will attempt to cling to and create fragile structural stabilities to reduce fear," Dr. Jack R. Gibb, a specialist in group process, has observed. "These apparently secure structures turn out to be made of sand."

Rigid rules invite infractions, which cause conflict and thereby intensify uncertainty and fear. Or the rules can incite rebellion in the form of apathy. The noninvolvement can lead to boredom and frustration and can worsen the members' distrust of one another.

The development of trust reverses this progression. As trust grows, people tolerate more and more uncertainty toward one another—the unpredictability is less and less threatening. "They become more spontaneous and less cautious," Jack Gibb has noted. "The boundaries of acceptance widen."

The following games are aimed at making you more aware of your level of trust, and helping you to become more trusting. All are nonverbal. For, like Emily Lynn Lewis, you really express trust for a person by entrusting him with your body.

Note: The "blind walk," which appears in the Invitation at the very beginning of this book, is a classic experience for building trust. Try it at any time, indoors or out, when you feel a need to develop closeness and trust with another person.

BIG LIFTS

► *Head Lift.* Lie on your back, and relax your head and neck. Have your partner lift your head and rotate it. This game is harder than it sounds. You are likely to find it extremely difficult to give control of your head to someone else.

► *Conveyor Belt* is best played in large groups, twenty or more. The crowd picks you up as high as possible and passes you overhead. Relax completely, and let yourself float on this sea of hands.

BACK FALL

► Fall backward into the arms of your partner. Intensify the feeling of falling by throwing your arms up and yelling as if you're going over a cliff.

Try not to catch yourself, but trust the fellow in back to catch you. Do this several times.

Chances are you'll start off reluctantly. When you allow yourself to do it, though, you'll feel exhilarated at the freedom and weight-lessness, and you'll be ever more trusting of the person who caught you in time.

This experiment can also point up when it is inappropriate to trust. Peter was in an encounter group in which he expressed a great deal of hostility toward Jack. When the group tried the Back Fall, Peter impulsively asked Jack to catch him.

Jack let him fall with a resounding thud, then added insult to injury by laughing. On reflection, Peter realized he had been naïve —it is unwise to depend on someone you have just antagonized: He may retaliate.

TEETER-TOTTER

▶ This is an especially good game for someone who seems reluctant to let himself go in a group. A circle of six or so people forms about him. He shuts his eyes and relaxes completely, letting himself be supported by the group. Members of the group pass him around the circle. He may be turned; he may fall or be pushed or pulled from one person to the next; he may be held and momentarily embraced. This exercise can often break through tension and stiffness in a group.

Virginia Streitfeld reports the results of this technique, which was used at a weekend gathering of people interested in what encounter techniques might have to offer the church. "There was little group feeling," she recalled. "The talk was mainly intellectual; most were guarding their feelings. Nothing was happening."

Then someone mentioned the trust circle. With a lot of silliness one of the more skeptical ministers was put in the middle. He began hesitantly falling against the group. At first, the group was slow in knowing what to do. Then they got the knack of catching him with their bodies and reversing his direction. They lifted him up and rocked him, then lowered him to the floor. The minister had not quite enjoyed the experience, not knowing what was expected of him. But others in the group decided it looked like fun and wanted a turn. At the end the group spontaneously turned to the first minister and gave him the experience again. This time he didn't worry about what he should do but just enjoyed it.

"By this time," says Virginia, "everyone was physically tired, but the good feelings were flowing, a real group spirit was formed and the skeptics began to see there might be something here."

ROCK-A-BY BABY

▶ Lie on your back, with your eyes closed and your face up. Have the other members (about six or eight) line up on either side of you and gently lift and rock you to and fro.

While this technique may be used as a game in which everybody is given a turn, it is much more meaningful and powerful if it occurs at a psychologically sound moment in the group, when it answers the needs of a particular person.

In one group a member by the name of Al burst into tears at one point. The group spontaneously lifted and rocked him, singing, "Rock-a-by ba-by on the tree-top. . . ." The leader got underneath to support him. Previously Al had been telling between sobs about his deprived childhood: His father was never home; his mother had to work. Now, Al's being rocked represented an idealized family scene: He was being comforted by his mother and supported by his father, while his brothers and sisters surrounded him.

Similarly, at the end of a weekend workshop, the leader, who had worked very hard, was surprised and pleased when a group of young people descended upon him and wanted to lift him. He was lifted and rocked; the gentle rhythm of the rocking made him feel serene and relaxed.

After being gently laid down, he tried to stand up but fell to the ground. A shirtless man in the group held him. "The experience was so powerful and regressive," the leader recalls, "that I buried my face . . . in his chest and for a while didn't know if he was a man or a woman."

Clark Moustakas wrote about the rocking experience in *Individuality and Encounter*: "The kind of tenderness this approach engenders is often radically unlike the early experiences of members of the group. Many . . . state that they cannot remember being held, cradled or rocked as very young children. . . . Almost consistently, people emerge from this experience high, alive, feeling wonderful. The motion, the rhythm, the flow, the gentle rocking, all contribute to a sense of elation and peace."

Games for Merriment

These games are just for fun. They can be hilarious. Try one of these games as a relief from a series of exercises involving grief, anger or fear. They have also proved useful in drawing together a group whose members have been ill at ease.

CHUCKLEBELLY

► Everybody lies in a circle on the floor. Each person lies with his head on the belly of someone else. The first person goes, "Ha." The second, "Ha-ha." The third, "Ha-ha-ha." And so on, around the group. Usually shrieks of resounding laughter ensue, and the effect heightens as people laugh at the laughter.

HUMAN CARPET

► Everybody lies on the floor side by side, with their shoes off. For snugness, they lie head to foot. The person on the end rolls on top of this human carpet. When he gets to the end, he lies down, and the next person goes, until everyone has a roll.

PEOPLE MACHINE

► In this game members of a group make themselves into a machine—with as many moving gears and levers as they can devise. One member starts by repeatedly doing a movement, like shaking a leg and making a sound. Another member joins himself to him and starts his own motion. A third attaches himself, and so on. Ultimately the group looks and sounds like a Rube Goldberg machine.

TANGLE

► Everyone stands side by side and clasps the hand of the person next to him. The person on one end of the row becomes the leader.

He starts weaving through the other people—between them, under their legs, around them—until he can take the hand of the person on the other end.

People Machine

Still holding hands, everyone follows him. There will soon be a horrendous tangle. The object of the game is to unravel the snarl and end up in a circle without unclasping hands. It may be necessary to appoint a traffic cop to call out who should lift up which leg or come around whose head.

PILE-UP

▶ Members of the group lie on their bellies in a large circle, heads pointing toward the center. With their eyes closed, they begin crawling toward the center. They will bump into one another or crawl over others. Everyone continues to crawl until he reaches the center, where a pile will start to form. When everyone is part of the pile, all open their eyes and look around.

SYMPHONY ORCHESTRA

▶ Make a piece of music as a group—but without using any instruments except your voices and bodies. One person may begin by slapping someone else's belly and buttocks while chirping. Another might join in by clapping a partner's hands and chanting. A third might click his teeth together, and so on. Change the rhythm and your action as the mood changes.

10

Games for Breaking Through Blocks

Maria was a closemouthed young woman. Occasionally she would mutter snide remarks about others in the group, but for the most part she stayed to herself, a formal, solemn wraith.

"What's troubling you?" a member asked.

"I don't want to talk about it," she replied. She remained aloof, speaking only infrequently and in an angry, choppy way.

Toward the end of the workshop she glanced at her watch and remarked loudly, "Well, this has been a huge waste of time."

Jason, the leader, recognized that there's more than one way to call for help. "Would you like to tell us what you're feeling?" he asked her.

"I'm feeling I should have stayed home and set my hair."

Jason suggested that she come to the middle of the group and say what was on her mind. Hesitantly, she sat in the center of the circle.

"Lie down and start letting the words come out," Jason said. "Talk about what the devil's going on with you. For all the time we've been together, you haven't let anything get in or out."

Maria rose to leave. She paused, then settled back down and whispered, "I've had this divorce, you see."

"Can't hear you," a group member called.

"*Fuck you, you bastard!*" Maria screamed.

And it began. With a rush she talked. About her ex-husband. About his brutality toward her. About her self-disgust at submitting to it. About their frenzied battles, violent separations and impassioned attempts at reconciliation. About his throwing her over in the most humiliating way he could think of.

"I came home and found him in our bed with a teen-age girl. 'I think she's home,' he told her, and proceeded to ignore me. I had to pack my suitcase in the same room while my husband was making it with another woman."

She moaned, "I've cut myself off from every other person. I don't want to be hurt again."

"Can you stay with this feeling?" Jason asked.

"It hurts."

"Where?"

"My arms. My legs. Ooh, my belly and head."

"Breathe deeply, and stay with the feeling. Breathe right into the feeling. Pant rapidly, deeply."

"Oh, my God!" groaned Maria. As her rigidity eased, she began to tremble violently. "I'm freezing."

She broke into deep, anguished sobs. Twice she tried to say something. She shook her head.

"I can't talk," she gasped, and surrendered to her sobbing.

"Let it all out," said Jason. "This is what you've been holding in all this time. This is the pain you've been afraid to feel." He massaged her abdomen. "Get down into your gut."

She sobbed convulsively. Her body became taut, as if on a rack, then relaxed into a rhythmic quiver.

Jason took her in his arms. Others in the group drew closer and touched her. When at last she looked up, the difference in her appearance caused some to gasp in wonder. Her face was softer, younger, more relaxed.

Maria smiled broadly and shut her eyes. "Holy Toledo!" she exclaimed. "There's a white light in there." She threw her head back and laughed. Others in the group, who had been crying with her, now joined her in her laughter.

She noticed tears in Jason's eyes. "Is this included in the price of the sessions?" she asked.

"How about sharing your good feelings with us?" he asked.

"Dance with me, Jason," she said. "You, too. And you." She bounded across the room, hugging and dancing a turn with each person.

She came to a young man in the group. "Hold me tight." Arms intertwined, they swayed in place. She hummed.

"I feel unlocked," she told him, her eyes closed.

"Do you still see that white light?"

She nodded.

"What is it?"

"Joy."

Ice Cubes in Your River

Maria had broken through a block, an obstruction in her personality that caused her to hold in, or suppress, her feelings. Her neurosis was manifested in everything about her: her rigidity, her dourness, her angry muttering, her sarcasm, her fear of again being hurt. The block shaped her, for it determined what she risked doing and dared not do lest she again be emotionally injured. The block dictated her appearance and manner, which in turn attracted some people and put off others.

Laura A. Huxley has spoken of "ice cubes in your river." Emotional blocks are like hunks of ice clogging up the river of your life. They jam you up, keep you from flowing smoothly. The block represents a frozen area of your personality, one which you no longer feel—and which is an obstruction to warmth and growth.

The purpose of this chapter is to help you melt those blocks. As in the previous chapter, most of these experiments are derived from group therapy and are likely to be most effective if performed in a group setting. A theoretical framework has been provided by Gestalt therapy, founded by Fritz Perls. Perls has divided the structure of the personality into levels, close in conception to the onionskin model of Dr. Fabian Rouke (see Chapter 7, "Games for Being Yourself").

The surface, or "phony" layer consists of the roles you enact to manipulate your environment. It is identical to what Dr. Helen Deutsch has called the "as if" person. You behave *as if* you're a big shot, *as if* you're inadequate, *as if* you're smart or stupid. The role dictates your actions, in denial of your self. (Maria was playing the role of Cold Bitch. Roles are discussed in some detail in Chapter 7, "Games for Being Yourself.")

Though these phony roles are painful, they are at least familiar and safe. Thus, they are undergirded by the second, or "phobic," layer. You may fear giving up a role and venturing into new territory—and the phobic layer represents your resistances: the myriad of ways you avoid giving up a role.

Confronted by the possibility of having to surrender a role, you may give forth objections about "why" you can't do such-and-such —get a job, tell off your parents, quit overeating. You may experience physical objections as well: losing your voice, developing a headache, suddenly needing to take to your bed. One young woman, who'd been sustained by playing Daddy's Little Girl, wanted to get married, yet didn't want to confront her father. She resolved the problem temporarily by having an automobile accident. This not only gave her time, but she was able to have her father and fiancé literally fight over her—one on either side of her hospital bed.

Rejection

As a child, you needed your parents' love and support much as a tree needs soil and water. If you received this in sufficiency when young, you may have become self-sufficient for life. But if you were denied this affection, if you perceived yourself as rejected, you may forever after have become vulnerable to fears of rejection.

A child can be desolated by the belief that his parents do not love him. Psychologist Judi Striano tells of a member of one of her groups who returned home from camp one summer to find that his parents had moved away without telling him. Another family was living in his apartment, and his parents had left no forwarding address. Eventually he tracked them down. They greeted him with: "How did you find us?" Forty years later the pain he felt still kept him up at night.

The pain of rejection can be the worst pain you will ever know, and—like a dog tortured to do tricks in a circus—you may jump through hoops to avoid it. You may, for example, deny your self. Parental love is experienced as love only if it is for you *as you are*. If you are manipulated into an image they can love, you will know it (though they may not)—and you will suffer fear of rejection if you dare express your self.

Similarly, a child who senses his parents' rejection seeks to know why. He may thus decide that he deserves the rejection—that he is unworthy of love or somehow inadequate. Self-denying and self-destructive, perhaps. But in the child's mind such explanations help him limit the threat he faces. "If I am no good," he says, "at least the *world* is not so bad." One young woman, who felt inadequate and rejected, solemnly postulated the following: "I must have done something very terrible in some former life to be so unhappy now."

The following experiments are painful. Why, then, should you take part in them? Because your feelings of rejection, and your fears of being rejected, are already inside you: ice cubes in your river. A value of these experiments is that they *do* bring out such pains—so that at last you can overcome them.

CASTAWAY

These games may help you come to grips with the worst kind of rejection: being completely cast away from the group, ignored, not taken seriously.

► *Leave the Room*. Choose one member the group is having difficulty reaching. Ask him to leave the room. Discuss him while he's gone. Then have him come back, but don't tell him what you talked about. This is more than likely to make him feel rejected, possibly violently angry. It may open up areas of feeling and action that will result in a smoother relationship with the group.

► *Blindman's Buff*. Sally McClure has devised a game in which one person in the group experiences what it would feel like if he were blind and in need of making contact with other people. The others in the group reject him and feel what it would be like for them to reject his need. They taunt, tease, insult and badger him but don't allow themselves to be caught.

Miss McClure reported one instance in which this exercise was used: "As the teasing became more intense and the taunts more cruel, the blind man became more and more wary and animal-like. He crouched, clutched wildly at the air, dashed this way and that."

▶ *Out in the Cold.* The group forms a circle. Each member in turn steps *out* of the circle. When it's your turn, wander about the room exploring how you feel in different locations. Focus on how it feels to step away from the group. You may feel intensely rejected, isolated, weak, even dead. On the other hand, you may be relieved and may feel freed. Are you happy or sad to be leaving? Do you feel the group is more, or less, complete without you?

Then return to the group, and focus on how you feel now. Do you feel whole again? Or do you feel as if you are destroying the unity of the group? Do you feel awkward or comfortable? Are you happy to be back?

As a group member, tune in to how you feel when someone leaves. Depending on how you feel about the person leaving, are you sorry for him? Are you gloating? Or do you possibly feel rejected as the person moves away? Some members may feel that the group has annihilated the one who's left and that they can abuse him. Others may feel that the person who's left is freer and stronger than the group.

WITHOUT SELF-CONSCIOUSNESS

A. M. Rosenthal was assigned to be a New York *Times* correspondent in Warsaw. Rosenthal brought his family and was settling into an apartment, when his young son spotted some boys his age playing on the street. Though he spoke no Polish, he went down to join them. The boys wouldn't let him play. Rosenthal watched his son pick up a stick and, successfully, demand his rights under the universal rules of boyhood to get in the game.

Without self-consciousness the youngster had set about fulfilling his need for people. Rosenthal recalls never being more proud of his son. His directness can serve as a model for many adults who feel the same need but are paralyzed by fears of rejection.

If you're crippled by such fears, these games may help you.

▶ *Breaking In.* One at a time, group members place themselves outside the circle. Once outside the circle, your job is to get in. The group's job is to try to keep you out—to try hard to keep you out, while you're trying hard to get in. If you do get in, you really become part of the group.

How do you try to get at the group? Push? Reason? Cajole? Trick? This may help you see the maneuvering you typically use to gain acceptance.

How do you feel keeping someone out? Superior? Exclusive? Strong?

If a member of the group appears to be left out of things and is not ready to break in and become a part of the group, the group can pick him up, carry him around, and bring him into the center of the group.

► *Breaking Out.* This is the other side of the same coin. The group stands around you in a tight circle with arms locked. The circle represents group tyranny, the forces of others which keep you from asserting yourself as an individual who neither craves acceptance nor fears rejection.

Your object is to get out. How do you respond to this challenge? Fearfully, perhaps with an urge to quit? Aggressively? Sneakily? One woman automatically got down on her hands and knees, and feebly tried to crawl through the others' legs. If she were more assertive, she feared, "the others would like me even less."

► *Ask for Acceptance.* In one encounter group a woman named Ina explained that she had been in a previous marathon and had felt rejected by the group. She had signed up for this workshop to prove to herself that she could master this upset.

She was on the verge of tears, but she choked them back. The leader had her go around the group and ask each person, "Will you accept me?"

Everyone said "Yes" and stood up and embraced her, and the tears started to flow. But she was still restrained and somewhat cold.

When she reached the leader, he said, "Yes, I will accept you, but not your holding back."

With this, her crying got stronger, and the leader encouraged her to let out her screams of pain.

"I was holding onto her wrists at the time and could feel the tremendous holding tension in her arms," he recalled.

Finally, Ina had a really good cry. Thereafter she became a part of the group.

SELLING YOURSELF

You may not only have a dread of being rejected; you may also project onto others your need to be accepted—and therefore burden yourself with people you don't like. These games give you experience in rejecting—in asserting *yourself* by selecting some people but not others—as well as in being rejected.

▶ *Nonverbal Rejection.* In a group invite or reject each other without talking. You can nod or shake your head, you can scowl, you can flirt, you can wink; you can invite or reject in any way you wish.

In a similar exercise nobody accepts anyone's invitation. You invite and are rejected; likewise, you reject the invitations of others.

▶ *High-School Dance.* The men line up on one side of a room, the women on the other. All choose a partner of the opposite sex from across the room. One at a time, the members walk across the room to the person chosen and nonverbally invite her to leave the line, and together they walk back to the end of the room. Those chosen are free to reject or accept. If the inviter is rejected, he walks back alone to his original position. One participant recalled: "My involvement was one of very real feelings, as I let several others go first; then I decided on an attractive girl and walked twenty feet across the room to her. I wondered if I would be rejected and, with about one hundred people watching, how I would respond. It was a very satisfying feeling not to be rejected."

▶ *Three's a Crowd.* Many people who fear rejection share a common memory from the jungle days of childhood: being deliberately excluded by playmates. This game recreates that situation and so gives you a chance to face up to several aspects of a rejection phobia.

Join with two others (no couples in this trio), and get to know each other nonverbally. For five minutes explore one another by touch, eyeball contact, hand-to-hand conversations, and so on.

Then, for another five minutes, talk among yourselves, with an eye toward which two of you should stay together.

At the end of this period decide which of you should leave. If the group is large enough, the rejects can form new trios and start again. Or a reject can join one of the surviving duos and see if he can displace one of the pair.

Here, from a feedback session, are the reactions of the members of one trio:

MARGE: At first I didn't want to play. I said, "I had enough of this insie-outsie crap in high school." You know, that's half a lifetime ago, and I'm still carrying it around with me.

DAN: Phil and I just assumed that one of us guys would go, so I started competing like mad for Marge. I'm appalled at how I played up to you, Marge, and how I gloated when you chose me over Phil.

PHIL: I'm also impressed with how Dan and I each felt we had to fight like two moose over a mate, instead of pairing off as male friends. But the thing that gets me most is how ready I am to quit. Almost as soon as I met Marge and Dan, I thought, "Who needs them?" I got as cold as a zombie and wasn't surprised when I was the one told to go.

MARGE: I felt terrible having to choose between Phil and Dan. Actually Phil's more my type of person, and I'd have preferred to choose him. But I didn't want to hurt Dan, who was trying so hard, while Phil didn't seem to care about me one way or the other.

DAN: I'm not surprised to hear Marge say that. Right after she chose me, I got to wondering if it was worth my trouble. I became aware of winning her with false credentials.

Fear

Fear occurs when pain, or the threat of pain, dominates a situation and produces in you a wish to escape or withdraw. Fear is a painful emotion. But it can be useful in protecting you from a dangerous condition, much as the pain of a burned finger can warn you of a fire. Fear of genuine hazards is logical, rational, normal and potentially life-preserving.

On the other hand, fear can be destructive and life-constricting. It can cause you to shy away from self-fulfilling experiences and can lead to frustration, dissatisfaction, hatred, deceit, resentment, greed.

Because fear is itself frightening, a frightened person often finds it difficult to examine his fears. How might you tell, then, if a fear is healthy or unhealthy? A healthy fear is exemplified for instance, when a man, meeting a bear in the woods, climbs a tree, hoping that the bear won't follow him. The bear departs, and after a short pause for recovery the man, too, goes on his way.

In sum, a healthy fear generally has the following characteristics:

• It is specific. The fear is limited to *this* bear in *this* situation. An unhealthy fear might extend even to bears safely behind bars in a zoo—or, by analogy, to all Negroes, all hippies, all policemen.

A healthy fear responds to a clear and immediate danger. An unhealthy fear causes you to react with fright to stimuli that are only remotely harmful, and this can exact a continuous—and needless—physical and mental toll.

• It is temporary, whereas chronic fearfulness leaves you so preoccupied with a fearful past or future that you have no time for living in the present.

• It can be expressed. Soldiers have found that the admission of fear can help relieve it and make army life more tolerable. Real courage, they have found, lies in functioning despite fear. Similarly, Abraham I. Beacher, of the Maimonides Medical Center, recalled treating civil-rights marchers in Selma, Alabama: "The ready admission of fear was very common, and it must have been healing—else how could they have overcome the frequent jailings, beatings and hosings? The admission of fear is a constructive and preserving emotion."

By contrast, members of street gangs are bound together through a camaraderie of alleged fearlessness. They must constantly prove their manliness and bravery in fights with other gangs. By thus denying their fear, they are on their way to anarchy and self-destruction.

DISCHARGE THE FEARFUL PAST

▶ Remember a situation in which you felt intense fear. Recall it in as complete detail as you can.

Then tune in to the physical sensations of your fear. An array of figures of speech is descriptive of physical disruptions fear can bring: You may suffer cold feet, cold sweat, butterflies in your stomach, shaking in your boots. You can be scared stiff, rooted to the spot, petrified, cold with fear. Your hair can stand on end, your knees knock, your blood turn to ice.

When you've identified your proprioceptive sensations of fear, try to see what they want to make you do. Do you have tense, shaky legs? Do you feel like running? Do so. Give in to the impulses you've long suppressed.

Are your shoulders raised, as if to ward off blows? Then perhaps you feel like hiding. Or pushing away the fearful images. Go ahead. In giving release to these pent-up sensations, you may at last dispel them.

Now play through the fearful situation again. Perhaps you've recalled encountering a bully in your childhood. You may have felt the impulse to run away and hide, and you may have done so. This time try to act in anger and in self-defense instead of from fear.

Thus, fantasize some way of conquering the bully—rush at him, beat him, shoot him, throw a poison dart at him. Then tune in to the proprioceptive sensations you now feel. You're likely to have overcome your fright.

You may similarly reconstruct in fantasy almost any fearful situation and remedy it in a fantasy solution, no matter how improbable. For example, if you felt cold fear at the approach of a car crash, in fantasy push away the oncoming car.

ATTACKING PRESENT FEAR

▶ The next time you feel fear, confront and attack it. You may be surprised to find that the fear has turned to anger. Psychiatrist Alexander Lowen has pointed out: "Fear, like anger, is an emergency situation that activates the sympathetic-adrenal system and mobilizes the musculature of the body. In anger, however, the organism attacks the source of pain; in fear, it withdraws and flees from it. The correspondence between the two emotions is such that if the direction of movement is reversed, one changes into the other. If a frightened person turns to attack, he will become angry and unafraid. When an attacking person starts to retreat, he will feel fear."

▶ One device for draining off fear is to have someone press with his thumbs on either side of your nose, just below the bones under the eyes. Open your eyes wide, and breathe deeply. Open your throat by saying "Oh-h-h-h." When there is an effective release, the sounds will climb and come out in rapid successions of "Oh, oh, oh," in involuntary staccato.

Leo appeared at a workshop, with eyes as big as owls. He was very frightened. The leader used the following technique to drain off some of the fear that had gotten frozen in his body: The group had him lie down, breathe heavily, open his eyes even wider and then asked him to scream. At the same time the leader pressed on his cheekbones. The first time, the scream did not come out too clearly. But then he spontaneously started to have the nightmares he had experienced when he underwent chest surgery at ten years old. He was asked to undergo this procedure a couple of times. Each time, the fear came out more clearly and was expressed more vividly. So much of the fear had been drained out of his face that a little while later one of the group members remarked how much brighter and younger he looked.

► Another device for draining off fear is to open your eyes wide and in a little childlike voice say, "I'm afraid," over and over again. You can wring your hands, cower or hide. Make your whole body reflect what you are saying.

Tune in to the physical sensations you are having, and exaggerate them. If your legs are shaking, make them shake harder. Make your whole body shake.

In one encounter group a young woman told the group she had been terribly frightened when she was momentarily blinded. Her sight returned quickly, and she'd never fully let out her panic at the prospect of remaining blind.

The leader encouraged her to let out the fear. The young woman sat cross-legged on a mat at the center of the group. "I'm afraid," she said quietly.

"I'm afraid!" the leader said more loudly.

"*I'm afraid!*" she responded. She repeated the words over and over. Each time they sounded more real. Soon she was wailing the words, then moaning and gasping. After a while all sound subsided.

Her face broke into a broad smile. She looked completely released from the fear of the experience—released and relaxed.

► When a person expresses fear, it often helps if someone in the group holds and comforts him. Andy was a young lathe operator, who had come to a group with his girl friend. He was more than fearful; he was terrified. There was a wild look in his eyes, he talked gibberish and he was shivering. The group brought him back into contact by having him go around the room and look everybody in the eyes. He calmed down and resumed contact. Then group members held him, quietly reassuring him.

When fear is released, it often results in feelings of joy. Howard was always frightened when the leader asked each group member to express his here-and-now feelings. On one occasion he was encouraged to stay with the feeling of fear, saying, "I'm afraid." Next to Howard was a warm, sympathetic fellow named Dan. He helped allay Howard's feelings of fear. Suddenly Howard seemed to break through the fear. He felt happier. Then joyful. He couldn't contain his joy. He leaped from his chair, grabbed Dan and pulled him to the floor. They rolled together from one side of the room to the other, laughing all the time.

Resentment

Resentment is another brooding sentiment, arising from a sense of personal injury. It is from the French *ressentir*—"to feel again," over and over continuously. Fritz Perls called resentment "the bite that hangs on."

In resentment you neither let up nor clear up the situation through an open expression of anger. Unexpressed anger feeds resentment. (For a discussion of resentment relative to anger, see Chapter 6, "Games for Letting Yourself Go.")

Resentment is also the obverse of guilt. The two virtually always go together. Any time you feel guilty, you resent the person you feel guilty toward. When you feel resentful, you want the other person to feel guilty.

MOTHER'S DAY

"Suppose somebody feels hostile toward his mother—and it seems to me that everybody has a real hostility against their mother—then, in order to get down to that place, I'll have people close their eyes and picture their mother in their mind's eye, and I'll hand them a pillow and say, 'Okay, now start swinging this pillow,' and they'll swing the pillow over their head and start banging it on the floor."

This unsentimental view of mothers has been expressed by a clergyman, Richard Lee, director of the Church of the Encounter, in California. In Dick Lee's church-cum-growth center you bang and scream until you've completely discharged your resentment against your mother (or some other person). Some people have banged pillows against the floor for an hour and a half, never stopping. One girl screamed constantly for forty-five minutes.

"Is she dead? Did you really kill her?" Lee will ask.

If you say, "I think so," Lee assumes you still have resentment inside you.

"You *think* so, sure," he says. "So keep banging!"

He'll ask again, "Is she dead?" until he finally gets the answer, "Yes, Mother's dead."

"Okay," he says, "now it's time to forgive her. Do you want to forgive her?"

▶ Lee asks you to name all the things you hate a person for: "I hate her for hitting me all the time when I was a kid." "I hate her for pushing a big wedding on me." Then he has you look at each of these resentments—and forgive the person for it.

Thus may you have a catharsis. If you get your feelings out, you will free yourself from an underground conflict. Furthermore, you can never go back and blame your mother again. Because, symbolically at least, she's dead inside you. You may feel a new urgency to be responsible for yourself.

In one of Lee's groups was an artist who was blocked and couldn't paint any more. He "killed" his mother. Then Lee suggested this further form of expressing resentment:

▶ He had the artist write a letter to his mother on three different days. When the letter was written, Lee said, "Okay, now tear it up. Tomorrow go back and write the letter again. Tear it up at the end of the next day, and write it again at the end of the next. Tear that up. Write it a fourth day, and if you want to mail that letter, okay. That's up to you."

The artist found that after he had followed Lee's advice, he had a much more meaningful relationship with his mother. He was free from her; he was no longer holding her responsible. He was allowing her to be just the person she was, and she could relax. She no longer had to be just what he was picturing her to be. They developed the beginnings of a loving relationship that had never been there before.

"The second thing that happened was that Mama then gave him back his balls," Lee recalls. "He began to get back some of his manhood, and he began to become extremely productive and creative in his art, and within a period of twenty-four hours he worked, worked, worked, and turned out some stuff that was the best, according to him, that he had done in two years."

► Another way of symbolically destroying an object of resentment entails your drawing a picture of someone you don't like. Then, voodoo-fashion, you do with it as you will.

In one group some people pounded their victims. Some burned the pictures. Some tore them up. Some hid them. One girl didn't know how to dispose of an old boy friend, so she gave him to another young woman, who took him and tore him up.

CLEAN OUT YOUR RESERVOIR

Dr. George Bach of Beverly Hills, California, whose book, *Intimate Enemy,* has popularized his marriage-counseling techniques for "constructive aggression," is a principal innovator of games for discharging resentment.

Bach has devised "rituals," forms of stylized fighting, in which you can dispel your resentment, while keeping your expression of feeling within reasonable bounds. Physical violence is *verboten,* but almost anything verbal goes. You thus get rid of the resentment, but you don't destroy the relationship or wind up with a black eye.

► *Virginia Woolf* is a Bach game for getting rid of your resentments and stereotypes in a rush of angry feeling. The game takes its name from the savage marital fighting in the Edward Albee play and movie *Who's Afraid of Virginia Woolf?* You can play it with your real-life adversary or with a stand-in.

This is a general insult exchange. You are not seeking a constructive resolution yet. Your objective is to spill out at last all the resentments, irritations and annoyances that have piled up for years.

If you are playing with a real-life antagonist (your spouse, for example), don't try to listen to each other. Resentments need no rational basis, and it would be pointless for you to try to answer each other's accusations. Seek to clean out the reservoir, not add to the dirty water.

The technique Bach has found most effective is to have the couple stand in front of each other and have a yelling confrontation. Start off with "I'm angry!" "Fuck you!" etc. Keep yelling things no matter how incongruous they may sound to others ("You put out and you never clean the canary cage!" one husband hollered). Before long you're likely to lose your intellectual control and let out—and thereby release—specific resentments that have long irritated you.

Most people pretend "little things" don't bother them. Yet they do, and as you yell epithets and push deeper, you're likely to dredge up muck you'd forgotten you'd buried.

► *Museum Trip.* You may be reluctant to bring up long-standing resentments, because they seem "outdated." Actually resentment respects no calendar. Time does not necessarily heal old wounds; it may merely add new wounds to them. An episode of a lifetime ago can set you seething today.

One way of dealing with old resentments is to ask your partner, "May I take you on a trip through my museum?" Thereby you acknowledge the vintage of your grievance and also open the way to its becoming a relic of the past. If the other person says yes, relate your beef.

This is an especially good experiment for husbands and wives. Sit as close as comfortable, look each other in the eye and alternate museum trips. Tell the first time you were irritated with your partner, the first time you were disappointed and so on, to the present.

Bach's wife brings out of her museum the first words she remembers George saying on seeing their second child in the delivery room. He remembers saying, "What a beautiful baby!" She recalls his blurting out, "That's one lousy maid you left me with!"

PUT THE PIECES BACK TOGETHER

Merely letting out your resentment is not enough. What's needed next are constructive ways of rebuilding a relationship. The following exercises will help you do so:

▶ *A Constructive Argument.* George Bach has devised a series of fighting rules for married couples in conflict, but they can be easily adapted for any two people with resentments against each other.

1. Make an appointment to fight. Many arguments are unproductive because only one person is doing the fighting; the other refuses to engage in the fight. So find an appropriate time for an argument—a time when you're not likely to be distracted.

2. Take turns expressing your resentments. Let one person talk for five minutes without interruption. Then the other has five minutes (or six or ten or whatever you decide together).

3. When you have finished stating your gripes, then have your partner repeat these gripes as fairly as possible. For example, a wife might say, "Do I understand correctly that you feel I ought to be home more, that I neglect you by not . . ." and so on. Her husband may correct some of these impressions. When he feels that she has stated his gripes against her fairly, she can go on to state her gripes against him.

4. Clearly state your expectations of each other. After all, when you resent something about a person, you are in a sense demanding another kind of behavior—a kind of behavior that you won't resent.

5. Determine together if your expectations are realistic and/or negotiable. Then try to come to a mutually satisfactory agreement about the future. Be as specific as possible about your future expectations and resolves.

This game can sometimes be played in trios, with one person acting as coach. His job is to help the fighting duo play according to the rules. He can time their griping periods and give plus and minus scores to each. Plus points are given for being specific, giving fair feedback before answering, negotiating in good faith. Minus points are given for phoniness, irrelevance, analyzing, hitting below the belt. Your score gives you an indication of the kind of fighting you're doing and how you can make it more constructive.

▶ *Haircut.* One way you might discharge a lot of resentment against someone—without causing a major crisis—is to give him a "haircut," a word taken from Synanon. Haircut is a game that follows formal rules. The person with the resentment asks the other, "May I give you a haircut?" The other can answer yes or no.

If he says yes, he must let the "barber" say what he wants without interrupting him. At the end of the barber's harangue, the person with the haircut must say, "Thank you." Then the barber can exact a penalty appropriate to the crime. (For example, an overbearing businessman was required to scrub the floors.) Thereafter, reverse roles.

If you were the barber, the other now gives you a haircut.

▶ *Enlarge Areas of Contact.* Think of ways of making relationships better, of expanding your knowledge and appreciation of another person. One young man, faced with this challenge, reported that he had a poor relationship with his parents and that he'd never had a frank discussion with them. On his infrequent visits to them he was unpleasant and uncommunicative, mostly out of resentment for the strict upbringing they'd given him. "I've never mentioned my feelings to them," he said.

Since "it *can't* make matters worse," he decided to confront them with his resentful feelings. They responded with equal candor. Soon they began to respond to each other as people—instead of as a son with resentments and parents with expectations. They found they had more in common than they'd ever expected.

11

Games for Happier Families

Family ties can be like a mountaineer's lifeline, which allows you to move with great freedom from a stable, secure base.

Or they can be like a noose around your neck.

You need to express your self, to fulfill your potential, in your family life at least as much as in your other relationships (see Chapter 7, "Games for Being Yourself"). Though a member of a family, you remain a unique individual, with traits and preferences that must be honored. You were born so and remain so with respect to your parents, your spouse, your children.

"All serious writers on the subject of ideal or healthy love have stressed the affirmation of the other's individuality, the eagerness for the growth of the other, the essential respect for his individuality and unique personality," Abraham Maslow observed in *Motivation and Personality*.

Maslow found such strong mutual respect much in evidence in his studies of self-actualizing people. In the "growth family"—the family whose members are encouraged in their striving toward self-actualization—the following are characteristic:

• Each person is respected as an independent entity and as a separate and autonomous individual.

• Members do not seek to use or control the others. Nor do they disregard the others' wishes or humiliate one another.

• Jealousy is absent. Maslow noted the "ungrudging pride of such a man in his wife's achievements, even where they outshine his."

• Women are regarded as partners and equals, as full human beings, as pals.

• Children, no less than adults, are allowed a fundamental, irreducible dignity. A child is treated with real respect.

Growth families are loving in the most satisfying and mutually fulfilling sense. As writer Harry Overstreet observed in *The Mature Mind:* "The love of a person implies not the possession of that person, but the affirmation of that person. It means granting him, gladly, the full right to his unique manhood."

Families, Open and Closed

There are marriages that seem happy even though they don't provide for the partners to function as individuals. Couples can work out relationships in which both of them feel better than they did when they were single. By limiting the range of their experience, they manage to function together and avoid conflict. Neither person can grow very much, but both of them feel safe.

This picture changes when children come along and disrupt the fine balance of the parents' needs and wishes. A new kind of therapeutic approach is based on the observation that troubled people generally come from troubled families. The person the family regards as a problem is most often the victim of an otherwise disturbed family situation.

In conjoint family therapy, as this new approach is called, a family is seen as a system. The members of the family constitute a set of interacting units, who together form the larger unit of the family.

A family can be a closed system or an open system. An open family system—a growth family—is characterized by the ability to accommodate change, and its members are able to express themselves openly.

In a closed family system everyone has a role to play and has to stick to it. Things can work only one way. Change is dangerous. The parent or child who disrupts this rigid equilibrium is the one who comes to be regarded as "our problem."

A closed family can seem to function smoothly, as smoothly as a ticking time bomb. Such a family invests a lot of energy in maintaining a rigid status quo. But rigid things easily shatter. With the passage of time change must come, if only because children get older and have an urgent need to lead their own lives.

The growth family, consisting of independent members, understands moods, preferences, change. The closed, constricting family tries to function as if these realities didn't exist. Just as a plant will creep along the ground if something blocks it from growing toward the sun, the closed family's differences go into hiding when they can't be expressed openly.

Often a seemingly minor crisis triggers the time bomb. A daughter wants to have her ears pierced. A son, to buy his own car. A father, to change jobs. A mother, to return to work. In families frozen into changelessness, change can ill be tolerated. A member of one such family said, "Other people's little showers are our hurricanes."

Bizarre episodes may occur, for example, over a son's adopting the current fashion of long hair. The hair, after all, is only hair, whatever attitude may lie in the head beneath it. But many parents act as if the few extra inches of hair were the same as the son's raising bees in his bedroom. In such families the hair is often a threat, mainly because it challenges the status quo. Stuart Wilson, a psychologist in Newport Beach, California, has observed: "The people who get uptight to an incredible degree about long hair are the people who value changelessness, who find it difficult to cope with change in their lives or anybody else's."

Parents and children alike may shy away from confronting family conflicts. (In this chapter "children" refers to grown offspring, as well as to small ones. Said a ninety-year-old mother about her sixty-eight-year-old son: "Newton has a big mouth for a kid.") The parents are often defensive and cling to the image of their family as perfect and happy except for a few minor problems. Family therapists, whom parents may consult as a last resort, are used to being told, "It's not that we really *need* you, you understand."

Some parents may recognize that the family is in conflict but see no reason to do anything about it. They may feel that their problems typify life, and that by trying to remedy the family's difficulties, they are seeking a fantasy world. Their belief may be that happiness and love are too much to expect; the "real" world consists of distrust and hostility—"Everyone's out for himself." They, therefore, accept emptiness and loneliness as ultimate realities.

A common reaction among children seeking family therapy is guilt over disturbing the family equilibrium and over exposing their parents to hurt. At the same time, the child may feel victimized by his parents, hate them for mistreating him and fear they will hurt him now.

In conjoint family therapy the whole family—not just the "problem," or the person who has problems—meets with the therapist. By encountering one another in this way, the family members are often able to open up systems that have long ago atrophied. The person with problems benefits, because the whole family comes to new realizations that make their life together more flexible. Observes Dr. A. Lisa Friedman, a family therapist: "The realization that there are better and less painful ways of . . . need fulfillment comes as a shock to families who, as one of my patients aptly put it, 'groove on a family's groove.' "

The following games may help you become aware of grooves in which your family is stuck:

FAMILY ARGUMENT

▶ To set up an experiment in which you can see how your family interacts, psychologist Daniel I. Malamud has suggested that you gather your family together for a simulated family argument. Think of something you might quarrel about—what to watch on television, what to do this weekend.

Behave as you might in a genuine family argument—but with this difference: Sit in a circle, and speak in order. Each person may say only one sentence when his turn comes. Continue until you reach some kind of resolution. Then discuss your responses.

What do you perceive about yourself and the others as the argument progresses? How do you feel when you are talking? When each other member of your family talks? Do roles or patterns emerge? Does one person always dominate? Submit? Who makes whom feel threatened? Angry? Ashamed? Resentful?

One family found that their arguments often began after Lois, the mother, made a demand in the name of order and routine.

"Anyone not at the table when dinner's ready doesn't eat," she would say. Or: "No more talcum powder in this house. It gets all over the bathroom floor."

The immediate reaction of Earl, her college-student son, would be near-total contrariness: "That's ridiculous," he would say. "Why can't everybody eat when he wants to?" Or he'd be sarcastic: "Maybe we shouldn't take showers, either."

Teen-age Iris would come to Lois's defense, often with a put-down directed at her brother: "I'd be delighted not to have to eat with you," or: "You don't take showers anyway."

Hank, the father, would then insist upon peace and quiet. "You behave yourselves," he'd tell the children. "I don't work hard all day to come home to a madhouse."

During an experiment of simulating an argument, all four members of the family fell into these familiar roles. Suddenly Lois had a realization: "I don't really mean what I say. I'm asking for double to settle for half." She went on to express an awareness of how her demands provoked Earl to take a counterposition. "I'm treating him like a child. So why shouldn't he react like one?"

Earl saw that his attitude was as uncompromising in its way as his mother's was in hers. "I'm responding automatically," he said. "I don't think; I just say no."

Iris admitted that though she often agreed with her brother, she would make a point of siding with Lois against him. "Because I know which side my bread is buttered on."

"Let's change the subject," Hank interrupted. Then, as the rest of his family laughed, he shook his head. "That's me," he agreed. "Peace at any price."

WHAT'S YOUR SYSTEM?

An open family system permits honest self-expression, even in conflicts. "Differences are viewed as natural," family therapist Virginia Satir has noted, "and open negotiation occurs to resolve such differences by compromise, agreement to disagree, taking turns, etc." In an open system you can say what you feel and think and can move toward growth without fear of destroying yourself or your family.

By contrast, in a closed family system you need to be dead to be your self. Differences are considered threatening, so everyone in a closed family is very cautious about what he says, lest a divergent feeling or thought cause the family to fly apart. Honest self-expression is virtually impossible. When it does occur, the other members of the family view the deviant as "sick" or "rebellious" and often close ranks against him. The limitations this imposes on growth are obvious. Says Virginia Satir: "I have found that emotional or behavioral disturbance is a certain sign that the disturbed person is a member of a closed family system."

To keep from rocking the boat, members of a closed family adhere to unwritten rules. For example, a family may have a rule prohibiting the direct expression of anger toward Mother. This rule constrains the family in handling a conflict. To the extent that the rules fail to fit the growth needs of each member, the family goes awry, and neurotic symptoms are likely to develop.

As a result of such constraining rules, Joan Ellen Zweben and Richard Louis Miller of the University of Michigan have observed, members of closed families often adopt characteristic patterns of behavior. These may also be viewed as modes of relating, or roles. Three of the most common are:

1. *The Placater*. No matter what the person thinks or feels, he attempts to tailor himself to fit the other at all costs. He thus annihilates his self. He says in effect: "I am always wrong [bad, sick or stupid]," implying that the other is always right, good, sane or bright.

In action he may sound like this: "Anything you would like, dear." "Of course I'll do those errands for you. I have my whole lunch hour free." "Don't you think it's better just to buy him the bike if he wants it?"

2. *The Attacker*. He responds in an assaultive way, by blaming, disagreeing, attacking. He annihilates the other as a distinct being, saying in essence: "*You* are always wrong [bad, sick or stupid]."

The Attacker may sound like this: "Why do you always ask me to suggest a place? You never make any suggestions yourself." "Isn't it just like you to want to go to the beach when I have my period!" "How come you never have my supper ready on time, the way other wives do for their husbands?" "If you weren't so busy all the time, we could have sex more often."

3. *The Evader.* He disrupts all significant exchanges of feeling by changing the subject or by otherwise diverting attention. He annihilates both his self and the other, with the thought: "I have no hope of our ever getting together in a mutually satisfying way, so let's keep it cool."

In response to a request to plan for a weekend vacation, an Evader may say: "Where is the vacuum cleaner?" "Have you seen my wallet?" "What a nice necklace." Or the Evader may use a nonverbal dodge—drop her knitting, spill his change, develop a headache.

In contrast with these three, there is a fourth type of role, which we will call the *Grownup.* He is most often nurtured in an open family and believes he and the others can exist as separate beings and still be together. His unspoken statement is: "There is a place for me and a place for you. We can each be ourselves and yet be together."

In effect, the Grownup commits himself, while including the other. He may say, for example: "I would like to go to the museum today. What would you like to do?" A Grownup husband may tell his wife: "I get furious when dinner is an hour late," and the Grownup wife may reply. "I get furious when dinner is on time and you aren't. Let's either move the regular time, or you call me when you'll be late."

The Grownup thus operates in a context of trust and respect for himself and the others in his family. Conflicts are negotiated on the basis of what fits a given situation. Being human, the Grownup is not always reasonable. But he is almost always emotionally expressive.

Joan Zweben and Richard Miller, drawing on the work of Virginia Satir, have devised "systems games," in which you act out each of the foregoing roles. Have a series of conversations in which you try to accomplish some task: Decide where to go for the day, or plan a vacation for the family. In these conversations have each person in the family play a particular role. Give everyone a chance to play every role, and correct each other if you forget to follow the rules. Set a time limit of perhaps ten minutes for each conversation.

▶ In the first discussion use only the Placater, the Attacker and the Evader. In the second discussion, only the Placater and the Attacker. In the third discussion have everyone play the Placater.

In all of these experiments throw yourself into the part—the role you are playing is important: a matter of life or death for the family. Feel free to express your part with actions and gestures, as well as with words.

This game often results in general merriment when you get fully involved. The repartee can sound like a comedy routine ("Let's go to the museum." "I hate the museum." "I hate the museum, too—how stupid of me to suggest that." "What so bad about the museum?" "Gee, I'm hungry." "I'm not hungry at all." "Me neither." "What's the capital of South Dakota?"). But while you're having fun, be attuned to familiar vibrations. Which of the roles seems to fit?

After you've finished the third discussion (in which everyone's a Placater), stop and share your feelings about how you felt as you played each role. Talk about your gut feelings—your proprioceptive sensations. A person who feels he must play the Placater may experience body tenseness, tight stomach, deep anger. An Attacker may experience body heat, shaking and headache. The Evader may feel he's drifting out of touch with the world.

▶ Finally, attack the same problem again, and all play Grownup. How does this feel different from the games that preceded it? From your real-life experiences? The first three games can show you what you might be doing. Being a Grownup may show you what you could be doing instead.

FAMILY SCULPTURE

Virginia Satir uses a game called Family Sculpture to demonstrate different kinds of relationships that can exist in families. In this living sculpture you create a three-dimensional representation of arrangements among parents and children. You portray physically what can take place emotionally. Often the participants respond as they would if these symbolic roles were real.

▶ Look over the following list of phrases. Choose the one that seems to describe your marriage. Try assuming these positions with your spouse. If the physical position reflects the nature of your relationship, it will probably *feel* familiar. Try the other positions, too.

Explore your proprioceptive sensations in each experiment. Discuss how you feel—about yourself, about the other person. What can you do in each position? What can't you do? What do you feel like doing?

Then add children to your family sculpture. How do they fit in? How does each child feel?

▶ *We Face the World Together.* Stand back to back, with your elbows linked. Pretend you're joined at the spine. You can look outward and present your front to the world.

If there is something one of you wants to do—cross the room, say—can you work out a way to do it? What if one of you wants to sit alone and read a book? You may feel protected, but also frustrated and cramped.

What happens to such a couple when children come along? At a demonstration Mrs. Satir chose six volunteers—a man and woman to play husband and wife, and two men and two women to be the children. She had the "husband" and "wife" face the world together, back to back, with their arms linked.

Then the first child was born. A volunteer "son" crawled between the parents' legs. Depending on which side the baby leaned toward, one of the parents would start to totter—the father here was a lit-

We Face the World Together

tle off balance. Mrs. Satir noted: "This is the kind of person who comes to me and says, 'After we had our first kid, everything went wrong.'"

The second child arrived. In order to stabilize the family, the child propped up the father. The third child came up and put her arms around her mother. The father still looked wobbly, and the fourth child helped hold him up.

By virtue of the children's support, the parents were now in a stable position. Alas, the whole arrangement was incredibly uncomfortable.

**By Virtue of the Children's Support,
the Parents Were Now in a Stable Position; Alas,
the Whole Arrangement Was Incredibly Uncomfortable**

The third-born child, whose arms were around the mother, could be called Mama's child. This Mama could be giving messages to the child that she is needed, Mrs. Satir observed. "And the child could be getting her self-worth from the fact—'I'm needed.' And look what would happen if she should back off—an empty space for Mama!"

In this arrangement the third-born couldn't see anybody but her mother. The father could only see the ones who were holding him up. The mother just had glimpses of those.

Reported the mother: "I'm having a little trouble breathing, and I feel trapped."

"I feel torn apart," said the father. "Also my back hurts, and I feel off balance."

The first-born chimed in: "I'm afraid to move because I'll knock the whole thing over." Indeed, locked in precarious mutual support, nobody felt he could move.

The first-born crawled slowly in the direction he was facing, then stood up on his own two feet. The family didn't collapse. But he said: "I don't want to go back in there."

Gradually the family unsnarled, until everyone was standing on his own feet, no one leaning on anyone else. Everyone breathed more easily. The wife let go of her husband's hand. "He'll probably still be there when I get back," she said, and walked a few steps to visit her children.

They all hugged one another. Finally the husband felt out of it and walked over to join them.

▶ *Master-Slave.* Wife, stand on a chair. Husband, on all fours in front of her, her foot on his back. Switch roles afterward. Note that if the husband wants to crawl away or rise up, the wife topples. Also note how little you see of each other.

Master-Slave

While demonstrating the Master-Slave position, Mrs. Satir remarked: "I'm sure you noticed that no one put the slave down there—he went by himself." Often a slave-husband will tell Mrs. Satir: "She put me there." Mrs. Satir asks: "How?"

One father playing the slave in a sculpture decided he couldn't take the weight of his wife and children on him. He crawled away and dumped them.

▶ *Only You and You Alone.* Stand face to face, belly to belly, with your arms around each other. What's available to the outside world? What if you want to do something on your own? A typical response from the other partner is: "I feel pushed around."

▶ *This Is Getting to Be a Drag.* Husband, stand up straight. Wife, get behind him, put your arms around his neck and hold on. What happens if the husband wants to cross the room? Maybe he feels strong and manly at first—but after five minutes? Wife, how do you feel? What if *you* want to go somewhere without changing this relationship? Try changing places.

Only You and You Alone   **This Is Getting to Be a Drag**

▶ *We Support Each Other.* Stand face to face, an arm's distance apart. Put the palms of your hands together, and lean on them. If one of you moves, the other is likely to fall flat on his face.

▶ *On a Pedestal.* Husband, stand on a chair. Wife, stand on the floor in front of him. Explore how you both feel. Then switch roles. One wife found: "We couldn't make eye contact. Before long, I resented that he was so above it all."

▶ *Swing Free.* Stand face to face, near enough to touch. How does this feel? Move toward and away from each other. Touch each other; come apart. Go your separate ways and return. Your marriage can approach this ideal.

If One of You Moves, the Other Is Likely to Fall Flat

Compare your feelings with how you felt in the other positions. If this is not the model of your marriage, you'll probably feel both better and somewhat anxious. If you're used to being stuck to your partner, it may make you uncomfortable to see him able to leave you and return. If one of you has been on a pedestal, you may find it unsettling to be on the same level—indeed, to level with each other.

Restoring Communication

A striking honesty marks self-actualizing relationships, Dr. Abraham H. Maslow has found.

In an open, self-fulfilling family you feel little need to be guarded, to conceal, to impress, to watch your words, to suppress your feelings. Rather, you can let your hair down. You can allow your faults, weaknesses and physical and psychological shortcomings be freely seen. You can say what you feel and be who you are.

People in a self-actualizing relationship, Maslow reported in *Motivation and Personality*, "can be themselves without feeling that there are demands or expectations upon them; they can feel psychologically (as well as physically) naked and still feel loved and wanted and secure."

By contrast, in closed, troubled families there are often near-total breakdowns in communication. "In watching these interactions," Dr. Lisa Friedman has said of her family-therapy sessions, "it is painful to see that the parents and children don't really know or understand each other. The needs, feelings of pain and sadness felt by both parents and children, have, for the most part, remained secret."

One trait of noncommunicating family members is that they *assume* their feelings are known and understood by the others. Then, commonly, they resent that their needs and wishes are being "ignored." Ian, a father of three teen-agers, was bitter because his children were "inconsiderate"—they planned their weekends around their friends, rather than around family activities.

"Why do I kill myself working for them if I never see them?" he complained.

But he had never told them that he wanted to spend a day with them. "They're supposed to know."

Ian's silence stemmed in large part from a wish to see himself and be seen as a "strong person" and "good provider." With the usual extremeness found in role playing, to admit that he wanted to be with his children—indeed, to admit to any needs or desires— was to be "weak." To take anything from his children (which was how he saw having their company on a Sunday) was to be a "demanding parent," the opposite in his mind of the kindly, benevolent paterfamilias.

When he finally said to his youngsters, "Let's all do something together this Sunday," they were surprised and embarrassed. They had long since gotten the idea that he was indifferent to them and would rather sit home and read the paper than go out with them. Their first outing together was more irritating than enjoyable—Ian had tried to plan every detail, then was annoyed when things went awry. Subsequent days out together have been more relaxed.

Among the things a child in a closed family is often "supposed to know," as if by ESP, is that he's loved. "It seems strange that some parents . . . believe that the children would just know they were loved and not need the love expressed and shown to them,"

Lisa Friedman remarked. The tragic results of keeping love a secret are illustrated in this exchange in a family seen by Dr. Friedman.

NEAL [*a twenty-one-year-old college student*]: I always felt you never wanted me. All of my life. That's the only feeling I ever felt. That you never wanted me.

MOTHER: I don't know where you got that idea.

NEAL: You put all sorts of ideas in my head, ever since I was little. Do you know that I remember you said to me that if I didn't behave and do what you wanted me to, you'd put me in a box and send me to Arizona? That's the kind of thing I remember.

[*He turns to his father.*]

I never had your love, Daddy. I let a man pick me up and play with me. That's how much I needed you, and you were never there. That's how much I regard myself as a person. Does that make you feel good?

FATHER: No. It makes me feel very bad.

NEAL: I'm glad, because you deserve to feel bad.

Such parents sometimes offer reasons for not demonstrating love for a child. "I don't want to spoil her," one mother explained. Said a father: "If I tell him I love him, he'll only use it against me."

Both these parents, and many like them, are loath to expose warm feelings like love, for fear they will be injured. They sense a threat and feel extremely vulnerable. Thus, they close up and are cold and unresponsive, even to their children.

Typically such parents are dictatorial. Feeling under attack, they perceive their youngsters as exposed flanks, through whom they may be embarrassed, inconvenienced, revealed or otherwise assaulted by the outside world. To reduce the threat posed on them through their children, they seek to control the children's behavior. A show of individuality, inevitable as a youngster grows, causes a family crisis. A common refrain among such parents is: "He was a wonderful baby, but now he's too independent." As a consequence, the child often feels guilty over his normal drives toward independence and falls far short of fulfilling his needs for self-expression.

HUMANIZING THE FAMILY

In troubled families parents and children don't often think of each other as human.

► They represent needs and threats to one another. In the welter of unfulfilled longings and of hurts and vulnerabilities they lose the perception of the others as persons. The parents and son in one family were asked to describe one another in one word or phrase.

Of his father the boy said, "Six dollars a week," the amount of his allowance. Of his mother: "A scouring pad."

The mother called her son "a dirty mouth"; her husband, "a busy bee."

The father said the son was "a pain in my heart"; his wife, "my salvation."

In not one of these descriptions is the other seen as a person. A role, an effect, a habit—but not a human being in the other's own right.

Family therapists often find almost magical effects resulting from parents and children opening up to one another as human beings. Here are some suggestions on how to bring your family closer together:

► *Air Your Grievances.* Clearing the air is necessary to resolve past hurts and resentments. The rage expressed by Neal at his parents in the foregoing discussion was actually a constructive first step.

Children and parents often surprise each other with their revelations. A parent may learn for the first time that his children don't believe he loves them. A child may find that his parents themselves feel injured and neglected—that they have looked to the child for feelings of importance or signs of love, which the child never gave.

The airing of grievances can put episodes in perspective. A teenage girl had an illegal abortion, arranged with the help of her parents. It was a traumatic event for the family but outwardly seemed to pass with the lightness of a snow flurry.

At last the girl accused her parents: "You don't care anything about me. You treated my abortion as if I were some tramp."

"You acted as if the abortion were a joke," her father replied. "Your mother and I didn't want you to laugh at our worry and concern."

As they talked over the abortion, they became aware of what it had meant to them all emotionally.

▶ *Discuss Family Background.* Children often resent the lives they were made to lead to fill their parents' needs. "What they want to know is why," Lisa Friedman has pointed out. "Why they were rejected, why their parents couldn't show love and outward affection, why they had to be constantly good to get attention, or why they felt forced to confront their parents with the worst behavior just to get any notice from them."

The reasons why are often found in the family's history. Dr. Friedman has found that family background information, no matter how terrible the parents think it is, proves to be welcomed by children. "Reality is less frightening than groping in the dark. Children often say, 'Why didn't you tell us?' The answers are always the same: 'We wanted to spare you.' 'You wouldn't understand. . . .'"

A child may say, "If you loved me, then why didn't you show it?"

The parent sometimes breaks down and cries, "I don't know how. Maybe because I never felt loved."

Notes Dr. Friedman: "And the children begin to understand that their parents, seemingly adults, are really little children themselves, and as children they could feel rejection by their parents and feel unwanted and unloved."

This awareness often marks an end to blame. The child can see that his parent was a victim. It was not the parent's fault.

Such a confrontation may end with the family sobbing in each other's arms, overwhelmed by the tide of feeling for one another. Neal's family, which had seemed so hopeless, ended such an encounter on the floor, with their arms around each other, sobbing and kissing. Said Neal: "Maybe now we know where it's at."

SENSITIVITY

"*Good morning,*" he says, and now it occurs to me that the word "morning," as he uses it, refers specifically to the hours between eight A.M. and twelve noon. I'd never thought of it that way before. He wants the hours between eight and twelve to be *good*, which is to say, enjoyable, pleasurable, beneficial! We are all of us wishing each other four hours of pleasure and accomplishment. Why, that's terrific! Hey, that's very nice! Good morning! And the same applies to "Good afternoon!" And "Good evening!" and "Good night!" My God! The English language is a *form of communication!* Conversation isn't just crossfire where you shoot and get shot at! Where you've got to duck for your life and aim to kill! Words aren't only bombs and bullets—no, they're little gifts, containing *meanings!*

—Philip Roth, *Portnoy's Complaint*

And there are other forms of communications as well. So much of family life is a matter of routine—eating at a certain time, watching favorite TV programs, getting ready to go to school or work—that people sometimes lose their sensitivity to each other. Words, touching, become automatic, empty of feeling.

▶ *Hand Talk.* Pair off with a family member. Close your eyes, and hold hands. Focus your attention on your partner's hands. First increase the pressure, then decrease it. Now open your eyes. Look at each other, and touch at the same time—without talking. Again, vary the pressure, and be aware of how this contact feels. The unarmored contact—through touching—will almost certainly make you feel closer.

▶ *All Channels Open.* Carry on a conversation with your family. Talk to one another normally, but without moving your heads at all. Now face someone and communicate only with your eyes.

Now close your eyes, and communicate with your family only by touching.

Finally, have a conversation in which you use all forms of communication—touch, speak and look at one another. Talk about what makes for satisfactory communication, about how you felt when different modes of expressing yourself weren't allowed.

CONDENSED CONVERSATIONS

▶ Sit facing your partner, and have a conversation using a single word at a time—a word that expresses how you are feeling toward your partner at the moment. It's likely to be frustrating. But once you get the hang of it, it can be very effective in cutting through the word muddle of most conversations.

One couple had been irritated and short with each other. A lot of loud words flew back and forth. They were encouraged to play this game. For a while they just looked at each other in silence.

Then she said, "Resentment."

Immediately he answered, "Guilt."

"Good," she said with satisfaction.

"Good?" he asked with a puzzled, hurt tone.

"No," she recanted. Then she smiled and said, "Warmer."

He said, "Better."

"Good," both said simultaneously.

► For a variation of this game say a sentence that expresses your here-and-now feelings toward your partner. Keep on repeating your sentence, listening to your partner's words, and see if your two sentences can meld.

In one case the man was saying, "I want to relate to you"; the woman, "I want to move with you and be quiet." The blends came out: "I want to movingly relate and be quiet with you," and "I want to quietly relate to you and move with you."

OPENING NEW LINES

► Virginia Satir has had couples try this series of experiments to open lines of communication.

1. First stand back to back, and talk to each other. "This is similar in form to some communications at home, with the wife in the kitchen, cooking, while her husband tries to discuss finances with her."

2. Then stand face to face, and look at each other without talking. What do you think your partner is thinking and feeling? In discussion, note how wrong your assumptions may have been.

3. Now eyeball each other, and communicate only with gestures and touches. See how much more gets through?

4. Close your eyes, and communicate without talking.

5. Eyeball each other, and talk without touching.

6. Finally, use all forms of communication—talk, touch and look at each other. Most people find they can't argue with each other without diverting their eyes and pulling back physically. Nor are you likely to mix your signals. The skin and eye contact puts you in touch.

GARBLED SIGNALS

Verbal communication takes place on at least two levels: the level of content (the words you actually say or hear), and the level of real meaning (what you're actually feeling when you talk; what you perceive the other person to be feeling when you listen to what he says). In open communication these two are the same. When you say, "Let's go to the movies," you mean you'd like to go to the movies with the person you're talking to, and he perceives that this is what you want to do.

When communication breaks down, you can say, "Let's go to the movies" and mean "God, if I have to sit here in this room with you for one more minute, I'll go crazy." And the person you're talking to may sense this incongruity. Your tone of voice, the expression on your face, your body tension—all will be out of keeping with your words.

Often the person sending out a static signal won't even realize what he's doing, because he's gotten into such a strong habit of communicating in this way.

▶ *What Do You Mean?* Try to communicate more directly—as both message giver and message receiver. As message giver, consciously make an effort to say what you mean. As receiver, tell your partner when you think you're getting a garbled signal. Family therapists sometimes have couples carry on a conversation, asking each other after every statement, "What do you mean?"

A husband said, "I'm hungry."

"What do you mean?" asked his wife.

"I'm bored."

"What do you mean?"

"I want to do something else."

"What do you mean?"

"I'd like to take a walk."

"What do you mean?"

"I want to be by myself sometimes."

He'd frequently felt the need to be alone, but he'd feared offending his wife. When he finally expressed this need, she understood, and the problem dissolved.

INTIMACY

Here are some experiments for opening communication between husbands and wives, and for bringing couples closer.

► *Intimate Talk.* Initiate a conversation about something you've never talked about before, or at least not in a great while. Then have your partner also broach an unopened subject. Have your discussions progress in depth of intimacy. At each stage of your talk symbolize your feelings of increasing intimacy by touching your partner's body, progressing in intimacy. If your partner is reluctant to talk about something you've suggested, don't press it. Instead, you might both want to discuss your feelings of unwillingness.

This game was played by a middle-aged couple whose love life had dwindled to nothing over the past year. They had trouble getting their intimate talk started and skirted important issues by staying with fairly safe topics. At last the wife confessed she was jealous of the freewheeling sex life of their college-student daughter. Her husband, it turned out, felt the same way. Bolstered by the success of this first venture into intimacy, they went on to discuss their own disappointing sex life.

Said the husband: "I don't suggest making love any more because I feel you're not interested."

"But that's just the way I feel," said his wife. "I feel aging and unattractive, and as if you don't want to any more. But," she added, "I am still interested."

Their intimate talk ended with their going to bed together for the first time in months.

► *Shampoo Your Partner.* Have him keep his eyes closed. Pour water over him. Close your own eyes from time to time, and simply feel the head, the suds, the washing motion of your hands. Rinse and dry his hair with a towel. Then comb it and smell it. Change places.

Then take a shower or bath together. Without rushing, take turns washing each other's body, sudsing every inch. Rinse and dry each other. If you'd like, oil and massage each other. These activities may also lead to sexual arousal.

It's a Wise Child

On "Sesame Street," an educational children's program, some puppets presented their own version of the popular TV show "To Tell the Truth." The announcer introduced a lovable little monster covered with fur. Facing him were the contestants: a lady puppet, a man puppet and a little-boy puppet.

"And now," the announcer said to the furry monster, his voice rising to a crescendo, "you are to find out *who is the mother of this family!*"

The little monster guessed the man puppet.

"That wasn't very good," said the announcer. "You should have been able to tell who the mother was from her voice and from the way she looked."

Then a deep voice sounded off-stage. "Are you ready to go home?" it said. The voice belonged to the monster's mother—a large masculine figure covered with curly fur, who growled as she dragged Junior away for dinner.

The petite lady puppet, of course, didn't look anything like a mother to the baby monster. The things the announcer thought were important meant nothing to him.

In your family the things you think are important about you may go unperceived. The things you've never noticed or thought about might be what characterize you to someone else in your family. Play these games with your spouse and children. They may provide surprises.

FAMILY PORTRAITS

Here are special ways of getting feedback from your family.

▶ *Stranger on a Train*. Imagine that a stranger is coming to visit you. He has never met your family, and someone is to meet him at the train. How would each member of your family describe the others? It isn't fair to say, "She'll have on her red coat." But impressions like "His suit will look as if he slept in it" are acceptable.

▶ *Biography*. Imagine that someone is writing a biography of each member of your family. What would each member say about the others in response to interview questions like: What are his likes and dislikes? What does he care about most? What kinds of things turn him off? What kind of person is he?

▶ *Self-Portrait.* After everyone has had a chance to describe everyone else, describe *yourself.* How would you tell someone to find you at the station? What would you tell your biographer?

Then discuss the differences that turn up between your self-impressions and your family's impressions of you. What have you found out about yourself?

▶ *Adjectives.* If you could choose just one adjective to describe each person, what would it be? Fill in the blank: "He [she] is the——one." Cheerful? Scowling? Shy? Domineering?

Write your adjectives down first, then share them. What adjective would you use to describe yourself?

▶ *Sculpting.* Go up to each member of the family in turn, and arrange his body in a position that seems to you to characterize something about him. Give the sculpture a title. One teen-age girl was frustrated in her efforts to sculpt her father in a characteristic pose. She couldn't get his foot in his mouth.

IDEAL FAMILY

▶ *Classified Ads.* What is your ideal family like? Answering this question may help you see what you feel is missing in your own family.

Dr. Daniel I. Malamud has suggested that you compose imaginary classified ads, headed "FATHER WANTED," "MOTHER WANTED" and so on, in which you describe, in twenty or thirty words, what you would like in a family member.

Then compose ads headed "SON [MOTHER, FATHER] AVAILABLE," in which you list *your* attributes. Tell the kind of relative you are and how you may improve.

A sample, written by a teen-age boy:

FATHER WANTED
To take youngsters seriously. Be attentive, warm.
Let son be himself. Listen without shouting.

SON AVAILABLE

Enthusiastic, warm and considerate when not hassled. Has lot
to learn, but willing. Assertive—sometimes too much so, but
rarely phony.

▶ *Pick a New Family.* This can be played best when two or more
families have gotten together. Your real family separates, and the
members unite with others to form new families.

The new family you choose doesn't have to correspond numeri-
cally to your real family—a child with five brothers and sisters can
choose to be an only child; a parent with two sons can choose two
daughters.

Once your new family is assembled, give yourself a new first
name, and make up a new last name for the family. Tell why you
chose one another to be your new family. Go around and tell each
member of your new family what you like and dislike about him.
Be sure to discuss how you felt about telling your new family members your likes and dislikes, and how it felt to be on the receiving
end.

From here on this is an open-ended game. The new family can
decide what they'd like to do as a family. A favorite version of this
activity is to play the family "systems games" with your new family
—with the members of the participants' real families as an audience. Discuss your feelings afterward with both your new family
and your old family.

How does your real family compare with your assumed one?
How realistic are your expectations concerning family members?

One father found that he soon provoked his new "son" and
"daughter" to rebellion with his suggestions. "They sounded like
my real boy and girl," he commented. "Moral: No kid likes the old
man butting in."

TURNABOUT

▶ *Role Switching.* By trading roles in your family, you can learn a
lot about how it feels to be in a different position in the family. Of
such experiments Virginia Satir has said, "In all of my experience
in using these games with many groups across the country, I have
never encountered a person who did not, once involved in a game
system, develop vivid 'gut reactions' to the roles he played."

Role switching is especially effective when you're having an argument. A five-year-old girl in a crabby mood was making it difficult for her mother to get her into her coat so they could go to the store. "All right," said the mother, "you be Mother, and I'll be Kate."

"Come put on your coat, Kate," said Kate.

"No!" screamed the mother. "No no no no no no!"

"We have to go to the store," Kate said. "Hurry up!"

"I don't want to go to the store! I want to stay here and watch television!"

Kate sat down, took her mother's hand, and said soothingly, "Now, dear, I know you don't want to go to the store. But if we don't go now, we won't have any food for dinner. I can't go off and leave you alone, because you're too little, so please put on your coat." The mother was suddenly aware that *she* was really re-experiencing what it's like to be dragged away from something you want to do.

Some parents find role switching useful as a way of teaching children about other points of view. Four-year-old Willie was jealous when his baby sister, Jenny, arrived. "Let's give Jenny away to Aunt Betty and Uncle Mike," he suggested.

"You be Jenny, and I'll be Willie," his father said. "Let's give Jenny away."

"You can't do that," protested Willie. "I live here!"

▶ *Spoon Feeding.* To learn what it feels like to be a dependent child, have your child or spouse feed you. Note how many ways there are of expressing emotion in a give-take relationship. Food (and analogously money, gifts, etc.) can be shoved in anger, or shoveled in because of guilt, and resisted out of resentment. Experience, too, the frustration that inevitably comes with dependence.

The Creative Family

▶ Think of as many descriptions as you can for this drawing:

In testing schoolchildren for creativity, psychologists Michael A. Wallach and Nathan Kogan asked this question about a number of such abstract drawings. A child's response was considered creative if he was able to think of many answers, and if his answers were original. For example, a common response to the above drawing was "a flower." A novel, creative response was "a lollipop bursting into pieces."

Wallach and Kogan found that you can encourage a child to be creative by giving him the freedom to express himself without fear of embarrassment. "Creative awareness," they said, "tends to occur when the individual entertains a range of possibilities without worry concerning how his self-image will fare in the eyes of others."

Creativeness is a universal characteristic of self-actualizing people, Abraham Maslow has observed. Maslow has postulated that creativeness is a "potentiality given to all human beings at birth," a fundamental characteristic common to human nature. The self-actualized person's creativeness seems to be akin to the naïve creativeness of unspoiled children. Most people lose this ability as they grow into the culture.

"But," noted Maslow in *Motivation and Personality,* "some few individuals seem either to retain this fresh and naïve, direct way of looking at life, or if they have lost it . . . they later in life recover it."

Creativeness is an attribute of the self-fulfilling family. Here are games for giving it new emphasis in your family life.

ADULT PLAY

Michael Wallach and Nathan Kogan found that successful creative thinking takes place in a mood of "playful contemplation." Playfulness comes naturally to children, and it's an attitude adults often lose altogether.

► One way to help yourself to the wondering child inside you is simply to be that child again: Play the way a child does, with involvement in what you're doing and lack of concern for what other people think.

What happens to you when you go into a toy store? Watch yourself or other adults next time. You'll find that most people pick things up and fiddle with them. If no one is watching, they'll pick out tunes on the toy piano, wind up mechanical toys and watch what they do, pile blocks the way they want to—yet few people will allow themselves to sit down at home and play the way a child does.

A happy, creative person is in touch with the child within him. Because adulthood brings so many new responsibilities with it, many people feel they must cut themselves off entirely from the pleasures of childhood. In giving up their dependence on their parents, they give up everything that made them happy as children. They throw the baby out with the bath water.

Workshop leader Marion Saltman has noted: "The concept that play is sinful still exists, even though it is not overtly expressed as it was only a generation ago. But the idea that all activity must be productive, be constructive, and be useful by the standards set by parents, teachers, and society is still very much with us."

Mrs. Saltman works with people to develop their potential through adult play, to help people re-experience themselves. She provides materials of the sort found in kindergarten. People are often self-conscious at first, like this woman quoted by Mrs. Saltman: "I felt enthusiasm when we sat down to play, but when I picked up the first block at random to do something, there was the feeling of 'What a ridiculous situation, and how did I get into this?' What will I do with the block? The inability to begin. It is stupid to pile blocks on one another if you don't know anything about architecture. *All the time* fingering the block. Then I placed one block on another; the structure grew, and I became totally involved with trying to decide on the right block and the best way to place it. It was exhilaration."

Play with things you enjoyed as a child: clay, building blocks, finger paints, dolls, toy soldiers. Play dress-up. Build snowmen or sand castles. According to Mrs. Saltman: "This is a unique, meditative . . . device for re-entering levels of earlier consciousness through the use of simple, tactile materials."

▶ Here is a variation in the same spirit. Join children in their games, the games you used to play. Throw yourself into them as you did as a child. A twenty-six-year-old woman sat down to play jacks with some little girls. "Suddenly memories came flooding back," she recalled. "I was completely caught up in the sounds and smells of my childhood, with the little girl I was then. It was a whole good way of feeling I'd completely forgotten about."

Dr. Herbert A. Otto told of two members of his Los Angeles Human Potentialities Training Group who engaged in spontaneous play with children on their street. They play jump rope, hopscotch, ring-a-lievio. Housewives came out of their homes to watch and laugh, then joined in with the comment, "I used to be an expert."

Soon the whole block was involved in the fun, creating a glow that persisted after all had returned to their homes.

FANTASY TRIP

In a book called *Put Your Mother on the Ceiling*, Richard de Mille urges parents to help their children develop their imaginative powers—and presents a series of games designed to do that. "There seems to be a permanent war going on between reality and imagination," he writes. "The battleground is childhood. On the side of imagination we have the child, eyes great with wonder, mouth issuing fantasies, misconceptions, and unreliable reports. Parents, teachers, the peer group, and the police are on the side of reality. They keep insisting on truth, accuracy, conformity, and obedience. . . . This is not a war to take sides in . . . reality and imagination can live in harmony."

▶ One of the ways to help a child keep his imagination alive and growing is to encourage him to take visualization fantasy trips. A child would enjoy playing some of the fantasy games in Chapter 7 ("Games for Being Yourself"). De Mille's book is full of instructions you can read to your child while he visualizes what is happening.

▶ For example, ask the child to picture his parents. Then have him picture two sets of parents, just alike. Have them grow smaller. Have them turn green. Put them up on the roof. Have a dragon come up and breathe fire at them.

Take all these steps gradually, and let the child tell you when he's ready to go on to the next one. If a child has trouble visualizing something, take it in steps. If he can't imagine someone floating up to the ceiling, have him imagine that birds are holding the person up, or balloons—and then have the birds or balloons go away, one at a time. If he can't imagine someone changing colors, have him imagine a little blue spot, then a bigger blue spot, then another one—until the person turns blue.

"One purpose of imagination games," de Mille wrote, "is to open up closed territory in the mind—to run the train of thought down some of the important common tracks and get rid of unnecessary defensive switches. The player learns to think thoughts and visualize events that at first may seem forbidding. He learns that the domain of his imagination is larger and safer than he thought it was."

BE AN ANIMAL

▶ Be an animal, suggests Laura A. Huxley in *You Are Not the Target*. It may help free you of some inhibitions.

Find a place where you will be undisturbed. Take some simple food (the kind of food the animal eats). Take off your clothes. Creep, crawl, gallop, fly. Growl, sing, hiss.

Express how you feel today. Be a bad animal. Be a gentle animal. Be frightening. Be sluggish.

RITUALS

Rituals are forms in which people can experience and express deep feelings. A ritual is a focusing lens for emotions. Weddings and funerals allow strong feelings, arising from marriage or death, to be shared and channeled. The ritual intensifies the feelings and gives them a beginning, a middle and an end.

In a family, creating and sharing a new ritual experience can be an exciting, strengthening experience.

Ann Halprin has pioneered a form of dance-cum-therapy in which people together evolve ritual experiences. She calls them myths. At her Dancers' Workshop Company in San Francisco, Miss Halprin conducts free-form sessions in which performers and audience create a dance based on themes central to human experience.

"I try to deal with ideas that are very common, basic, and ordinary," says Miss Halprin, "—sensuality, sexuality, conflict, aggression, celebration, bewilderment, the sharing of tragedy." The whole idea is to "allow people to get in touch with their own resources" by means of "an experiment in mutual creation."

You and your family can adapt some of Ann Halprin's dance techniques to release your buried creativity.

► *Make a Myth.* Decide on a universal theme for each session. Ann Halprin suggests Atonement, Maze, Dreams, Masks. Also try Birth, Death, Confusion, Hard Work, Frustration, or try inventing your own.

Participants first find their own pattern of movement to express the theme, then interact with each other in a spontaneous group ritual.

► *Create a New Environment.* This is another exercise in creativity developed by Miss Halprin. Collect a big assortment of junk: boxes, sheets of plastic, musical instruments, pieces of clothing, lights, ladders, ropes—anything you think you can use to create a new environment.

Take these things into a room. Divide the family in half, and send one group out.

Those remaining have fifteen minutes to alter the environment by redecorating and by reshaping space. Make it an environment you can interact with. You can pile things up to be climbed on and crawled under. Flash lights. Turn on radios and TV's. Sing and dance.

When the others return, have them move through the new environment creatively, reacting to it and changing it. The purpose is for all of you to see things in new ways. After fifteen minutes the first group goes out. The second group now destroys the old environment and, using the same materials, creates a new one.

Often the experience takes on a primitive, archetypal quality. One of Ann Halprin's groups spontaneously embarked on a ceremony that closely resembled a primordial ritual of birth, ordeal, sacrifice and finally triumph of life and vitality. The door to the room was blocked, so that each entrant had to be pulled through an opening. He was passed overhead from hand to hand by a line of men and then placed against an upright board covered with shiny plastic. Here he was held, and bright light was focused on him.

He then crept into a huge cardboard box, and people pounded on the outside of it. He escaped from the din to a convoluted tunnel made of paper cloth and boxes. This led to a chamber in the center of the room, underneath a tower, formed by scaffolding. At last, the "initiate" (as the group came to regard each person going through the maze) went out an opening and burst free of the enclosure.

When it was Ann Halprin's turn to go through the maze, the crowd shouted, "Sacrifice! Sacrifice!" Recalls Miss Halprin: "They held me against the wall, put me in the cave, and handed me up to the top of the tower. The whole room then broke into joyous dancing. The emotional result was tremendous exuberance and awe, which was frightening to some, for we had really participated in 'mysteries'!"

12

Invent Your Own Games

Part of the adventure of games lies in creating new ones to fit your needs.

Devising new experiments, or improving old ones, can be exciting—and can itself be an activity leading to growth. "Too often," the *Esalen Newsletter* has written, "particular philosophies and religions—and science, too—limit the development of man's potential by foreclosing upon insight and practice. But we in this field are committed to keeping an open forum." The many activities in this book follow, for the most part, only a few general principles.

1. *Tune in* to the need for inventing new games. While playing growth games, be aware that one activity or discussion can lead to a new game. For example, in a discussion following a game that involved participants' reaching out to each other, one woman mentioned that she had felt afraid of being rejected. Other people realized that this had been part of their experience, too, so the group decided that instead of just talking about it, they would explore this experience.

2. *Brainstorm.* Once you've hit on something you want to play a game about, come up with free associations of the idea: Think and talk about things like "What does this remind me of?" "What can I (we) do to exaggerate this feeling?" A workshop group was playing a game in which participants took turns trying to break into a circle of other people. Some of the players devised a new variation of the game—which they called Turnstile—in which two players

linked arms and kept turning around while a third player tried to break in.

In the group that was discussing fear of rejection one player remembered how anxious he'd always been as a child when teams were being chosen for a game, so the group devised a game called Choosing Up Sides. Two captains were arbitrarily appointed to pick teams—not for any particular purpose, but just as a way of exploring the feelings of the people who were waiting to be picked —and the captains' feelings in picking them.

3. *Be simple.* Give clear instructions. If the instructions take more than a minute or two, the game is probably too complex. If there are progressive stages to an experiment, introduce each stage only when the players seem ready for it, not all at once at the outset.

Beware of any game so complicated that playing it detracts from the effect you want to get. One practitioner devised a game called Magic Shop, a kind of auction in which participants offered whatever they chose and haggled with a "shopkeeper" for "love," for "freedom from guilt," and so on. The idea was sound—it helped put desires in order of priority. But in practice the activity tended to get confusing, and too much mental activity was required to determine whether "myself" could be exchanged for "freedom from guilt," for "happiness," for "love."

4. *Bring forth clear-cut responses.* Games can help the player focus on individual elements of his personality. A good game evokes a particular type of response, whereas games with ill-defined goals are rarely effective.

During the introduction of a game players nearly always have in mind the question: "What's supposed to happen?" If you can't answer this question in a few words—perhaps by citing (but not pushing) possible responses—your game may well be too muddy in its objectives.

5. *Capture an unfamiliar perspective.* A good game gives you the sort of surprise you get from suddenly confronting yourself in a triple mirror. The game needs to be involving, if not enjoyable, and novel enough to circumvent your stereotyped responses. In Game Land the following general principles apply:

• Everything is in the here and now. This approach brings feelings to the present, where they can be dealt with (as discussed in

Chapters 3 and 10). If you refer to a past event, tell about it in the present tense. If you speak of someone, address him directly as if he were here right now.

• What's hinted at is made explicit. "How do you mean?" and "For example?" are questions that bear repeating. The better to get further and further away from the verbal abstractions, and closer and closer to the emotional reality. Emotion gets expressed. Proprioceptive sensations (Chapter 5) get spelled out.

• Fantasies are valid. Daydreams, intuition, imagination—all are manifestations of your personality and therefore are at least as real as, say, reason and thought in the intellectually oriented "real" world.

• Figures of speech are expressed literally. Instead of making a put-down remark, walk over and physically put the person down. If you feel a need to lean on someone, actually lean on someone and experience what that feels like.

• Exaggerations are the norm. This helps bring a sensation to awareness. If you're timid, feel supertimid. If your jaw is tight, make it supertight.

• Reach a happy medium. By emphasizing one extreme, then the other, you can oscillate to a point of equilibrium. To relax a muscle, squeeze it—then stretch it. After being supertimid, be superbold.

Fare Well

You've got to stand up for your self.

Strong pressures oppose your growth, for people cling to the familiar. Family and friends rarely want you to change. They know you as you are. They have a vested interest in keeping you that way.

Your past may hold you captive. You may react to everyday situations out of habit. In a clinch your automatic response is likely to be a role that is familiar but phony.

▶ In seeking to fulfill your potential, every situation, every day, can be a challenge. A hundred times as you go through each day, ask yourself, are you acting as you'd really like to? Or are you acting as you're used to?

In Yoga you go as far into a position as you comfortably can without straining—and then you push just a little. By doing this regularly, each time you can go a little farther. Similarly, each time you face up to a situation—and act in a way that's *you*—it becomes easier the next time.

For longer and longer periods each day make a conscious effort to be the kind of person you'd like to be. You will change if you take charge.

You make your own opportunities, and you are responsible for your own failings. Good luck.

Continue the Experiment

"The encounter and other groups that have an orientation of exploration . . . do not lead to old answers but to new puzzles, new problems, new modes of experience, new perspectives, and subsequently provide a possible . . . footing from which one may reach for new answers and new skills." So wrote Donald H. Clark in a report to the Carnegie Foundation on a study of sensitivity training in education.

If you've gotten something out of this book—an insight or a better sense of your body or a good time—you may care to continue the experiment by participating in one or more of the wide assortment of group experiences offered by the Human Potential Movement.

Most of these activities are sponsored by "growth centers," the new institutions that have sprung up to serve as workshops for the Human Potential Movement. A landmark in the development of humanistic psychology was the founding of Esalen, the first growth center.

In 1961, in a speech at the University of California at Berkeley, Aldous Huxley criticized the American educational system's emphasis on the verbal-rational side of man. Huxley complained that the schools were neglecting the affective domain, which includes feelings, senses, interpersonal relationships and spiritual needs. To correct this imbalance, Huxley urged the creation of college courses in such nonverbal humanities as introspection, sensory awareness and meditation.

Michael Murphy, a Stanford psychology graduate, who had recently returned from eighteen months at an ashram in India, was impressed by Huxley's ideas. Murphy's interest in meditation and other techniques for expanding consciousness was shared by Richard Price, a close friend, who studied Eastern philosophy at the American Academy of Asian Studies in San Francisco.

"In the fall of 1961," Murphy recalls, "Dick and I decided to found a center for experimentation and education in the affective domain. We hoped to provide a forum for people exploring the potentials of human existence that would balance the verbal-rational orientation of existing institutions.

"For our center we used the Big Sur Hot Springs, a lodge and resort on the Monterey coast that was owned by my grandparents. We called our center the Esalen Institute, after the Indian tribe that once camped around the hot springs."

Esalen's achievements have been as spectacular as its setting, a wooded cliff over the Pacific. At least 50,000 people have participated in its programs, and it has stimulated the establishment of about 100 other growth centers across the country.

Growth centers are the laboratories and research centers—the practical arm—of the Human Potential Movement. Esalen, the first fully elaborated center to develop as an ongoing concern, is the prototype—but because of the highly experimental nature of the movement, there is a lot of variety. Some centers, like Esalen, are physically magnificent; others may run ongoing programs but have no permanent setting.

The Aureon Institute in New York, the oldest East Coast center, maintains a Manhattan office and arranges lectures, seminars and workshops at various locations. It has a retreat in the mountains near Woodstock, New York. Far from being in rural settings, other big-city centers have the utilitarian air of settlement houses. Most growth centers have been independently founded as nonprofit organizations, though a few have developed in association with other institutions, principally churches and universities.

The diversity of the growth centers reflects the freewheelingness of the Human Potential Movement. Humanistic psychology is nothing if not eclectic. Most of the people active in the field have formal credentials in psychology and education—but they are quick to acknowledge that psychologists, psychiatrists and teachers hardly have a monopoly on the understanding of man. Thus, growth-center programs have been given by such ultra-Establishment figures as Abraham Maslow, former president of the American Psychological Association; B. F. Skinner, pre-eminent in behaviorism; and M.D.'s prominent in the American Psychiatric Association and American Medical Association. At the same time, implicit in the Human Potential Movement is the belief that many practitioners outside the conventional helping professions have a contribution to offer.

Teachers of Zen and Yoga share growth-center schedules with practitioners of a large number of other unorthodox fields. A considerable amount of work is done in sensory awareness. Humanistic psychologists also tend to give the relationship between mind and body substantially more attention than do psychologists at large, and more than is customary throughout the profession welcome the participation of dance therapists, masseurs and the like.

More than half of any growth center's schedule is likely to be made up of group sessions, which are strikingly different from traditional group therapy. Customarily, patients in traditional group therapy meet regularly over an extended period of time, generally in the presence of a professional therapist, who may or may not be treating them individually as well. Their contact with each other is usually exclusively verbal, and the therapist maintains his role as a nonparticipant. A growth-center group may meet only once— perhaps for an evening, day or weekend—and their activities may range from verbal explorations of feelings about themselves and each other to long sessions of purely nonverbal contact. In general, there tends to be a lot more physical activity, and the leader joins in as well as providing direction.

In the following listing of growth centers you may find the name and address of an organization to get in touch with for information about activities in your area.

Major Growth Centers in the United States

ARIZONA
Arizona Training Laboratories for
  Applied Behavioral Science
Box 26660
Tempe 85282

CALIFORNIA
Northern
Berkeley Center for Human
  Interaction
1820 Scenic

Berkeley 94709
(415) 845–4765

Blue Mountain Center of
Meditation
1960 San Antonio
Berkeley 94707

Bridge Mountain Foundation
2011 Alba Road
Ben Lomond 95005
(408) 336–5787

Casaelya
2266 Union Street
San Francisco 94117
(415) 567–7961

The Center
Box 3014
Stanford 94305
(415) 327–7686

Center for Human
Communication
120 Oak Meadow Drive
Los Gatos 95030
(408) 354–6466

Center for Interpersonal
Development
3127 Eastern Avenue
Sacramento 95821
(916) 454–6188

Esalen Institute
Big Sur 93920
(408) 667–2335

Esalen Institute
1776 Union Street
San Francisco 94123
(415) 431–8771

Explorations Institute
Box 1254
Berkeley 94701
(415) 548–1004

Gestalt Therapy Institute of
San Francisco

1719 Union Street
San Francisco 94123
(415) 776–4500

Human Dynamics Workshop
Box 342
Boulder Creek 95006
(408) 338–3926

Humanist Institute
1430 Masonic Street
San Francisco 94117
(415) 626–0544

Institute for Creative and Artistic
Development
5935 Manchester Drive
Oakland 94618
(415) 653–9133

Institute for Group and Family
Studies
347 Alma
Palo Alto 94301
(415) 327–5431

The Institute for Multiple
Psychotherapy
3701 Sacramento Street
San Francisco 94118
(415) 752–3564

Pacific Training Associates
3516 Sacramento Street
San Francisco 94118
(415) 346–0770

San Francisco Venture
584 Page Street
San Francisco 94117
(415) 626–6776

S.E.L.F. Institute
40 Hawthorne Avenue
Los Altos 94022
(415) 948–9318

Self-Other Systems Institute
1605 Broderick Street
San Francisco 94115
(415) 922–7077

Society for Comparative
Philosophy, Inc.
Box 857
Sausalito 94965
(415) 332–5286

Sweet's Mill
Auberry 93602

Tahoe Institute
Box 796
South Lake Tahoe 95705
(916) 544–5003

Well-Springs
2003 Alba Road
Ben Lomond 95005
(408) 336–8177

Southern
Center for Studies of the Person
1125 Torrey Pines Road
La Jolla 92037
(714) 459–3861

Dialogue House Associates, Inc.
Box 877
San Jacinto 92383
(714) 654–2625

Elysium Institute
5436 Fernwood Avenue
Los Angeles 90027
(213) 465–7121

Emotional Studies Institute
775 Camino del Sur C–2
Goleta 93017

Gestalt Therapy Institute of Los
Angeles
1029 Second Street
Santa Monica 90403
(213) 276–2818

Gestalt Therapy Institute of San
Diego
7255 Girard Avenue
La Jolla 92037
(714) 459–2693

Human Potential Institute
2550 Via Tejon
Palos Verdes Estates 90274
(213) 376–8533

Human Resources Institute
7946 Ivanhoe Street
La Jolla 92037
(714) 459–3664

Human Resources Institute
1745 South Imperial Avenue
El Centro 92243
(714) 354–3501

Institute for Personal
Development
School of Social Sciences
University of California
Irvine 92664
(714) 833–6336

Kairos
The Ranch
Box 350
Rancho Santa Fe 92067
(714) 756–1123

National Center for the
Exploration of Human
Potential
8080 El Paseo Grande
La Jolla 92037
(714) 459–1484

Topanga Center for Human
Development
Box 480
Reseda 91335
(213) 349–4443

Western Center Consultants
9400 Culver Boulevard
Culver City 90230
(213) 836–5452

COLORADO
Evergreen Institute
2244 South Albion Street

Denver 80222
(303) 798-6351, 255-0554

Rocky Mountain Behavioral
 Institute
12086 West Green Mountain
 Drive
Denver 80228

FLORIDA
The Center of Man
Micanopy 32667
(904) 466-3459, 466-3351

The Han Institute
501 South Ocean Boulevard
Boca Raton 33432
(305) 391-5840

Heliotrope
Box 9041
Fort Lauderdale 33312

Maitreyan Foundation
220 S.W. Second Street
Boca Raton 33432
(305) 395-7573

Miami Tour & Growth Center
1329 Pennsylvania Avenue
Miami Beach 33139

GEORGIA
Adanta
1298 Talcott Place
Decatur 30033

Atlanta Workshop Institute for
 Living-Learning
3167 Rilman Road, N.W.
Atlanta 30327
(404) 233-4414

Keystone Experience
Department of Psychology
West Georgia College
Carrollton 30117

HAWAII
Human Explorations Program
Box 1145
Kaneohe 96744

IDAHO
Star Weather Ranch Institute
Box 923
Hailey 83333

ILLINOIS
Forest Growth Center
555 Wilson Lane
Des Plaines 60016
(312) 827-8811

Human Resource Developers, Inc.
520 North Michigan Avenue
Chicago 60611
(312) 644-1920

Oasis
Stone-Brandel Center
1439 South Michigan Avenue
Chicago 60605
(312) 922-8294, 267-9200

Ontos, Inc.
40 South Clay
Hinsdale 60521
(312) 325-6384

Seminars for Group Studies
Center for Continuing Education
University of Chicago
1307 East Sixtieth Street
Chicago 60637
(312) 288-2500

INDIANA
University Associates
Box 24402
Indianapolis 46224
(317) 637-7140

IOWA
Center for Creative Interchange

602 Center Street
Des Moines 50309
(515) 243–5692

University Associates
Box 615
Iowa City 52240
(319) 351–7322

MARYLAND
Human Resources Institute, Inc.
Box 3296
Baltimore 21228

Orizon-Johns Hopkins
Group Training Center
Baltimore 21205

MASSACHUSETTS
Associates for Human Resources
Box 727
Concord 01742
(617) 369–7810

Human Relations Center
Boston University
270 Bay State Road
Boston 02215

Institute for Experimental
Education
Box 446
Lexington 02173
(617) 862–0869

MICHIGAN
Cranbrook Center for
Human Resources
380 Lone Pine Road
Bloomfield Hills 48013

Inscape
2845 Comfort
Birmingham 48010
(313) MA 6–2384

Outreach
University of Michigan

554 Thompson
Ann Arbor 48104
(313) 764–1817

MINNESOTA
Domus
2722 Park Avenue
Minneapolis 55407
(612) 332–5333

Kopavi, Inc.
1462 Wilson Avenue
St. Paul 55106
(612) 776–9728

Training Consultants
International
7710 Computer Avenue
Minneapolis 55435

Uomes
110 Anderson Hall
University of Minnesota
Minneapolis 55455
(612) 373–2851

MISSOURI
Communication Center No. 1
1001 Union Boulevard
St. Louis 63113
(314) 863–7267

Midwest Personal Growth Center
200 South Hauley Road
Clayton 63105
(314) 863–8476

Omega
Human Potential
Unity Village 64063

People
4340 Campbell
Kansas City 64110
(816) 561–6847

NEVADA
Vida
1934 East Charleston Boulevard
Las Vegas 89104
(702) 384-4844

NEW HAMPSHIRE
Cumbres
Box C
Dublin 03444
(603) 563-7591

Human Resources Development
Hidden Springs
South Acworth 03607

NEW JERSEY
Laboratory for Applied Behavioral
    Science
Newark State College
Union 07083
(201) 289-4345

Plainfield Consultation Center
831 Madison Avenue
Plainfield 07060
(201) 757-4921

Princeton Associates for Human
    Resources
341 Nassau Street
Princeton 08545
(609) 921-2727

NEW YORK
Anthos
24 East Twenty-second Street
New York 10010
(212) 673-9067

Aureon Institute
71 Park Avenue
New York 10016
(212) 532-6380

Awosting Retreat
315 West Fifty-seventh Street

New York 10019
(212) 765-4670

Community Consultation Services
285 Central Park West
New York 10024
(212) 873-3668

Dialogue House Associates, Inc.
45 West Tenth Street
New York 10011
(212) 228-9180

Human Dimensions Institute
4380 Main Street
Buffalo 14226
(716) 839-3600

Sentio
247 West Seventy-second Street
New York 10023

Wainwright House
Milton Point
Rye 10580
(914) 967-6080

W.I.L.L. (Workshop Institute for
    Living-Learning)
333 Central Park West
New York 10025
(212) 865-5790

NORTH CAROLINA
Piedmont Program
Box 6129
Winston-Salem 27109

OHIO
Amare: The Institute of Human
    Relatedness
Box 108
Bowling Green 43402

Antioch Group for Human
    Relations
Antioch College
Yellow Springs 45387
(513) 767-7331

Gestalt Institute of Cleveland
12921 Euclid Avenue
Cleveland 44112
(216) 421–0469

Shadybrook House
Rural Route 1
Mentor 44060
(216) 255–3406

OKLAHOMA
Oklahoma Growth Center, Inc.
4608 Harvey Parkway
Oklahoma City 73118

OREGON
Seminars in Group Process
7433 West Garden Home Road
Portland 97223
(503) 244–8806

Senoi Institute, Inc.
Route 2, Box 259
Eugene 97401
(503) 747–4311

PENNSYLVANIA
Athena Center for Creative Living
2308 Smith Avenue
Aliquippa 15001

Bucks County Seminar House
Erwinna 18920
(215) 294–9243

Center for the Whole Person
1633 Race Street
Philadelphia 19103
(215) 563–4560

Institute for Living, Inc.
300 South Nineteenth Street
Philadelphia 19103
(215) 546–7344

Pendle Hill
Wallingford 19086

Spruce Institute
1828 Spruce Street
Philadelphia 19103
(215) 546–6184

SOUTH DAKOTA
Center for Human Growth
113 North Yale
Vermillion 57069

TEXAS
Espiritu
1214 Miramar
Houston 77006
(713) 528–3301

Hara, Inc.
7322 Blairview
Dallas 75230
(214) 361–7444

The Laos House
700 West Nineteenth
Austin 78701
(512) 477–4471

VERMONT
Sky Farm Institute
Maple Corner
Calais 05648

WASHINGTON, D.C.
Mid-Atlantic Training Committee
Suite 325
1500 Massachusetts Avenue,
   N.W. 20005
(202) 223–4763

N.T.L. Institute for Applied
   Behavioral Science
1201 Sixteenth Street, N.W.
   20036
(202) 223–9400

Orizon Institute
2710 Thirty-sixth Street, N.W.
(202) 298–6757

Quest
627 G Street, S.W. 20024
(202) 554–4189

WISCONSIN
Cambridge House
1900 North Cambridge Avenue
Milwaukee 53202
(414) 272–4327

Major Growth Centers in Other Countries

AUSTRALIA
Australian Institute of Human
  Relations
c/o S. D. Forsey
14 Webb Street
Altona 3018 Victoria

BELGIUM
M. Ferdinand Cuvelier
179 Passtraat
Geel

CANADA
The Centre for Continuing
  Education
York University
E. G. O. Programme
4700 Keele Street
Downsview 463, Ontario

Claremont Experiment
Box 123
Weston, Ontario
(416) 247–2470

Cold Mountain Institute
Box 4362
Edmonton 60, Alberta

The Gestalt Training Institute
  of Canada

Lake Cowichan, Box 39
Vancouver, B.C.

Shalal
750 West Broadway
Vancouver, B.C.

Strathmere
North Gower, Ontario
(613) 489–3768

Synergia
Box 1685, Station B
Montreal 2, Quebec
(514) 488–9901

Toronto Growth Centre
Box 11
Downsview, Ontario

Toronto Growth Centre
43 Eglinton Avenue, East
Toronto, Ontario

ENGLAND
Ananda Centre Ltd.
54 Marshall Street
London W. 1

Centre for Applied Social
  Research
The Tavistock Institute for
  Human Relations
Belsize Lane, London N.W. 3

Centre House
The Centre Community
   Association
10 A Airlie Gardens
Kensington, London W. 8

Quaesitor
Vernon Lodge
Vernon Road
Sutton, Surrey
643–1834

MEXICO
Athena Center for Creative Living
Apartado Postal 85
San Miguel de Allende
Guanajuato

Tarango-Centro de Desarrollo
   Humano
Norte 59, #896
Industrial Vallejo
Mexico D.F. 16

Yolotli
Sierra Vertientes 365
Mexico D.F. 10
40–07–52

WEST GERMANY
Christopher Wulf
DIIPF
Box 900280
6 Frankfurt 90
Schloss Strasse 29

For Further Information

If you are interested in the Human Potential Movement, you can do no better than to join the Association for Humanistic Psychology (584 Page Street, San Francisco, California 94117).

The association's annual meeting is the prime gathering together of practitioners and theoreticians in the field and includes experiential (*i.e.*, group participation) sessions, as well as demonstrations and discussions. The association's *Newsletter* is a fine forum for news and opinion. Chapters springing up in major cities have their own newsletters and programs, which may interest you.

When joining the association, you may also sign up for the best periodical in the field: the *Journal of Humanistic Psychology*, a literate and generally nontechnical semiannual. You may also subscribe to the *Journal* alone (2637 Marshall Drive, Palo Alto, California 94303).

Also recommended is the *Journal of Transpersonal Psychology* (Box 4437, Stanford, California 94305), which covers such areas as meditation, mystical experiences and altered states of consciousness.

Psychology Today (Box 60407, Terminal Annex, Los Angeles, California 90060) frequently publishes articles relating to humanistic psychology.

The following annotated bibliography contains books most recommended for further reading.

Annotated Bibliography

Humanistic Psychology

Bugental, James F. T., ed., *Challenges of Humanistic Psychology*, New York, McGraw-Hill Book Co., 1967. An excellent presentation of the people, the ideas and the methods in the field of humanistic psychology. Includes writers from the humanities, as well as practitioners of existential therapy and the basic encounter group.

Farson, Richard E., ed., *Science and Human Affairs*, Palo Alto, Cal., Science & Behavior Books, 1965. Contains twelve lectures given from 1961 to 1964, under the sponsorship of the Western Behavioral Sciences Institute. A valuable set of papers by distingished students of human affairs on new concepts in the behavioral sciences and new approaches to the study of human problems. Includes an article by Aldous Huxley.

Gustaitis, Rasa, *Turning On Without Drugs*, New York, Macmillan Co., 1969. Written by a journalist, this is one of the best "I was there" pieces about the Human Potential Movement to date. This personal account of one woman's experiences in expanding her consciousness ranges from her attendance at Esalen workshops and visits to other innovative centers in California, to Charlotte Selver's sensory-awareness classes.

Howard, Jane, *Please Touch*, New York, McGraw-Hill Book Co., 1970. A *Life* reporter chronicles her year's experience in some twenty workshops given by leaders of the Human Potential Movement—a trip starting with her assignment to cover an Esalen workshop in January, 1968. Written in a witty, subjective but sharp-eyed manner. A good guide to the movement.

Jourard, Sidney M., *Disclosing Man to Himself*, Princeton, N.J., D. Van Nostrand Co., 1968. The meaning of self-disclosure, which was explored in Jourard's first book, *The Transparent Self*, is here further investigated through original essays and reprints of articles that have appeared elsewhere.

Jourard, Sidney M., *The Transparent Self*, Princeton, N.J., D. Van Nostrand Co., 1964. One of the key figures in humanistic psychology, Jourard has brought together a series of lectures and papers centering around the theme of self-disclosure.

Maslow, Abraham H., *Motivation and Personality*, New York, Harper

& Row, 1954. A landmark. It is in this book that you will find the only complete description of Maslow's famous study on self-actualizing people—the study that has had an incalculable influence on the Human Potential Movement.

Maslow, Abraham H., *Toward a Psychology of Being,* Princeton, N.J., D. Van Nostrand Co., 1962. Get the second edition, because it contains Maslow's famous eupsychian list of groups, organizations and journals interested in humanistic growth. This book contains revisions of lectures and papers given from 1954 to 1962 on peak experiences, growth motivation and self-actualization psychology.

Rogers, Carl R., *Person to Person: The Problem of Being Human,* Barry Stevens, ed., Lafayette, Cal., Real People Press, 1967. An unusual book of essays by professional therapists from an existential or humanistic orientation that have been set in a context of the personal associations and feelings of the editor, Barry Stevens, a high-school dropout. Barry is an "amateur" who wrote the material linking these papers while a guest at the Western Behavioral Sciences Institute. Contains three of Rogers' key papers.

Severin, Frank T., ed., *Humanistic Viewpoints in Psychology,* New York, McGraw-Hill Book Co., 1965. The first comprehensive position statement about the new humanistic development in psychology. Brings together the viewpoints of its most articulate spokesmen.

Sutich, Anthony J., and Vich, Miles A., eds., *Readings in Humanistic Psychology,* New York, Macmillan Co., Free Press, 1969. A carefully chosen selection of the best articles from a decade of publication of the *Journal of Humanistic Psychology.* The editors were the editors and associate editor of the *Journal,* which is the chief organ for publishing theoretical and applied contributions in the area of humanistic psychology.

Human Potentialities

Leonard, George B., *Education and Ecstasy,* New York, Dell Publishing Co., Delacorte Press, 1968. A passionate and compassionate statement about the present damming up of human potentialities in the educational system, and a description of innovative schools and communities that might lead to the school of the future, which Leonard graphically describes. An exciting book that celebrates the joy, the unity of learning and living—with practical suggestions on how our schools can make this vision a reality now.

Murphy, Gardner, *Human Potentialities*, New York, Basic Books, 1958. One of the great American psychologists describes "the three human natures" of man and the unprecedented acceleration of all the sciences in recent years, which can open the way for free expression and fulfillment of potentialities. A philosophical and inspiring vision.

Otto, Herbert A., ed., *Explorations in Human Potentialities*, Springfield, Ill., Charles C Thomas, 1966. In this volume the subject of human potentialities emerges as a distinct area of research. It is chiefly Otto who has popularized the idea that healthy people operate at only 10 to 15 per cent of their potential. Thirty-five professionals from the various behavioral sciences have contributed original papers.

Otto, Herbert A., ed., *Human Potentialities: The Challenge and the Promise*, St. Louis, Mo., Warren H. Green, 1968. Published two years after *Explorations in Human Potentialities*, this volume on human potentialities describes specific methods of growth and has selections from active researchers who had not been anthologized before, such as Alexander Lowen and Michael Murphy.

Self-Help

Huxley, Laura A., *You Are Not the Target*, New York, Farrar, Straus & Giroux, 1963. In the form of thirty-three "recipes for living," this book by Aldous Huxley's wife shows great wisdom and offers practical suggestions for coping with life. One of the most original and insightful self-help books.

Malamud, Daniel I., and Machover, Solomon, *Toward Self-Understanding: Group Techniques in Self-Confrontation*, Springfield, Ill. Charles C Thomas, 1965. Includes more than sixty group experiments that have evolved out of adult university extension classes of thirty to sixty students. Can also be used as a manual.

Otto, Herbert A., *Guide to Developing Your Potential*, New York, Charles Scribner's Sons, 1967. Introduces the concept of keeping a potentialities "workbook" and includes many suggestions and ideas for developing one's potential through the use of field trips, action programs, specific exercises and the like. In simple language Otto delineates the nature of human potentiality, factors that impede potential and methods for releasing potential.

Otto, Herbert A., and Mann, John, eds., *Ways of Growth: Approaches to Expanding Awareness*, New York, Grossman Publishers, 1968;

paperback, New York, Viking Press, 1969. Brings together methods
for fostering personal growth in normal individuals from the fields
of psychotherapy, education, art, psychology and religion. Not altogether a how-to-do-it book, but some articles do describe approaches a layman can use.

Consciousness Expansion

Assagioli, Roberto, *Psychosynthesis*, New York, Hobbs, Dorman & Co.,
1965. A manual of principles and techniques assembled by an
Italian psychiatrist who is trying to synthesize procedures and goals
from several schools of psychotherapy. A source book for the
pioneering work of European psychiatrists in the guided daydream
and other visualization methods, which the psychosynthesists have
helped introduce to America.

De Ropp, Robert S., *The Master Game*, New York, Dell Publishing
Co., Delacorte Press, 1968; paperback, New York, Dell Publishing
Co., Delta Books, 1968. Looks at life in terms of games, the master
game being the pursuit of cosmic consciousness—of a true awakening. Really puts the drug experience in a proper perspective. Contains a clear exposition of the Gurdjieffian system. A very wise
book.

Herrigel, Eugen, *Zen in the Art of Archery*, New York, McGraw-Hill
Book Co., 1964. A major Zen classic that is particularly good in
getting across the elusive ideas of Zen through the medium of the
author's concrete experience with archery, which is regarded in
Japan as a religious ritual, as well as a sport.

Huxley, Aldous, *The Doors of Perception* and *Heaven and Hell*, New
York, Harper & Row, 1956; paperback, 1963. An unsurpassed description of the psychedelic experience. Written by the writer-
philosopher who has inspired, with his lectures and writings, so
many researchers in the new science of altered states of consciousness.

Jung, Carl, *Man and His Symbols*, London, Aldus Books, 1964; paperback, New York, Dell Publishing Co., 1968. The last piece of
work undertaken by Jung before his death in 1961. There has not
yet been written a book in English on the practice of imagery in
man. Until one comes along, this handsome book, which deals
nontechnically with the imaginative life of man around the globe,
will be a valuable aid.

Kapleau, Philip, ed., *The Three Pillars of Zen*, New York, Harper & Row, 1966; paperback, Boston, Beacon Press, 1967. One of the best books to deal with Zen, because it includes, in addition to the usual metaphors and anecdotes, a number of case illustrations.

Reps, Paul, *Zen Flesh, Zen Bones*, Rutland, Vt., Charles E. Tuttle Co., 1957; paperback, New York, Doubleday & Co., Anchor Books, 1957. A collection of Zen and pre-Zen writings, prepared in collaboration with Nyogen Senzaki, a Buddhist monk and scholar. Includes four books: *101 Zen Stories*, the experiences of Zen teachers over a period of five hundred years; *The Gateless Gate*, Mu-mon's classic commentary and collection of koans; *10 Bulls*, an illustrated commentary on the stages of awareness leading to enlightenment; and *Centering*, a Sanskrit manuscript that may be the root of Zen.

Schultz, J. H., and Luthe, W., *Autogenic Therapy*, Vol. 1, *Autogenic Methods*, New York, Harcourt Brace Jovanovich, Grune & Stratton, 1969. Originating in Germany, autogenic therapy, for some inexplicable reason, has never caught on in the United States. It has long been tested (for more than half a century) and researched (in more than 2,400 publications). This volume contains methodically worked-out self-hypnotic verbalizations for calming the body. Meditative exercises are also included. Particularly good are the exercises to develop the kinds of color visions that can come from taking drugs.

Tart, Charles T., *Altered States of Consciousness*, New York, John Wiley & Sons, 1969. Treats subjective experience from a scientific viewpoint. Thirty-five technical papers illustrate a variety of altered states of consciousness and their effects. Describes some of the techniques, both ancient and modern, for producing these states. Contains two out of the three published experimental studies on meditation. A good combination of humanistic and scientific approaches to the nature of human consciousness.

Watts, Alan W., *The Way of Zen*, New York, Random House, Pantheon Books, 1957; paperback, New York, Random House, Vintage Trade Books, 1967. A leading interpreter of Zen in the West, Watts has written a highly readable book intended for both the casual reader and the student. The author has also written many other books (nineteen to date) on Zen and other related topics.

Body Approaches and Sensory Awareness

Gunther, Bernard, *Sense Relaxation Below Your Mind*, New York, Macmillan Co., Collier Books, 1968. A picture book on sensory awakening, as developed by Gunther in workshops at Esalen. The explicit directions and suggestions enable the reader to try out the procedures himself.

Lamb, Warren, *Posture and Gesture*, London, Gerald Duckworth & Co., 1965. An introduction to the study of physical behavior by an English researcher who has been influenced by a system for codifying human movement, invented by Rudolph Laban, a German choreographer. Contains some essays on posture and gesture, which are most illuminating.

Lowen, Alexander, *The Betrayal of the Body*, New York, Macmillan Co., 1967; paperback, Macmillan Co., Collier Books, 1969. In this, his third book dealing with bio-energetic analysis, Lowen describes the exercises that are used in his body-oriented therapy. A major work on the relationship of personality disturbance to muscular tension and impaired breathing.

Pesso, Albert, *Movement in Psychotherapy: Psychomotor Techniques and Training*, New York, New York University Press, 1969. One of the first systematic efforts directed toward the use of the body and body movements for educational and therapeutic ends. The exercises for psychomotor training may be familiar to those who have worked with dance. While this book is basically a teaching manual for psychomotor therapists, many group leaders should find portions of the book useful in understanding and working with body movement in groups.

Creativity

De Mille, Richard, *Put Your Mother on the Ceiling: Children's Imagination Games*, New York, Walker & Co., 1967. A particularly fine preface on reality and imagination. It provides a good background for a great number of visualization games for children.

Gordon, William J. J., *Synectics*, New York, Harper & Row, 1961; paperback, New York, Macmillan Co., Collier Books, 1968. One of the key works on brainstorming through the use of analogies and metaphors, in particular, to foster creative and original ideas in order to solve difficult problems.

Koestler, Arthur, *The Act of Creation*, New York, Macmillan Co., 1964; paperback, New York, Dell Publishing Co., 1967. Examines the common factors in scientific, artistic and comic creativity. A valuable compendium of scientific and psychological information for the layman. Makes sense of the mystery of creative genius.

Osborn, Alex F., *Applied Imagination*, New York, Charles Scribner's Sons, 1963. Group brainstorming and much of education for creativity originates with Osborn. Makes the key point that judgment must be separated from perception and delayed if the delicate bud of creativity is to flower. A practical, rewarding book.

Spolin, Viola, *Improvisation for the Theater*, Evanston, Ill., Northwestern University Press, 1963. The basic text on theater games by their founder. Contains more than 200 such games in manual form, and practical exercises to enhance improvisational abilities and release inner creativity. Written for the teacher rather than for the general reader.

Torrance, Ellis P., *Guiding Creative Talent*, Englewood Cliffs, N.J., Prentice-Hall, 1962. An outstanding specialist in creativity research, especially as it applies to the education of children, Torrance demonstrates with several studies how children sacrifice creative talents in our present educational system.

Encounter Groups

Bradford, Leland, Benne, Kenneth, and Gibb, Jack, *T-Group Theory and Laboratory Method*, New York, John Wiley & Sons, 1964. The best book to date for an understanding of the historical and philosophical perspectives from which the T-group arose. Also contains essays by nine experienced T-group trainers. Surveys research in the field and contrasts the T-group method with group therapy and other forms of group discussion. Edited by three of the most important pioneers.

Burton, Arthur, ed., *Encounter: The Theory and Practice of Encounter Groups*, San Francisco, Jossey-Bass, 1969. Devoted exclusively to the encounter group, this is the first book to cover the subject. A good start in describing and analyzing the variety and potential of this new vehicle for social change. Unusual in the amount of self-revelation that appears in these scientific papers.

Moustakas, Clark, *Individuality and Encounter*, Cambridge, Mass., Howard A. Doyle Publishing Co., 1968; paperback, 1968. Moving descriptions of feelings of loneliness, acceptance, love and suffering (both his own and others') in encounter groups that the author has conducted in several growth centers. No one appears to write more poignantly than Moustakas about the tender, loving moments that occur in an encounter group.

Reid, Clyde, *Groups Alive, Church Alive*, New York, Harper & Row, 1969. Out of personal experience the author, a minister, offers advice on integrating the encounter group into the church. A practical presentation of the principles of group process, which should be helpful not only to leaders of small groups, but also to the person who wants to learn about group dynamics.

Rogers, Carl R., and Coulson, William R., eds., *Freedom to Learn,* Columbus, Ohio, Charles E. Merrill Books, 1969. This distillation of Rogers' thirty-five years of experience in experimenting with the learning process in education provides a plan for self-directed change in an educational system through the use of encounter groups. Describes the beginning of an actual attempt to put this plan into practice in the Immaculate Heart school system in Los Angeles.

Schutz, William C., *Joy: Expanding Human Awareness*, New York, Grove Press, 1967. The book that helped put Esalen on the map. A description of the variety of nonverbal methods that Schutz has appropriated from various sources to enliven and enrich the T-group and turn it into the more freewheeling encounter group.

Gestalt Therapy

Fagan, Joen and Shepherd, Irma Lee, eds., *Gestalt Therapy Now*, Palo Alto, Cal., Science & Behavior Books, 1970. A new generation of Gestalt therapists reports on recent developments in the theory, techniques and applications of Gestalt therapy. The most up-to-date statement on what has happened with Gestalt therapy since Fritz Perls's original presentation, *Gestalt Therapy* was published in 1951.

Lederman, Janet, *Anger and the Rocking Chair*, New York, McGraw-Hill Book Co., 1969. A prose-poetry account of the use of Gestalt awareness methods with negativistic children in an elementary school. Simple and instructive, it illustrates the effectiveness of these methods, especially the creative handling of negativism, in a classroom context. Has profound implications for the entire educational scene.

Perls, Frederick S., *Gestalt Therapy Verbatim.* Lafayette, Cal., Real People Press, 1969. Contains verbatim transcripts of complete Gestalt-therapy sessions conducted by Fritz Perls, along with some expositions of his theories. This book is the next best thing to having seen Fritz in action or seeing the films made of his work before his death early in 1970.

Perls, Frederick S., Hefferline, Ralph F., and Goodman, Paul, *Gestalt Therapy*, New York, Julian Press, 1951. (Republished, New York, Delta Books, 1965.) Contains the original basic formulations of Gestalt therapy. While this book is less clear than others, there are still many procedures of practical value to be found here. Introduction is particularly good.

Shostrom, Everett L., *Man, the Manipulator: The Inner Journey from Manipulation to Actualization*, Nashville, Tenn., Abingdon Press, 1967; paperback, New York, Grosset & Dunlap, Bantam Books, 1968. A popularized version of some of the key ideas of Maslow and Perls. Takes the reader on the journey from manipulating behavior to actualizing behavior.

Marriage and Family

Bach, George R., and Wyden, Peter, *The Intimate Enemy: How to Fight Fair in Love and Marriage*, New York, William Morrow & Co., 1969. On marital fighting, both fair and foul. This highly original and readable book gives principles, fight styles and 122 case histories that point the way to using domestic quarrels constructively.

Lowen, Alexander, *Love and Orgasm*, New York, Macmillan Co., 1965; paperback, New York, New American Library, Signet Books, 1967. An introduction to the theory and techniques of "body work," stemming from Reichian therapy, as it relates to love and sexuality. Includes several long case studies, with therapeutic procedures in the treatment of sexual pathology.

Otto, Herbert A., *More Joy in Your Marriage*, New York, Hawthorn Books, 1969. In this book the author, founder of the National Center for the Exploration of Human Potential, offers an abundance of methods, games and action programs to enliven and enrich a marriage.

Rogers, Carl R., *On Becoming a Person*, Boston, Mass., Houghton Mifflin Co., 1961. A leader of the movement shares his personal experiences as a man, a father, a husband and a psychotherapist as they relate to living in today's rapidly changing world.

Satir, Virginia, *Conjoint Family Therapy*, Palo Alto, Cal., Science & Behavior Books, 1967. This volume summarizes a philosophy about the family and the communication process. Most of it is written for professional helpers, but the last chapter is "must" reading for everyone. It introduces Mrs. Satir's original communication and systems games, which will be expanded in a forthcoming book, *The People Makers*.